ONE STOP
Company Secretary

C000165659

ONE STOP

Company Secretary

An A–Z guide to keeping your company legal

Seventh edition

DAVID MARTIN

icsa.
Publishing

Published by ICSA Information & Training
16 Park Crescent
London W1B 1AH

Typeset in 10 on 12.5 pt Meridien by Hands Fotoset, Mapperley, Nottingham
Printed and bound in Great Britain by Hobbs the Printers Ltd, Totton, Hampshire

British Library Cataloguing in Publication Data
A catalogue record for this book is available from the British Library.

ISBN: 978 1860 724633

Contents

Preface

Each year in presenting around 80 seminars in the UK, I have the pleasure of addressing and listening to around a thousand directors and company secretaries. They represent organisations on whom the wealth and success of the nation depends and their prime roles are to maintain the success of their companies, in the process creating employment and making profits, the tax on which funds society's needs. They are required to operate within an increasingly complex legislative regime perpetrated by law initiators, some of whom seem unable to understand business in general and the operation of limited liability companies in particular. Indeed, the vast majority of those responsible for this legislative minefield have never run a business, operated at a senior level in one, or even have any personal first-hand experience of business. Yet they expect those that do have that experience not only to run their organisations but also to comply with around 3000 additional laws each year creating, in passing, a legislative morass which is so complex it is doubtful if any of those responsible for their business could honestly state that it is and they are entirely legally compliant. Ignorance of the law is no excuse and someone in each organisation needs to be responsible for this compliance facet of company existence. DBIS announced in mid 2011 that there were then 22,000 business statutes in force.

The person who should try to keep the company and its directors legally compliant is the company secretary, whose position as 'keeper of the company's conscience', legal interpreter and adviser and board's confidant, is vital. Quite a task given the legal scenario set out above, to which is added the need to deal with the considerable challenges in the Companies Act 2006. Prior to enactment, CA06 had undergone a gestation period of 11 years, during which period many millions of words were spoken and written (and reinterpreted and rewritten). What was eventually enacted is a monster, being the largest single piece of legislation then passed by the UK Parliament.

During that process the idea of companies being able to operate without a company secretary was mooted, thereby removing the person who is:

- the focal point for legal matters and interpretation;
- the person to whom the board have every right to look for guidance on matters legal;
- the logical point of contact for third parties with the legal person that is a limited liability company;

- the custodian of the board's confidential data or 'secrets' (from which the word 'secretary' is derived);
- the logical person to construct the legally required written record of board meetings (i.e. the minutes, which may assume an even greater importance as a result of the right to launch derivative claims given to shareholders under CA06); and
- in essence, the keeper of the company's conscience.

Many of those involved in the consultation process pointed out this concept of 'doing without' the company secretary was dangerous. Abolitionists might have been wise to have considered the New Zealand experience. Nine years after companies were given the option of not having a company secretary, only just over 5 per cent of New Zealand companies have done so! This is entirely understandable since if there is no appointed company secretary, the duties normally undertaken by such a person must still be fulfilled – ideally by a director, even though the two jobs have entirely different parameters and pressures.

When many years ago, I was qualifying for the ICSA examinations, I sought unsuccessfully to find a practical guide to enhance the theoretical nature of the course studies and to help me understand the practical day-to-day requirements of a company secretary. This title (revised for the seventh time) is the result of those years of hands-on experience of actually doing the job for a variety of companies (both in-house and for my clients), and is very much the title I sought all those years ago. It is aimed at those seeking practical hands-on guidance and is designed for those who undertake the role of company secretary as add-on responsibilities to other administrative duties, and yet lack any formal training in this area to help them cope with these challenges.

The book is written in ordinary everyday English and is arranged in the expanded index format so that a reader should instantly be able to find user-friendly guidance to specific subjects. As a plain guide to both traditional and new requirements such content should suffice in over 90 per cent of the cases where guidance is required. In the other areas it would be wise to seek specific legal advice – in which case the book should enable the reader to ask the right question, without which there is little hope of ever obtaining the right answer. I hope it is helpful in undertaking a fascinating role.

David M Martin
Buddenbrook Consultancy
June 2011

Using this book

I   Using the expanded index format allows each subject to be dealt with comprehensively but also leads to some duplication in other sections, to which attention is drawn by setting the name of the referral section in upper case e.g. 'see AGENDA'.

2   Throughout, a public limited company is referred to as 'PLC'; a private limited company as 'LTD'; the Registrar of Companies at Companies House as 'CH'; a Single Alternative Inspection Location as 'SAIL'; the Employment Appeal Tribunal as 'EAT'; the Department for Business, Innovation and Skills as 'DBIS'; and the various Companies Acts as 'CA' followed by the last two digits of the year they were enacted, thus the Companies Act 2006 is 'CA06'.

3   'Traded companies' refers to PLCs whose shares are listed on the main Stock Exchange. 'Non-traded companies' includes other quoted PLCs (on the Alternative Investment Market) plus unlisted/unquoted PLCs and all LTDs.

4   CA06 allows optional dilutions (e.g. LTDs are not obliged to appoint a company secretary, do not need to hold an Annual General Meeting (AGM), only need give 14 days' notice of special resolutions etc.). Such dilutions can, however, only be used providing the Articles are silent about them or do not prohibit them. Thus if the Articles refer to an LTD holding an AGM each year then it must (unless it changes its Articles) continue to do so. CA06 does not overrule a company's Articles as far as these dilutions are concerned.

5   CA06 applies to all companies now being formed, which may pose a challenge to those administering companies formed under a previous CA if they do not amend the Articles of existing companies to bring them into line with the format and content of those of new companies. Thus an objects clause is no longer necessary (other than for charities). However, such clauses appear in most of the Memorandums of companies formed under earlier legislation. Although CA06 stipulates that these objects clauses are now 'deemed' to form part of the Articles of those companies, no action is required and thus those companies' Memorandums will continue to contain objects clauses.

6   Traditionally, any meeting other than a company's AGM has been called an Extraordinary General Meeting (EGM). CA06 specifies that meetings other than the AGM are simply called General Meetings. However, most companies registered under CAs prior to CA06 have

Articles based on drafts in those Acts (e.g. Table A of CA85) which refer to EGMs. CA06 does not override the Articles and thus unless (and until) the Articles of those existing companies are changed, requirements regarding holding an EGM continue to apply.

7   Since 1856 each company's constitution has been comprised of a Memorandum and Articles. A CA06 company has a Memorandum (which cannot subsequently be altered) consisting only of its country of registration, number, address, and details of the promoters. If such a company wishes to adopt 'objects clauses' they must be put in the Articles (now referred to as the company's 'Constitution'). When existing companies change their Articles they will be required to incorporate their objects clauses in the revised Articles.

8   References to Table A of CA85 apply only to companies registered under that Act and/or which have adopted those regulations.

9   The current definitions of 'companies' sizes' are:
Small: Does not exceed two of the following criteria:
■ turnover: £6.5 million net;
■ balance sheet aggregate: £3.26 million;
■ 50 employees.
Medium-sized: a company that exceeds the parameters for a small company but does not exceed two of the following criteria:
■ turnover £25.9 million net;
■ balance sheet aggregate £12.9 million net;
■ 250 employees.
Large: exceeds the medium-sized parameters.

10   All references to companies (other than in case studies) are for example only and not representative of any real company

11   The attention of listed PLCs is drawn to the various guidance notes issued by the Financial Reporting Council (FRC); as well as to information issued by the Institute of Chartered Secretaries and Administrators (ICSA).

12   The Financial Services Authority (FSA) is expected to be broken up during 2012 with regulatory oversight of the financial markets reverting to the Bank of England. There will be two new organisations – the Consumer Protection and Markets Authority (possibly encompassing the enforcement unit of the FSA) and the Prudential Regulatory Authority.

13   Use of the masculine includes the feminine.

14   Opinions expressed in this book are those of the author – not of ICSA.

Table of cases

Agenda and notice

INTRODUCTION

A meeting has been described as a 'maze' with an agenda being the map for the best route through it, whilst also providing control of the content. If meetings are not convened properly by means of a notice and agenda, and attended by the required QUORUM, decisions may be invalid and the meeting will fail to achieve its purpose(s). The specimen sets of Articles that accompany CA06 each state *every director must be given reasonable notice of a meeting of directors'*. Such notice is meaningful only if the matters required to be considered are listed and, although this may not be so vital for routine general meetings, advance planning is essential.

Board meetings

Agendas need careful consideration and compilation, which experience suggests is often not the case. The benefits of a detailed agenda include:

- guidance through the meeting's 'maze';
- assistance to the chairman in achieving the meeting's aims;
- guidance to all participants of what is required to be achieved; and
- (an invaluable benefit for the company secretary!) a first draft of the legally required record of the meeting – the MINUTES.

Example	Detailed board agenda
	ANY COMPANY LTD
	For a meeting of the Board to be held on Thursday 30th March 2XXX in the Boardroom at 10.00 a.m.
	Apologies for absence
	1 MINUTES of Board Meeting held on 29th February (copy attached).
	2 DIRECTORS' INTERESTS – review entries since last meeting. →

Example	Detailed board agenda – *continued*

3 RISK – consider attached review of reassessment of risks identified which could impact the company.

4 SHARES
   a) Resolution to approve share transfers in favour of Mr PQR.
   b) Consider recommendation that share registration work of the company be placed with Share Registrars Ltd. (Report and contract attached.)

5 FINANCE
   i) Consider Management accounts to 28th February 2XXX. (Complete set to be distributed by Finance Dept by 25th March.)
   ii) Consider recommended change to calculation of depreciation charge. (See attached report from Finance Dept on effect.)
   iii) Capital expenditure
      a) Proposed purchase of (units).
      b) Capex project 13/2XXX.
   iv) Cash flow. (Projection for remainder of 2XXX attached.)
   v) Bank Mandate – new format. (See attached draft.)
   vi) Borrowings. (The secretary will table a report concerning negotiations with the bankers regarding sourcing additional borrowing.)
      Draft resolution required to be adopted: THAT the chairman and Mr UVW be and they hereby are empowered to sign such documents and take such actions to provide the company's bankers with the documentation they require in order to facilitate the advance of the additional borrowing requirement.

6 CURRENT TRADING
   Managing director's report (see enclosed confidential report).

7 PERSONNEL
   a) Wage negotiations for review 1st July 2XXX. (See report from divisional director (personnel) attached.)
   b) Impact of recent employment protection legislation. (The secretary to table report at meeting with recommendations to be tabled.)

8 PROPERTY
   i) Board approval required for items X, XX, XXX in attached report.

Example	Detailed board agenda – *continued*
	ii) Progress on sale (facility).
	9 SAFETY MATTERS
	i) General report (attached).
	ii) Report re [new project] implementation.
	10 SEALING
	Approval required for items XX to XX
	11 BOARD MEETINGS IN 2XXX
	Consider additional dates as follows 28th April, 30th May, 30th June, 28th July, 31st August, 29th September, 25th October, 23rd November, and 21st December.
	Note: *In MINUTES there is an example of the record of the meeting convened by this agenda.*

Such a detailed agenda seeks within itself to aid the efficiency of the meeting. Suggesting a form of words for a formal resolution such as is shown in item 5 (vi) may save valuable board time if such a resolution has to be drafted on the day. If the agenda and the reports tabled are kept with the minutes it can also show what information was before the board at the time of the decision-making process.

Annual General Meeting (AGM)

Every PLC must hold an AGM each year within six months of the company's FINANCIAL YEAR END, but under CA06, LTDs are no longer required to hold an AGM, unless their Articles, their shareholders or members (or the directors) require it. If an LTD does need an AGM, it must be held within 10 months of the company's year end. Everyone entitled to attend must be given adequate notice of the meeting.

Specified days' notice must be given to convene the AGM of a PLC, which can only be waived in whole or part if all the members agree (see GENERAL MEETINGS). Normally, notice required is 21 days but this can be reduced to 14 if the shareholders have agreed and the company offers to all its shareholders the *'facility for shareholders to vote by electronic means'*.

Under CA06, the AGM of an LTD requires 14 days' notice although the Articles must be checked in case a longer period (e.g. 21 days) is required. Notice for an LTD's AGM can be waived if 90 (which the Articles can increase to 95) per cent of the voting strength of the members agree.

Whilst accidental failure to give notice to one or more members will not usually invalidate the meeting, every effort should be made to ensure that members' addresses are kept updated. With the authority of their shareholders, companies can now serve such notices on their members by electronic means – email or fax.

Case study	Faxed notices of AGM
	In *PNC Telecom plc v Thomas* the Court held that it was valid to serve notice of a meeting by fax. This was the first occasion on which this matter was challenged in Court.

At the meeting standard business can be conducted, although this does not prevent other business being considered. The Articles should be checked for requirements. If business other than that covered in the draft agenda below is to be considered then full details must be given; for example, a special resolution or special notice of an ordinary resolution require specific periods and types of notice.

Example	Draft agenda for an AGM
	ANY COMPANY LTD
	NOTICE
	Is hereby given that the
	XXTH ANNUAL GENERAL MEETING
	of the members of the Company will be held at 9.30 a.m. at the [registered office] on Friday, 14th March 2XXX, for the purpose of considering the following business:
	1 Notice of Meeting.
	2 Apologies for absence.
	3 Directors' report for the year ended 30th September 2XXX.
	4 Profit and Loss a/c for the year ended 30th September 2XXX and Balance Sheet as at that date.
	5 To consider and if thought fit authorise payment of a final dividend of X% (Y pence per share) to ordinary shareholders on the register as at [date]. ➔

Example	Draft agenda for an AGM – *continued*

6   Retirement and proposed re-appointment as directors of:
a) Ms C Smith
b) Mr B Jones
who retire by rotation and, being eligible, offer themselves for re-appointment.

7   Retirement and proposed re-appointment as a director of Mr A Robinson who was appointed a director on 1st January 2XXX and retires and offers himself for re-election.

8   Appointment and remuneration of auditors.

By order of the board

[Name]

Secretary   15th February 2XXX

A member entitled to attend and unable to do so may appoint a proxy to vote in his place. Such proxies should be sent to the Registered Office of the company to arrive not later than 48 hours before the commencement of the meeting.

Notes

1   When issuing the notice of the meeting, if the company secretary is also a director he should sign 'On behalf of the board', otherwise the meeting is convened 'By order of the board'.

2   The ARTICLES of some companies require a proportion of the board to retire ('by rotation') at each AGM and to offer themselves (if they wish and are eligible) for re-election. However, if the Articles incorporate reg. 84 of Table A of CA85, only non-executive directors are required to retire by rotation. Experience indicates that many LTDs operating under such rules do not realise this and require rotation by a proportion of both executive and non-executive directors!

3   Any director(s) who has/have been appointed since the previous AGM must retire at the next following AGM and may (if they wish and are eligible) offer themselves for re-election, thus ensuring that members' authority is eventually obtained for all board appointments.

4   Special rules apply regarding the appointment at a general meeting of anyone other than the retiring AUDITORS.

5   Only members and auditors have a right of attendance at a general meeting, although non-shareholding directors have a right of attendance (and to address the meeting) should their REMOVAL be proposed.

General Meetings

CA06 specifies (but only for companies formed under that Act or those that change their Articles) that meetings of members other than the AGM are simply called general meetings (GMs), although the requirements are identical to the previous requirements for Extraordinary General Meetings. Most pre-CA06 companies have used as a base for their Articles pro forma drafts accompanying previous CAs – e.g. Table A of CA85 – and such drafts (and often the Articles of those companies adopting them) refer to EGMs. CA06 does not override the Articles of companies formed under earlier legislation and thus unless (and until) the Articles of those existing companies are changed, the requirements regarding EGMs (which are the same as those for GMs) apply.

GMs are usually convened for specific purposes, although there is nothing to stop such business being conducted at the AGM if the timing is appropriate and providing any special rules regarding the business to be considered are adhered to.

Example	Draft agenda for a GM or EGM

ANY COMPANY LTD

NOTICE

Is hereby given that a(n)

(EXTRAORDINARY) GENERAL MEETING

of the members of the Company will be held on Wednesday 18th June 2XXX at 11 a.m. at [registered office] for the purpose of considering the following business:

1   Notice.

2   Apologies for absence.

3   SPECIAL RESOLUTION: that the share capital of the company be and it hereby is increased from £10,000 to £2,000,000 by the creation of
   a) 990,000 new ordinary shares of £1 each ranking in all respects *pari passu* with the 10,000 existing ordinary shares of £1 of the company,
   b) the creation of 1,000,000 [X]% net p.a. Cumulative Redeemable Convertible Preference Shares of £1.

4   SPECIAL RESOLUTION: that the name of the company be changed to ANY OTHER COMPANY LTD.   ➔

Example	Draft agenda for a GM or EGM – *continued*
	By order of the board [Name] Secretary 20th May 2XXX

Notes

I An (E)GM normally requires 14 days' notice, but longer notice may have to be given if a special resolution is to be considered. Although under CA06 only 14 days' notice (formerly 21) is required of special RESOLUTIONS, a pre-CA06 company's Articles may require a longer period.

2 To be passed at a meeting a special resolution requires a minimum support of 75 per cent of the votes cast (whether present or by proxy) and must be filed with CH within 15 days of being passed. In filing, a specified layout must be followed. If a special resolution is required to be passed using the written resolution alternative it requires support of 75 per cent of *all* the votes – not of the votes cast, as at a meeting.

Allotment and transfer of shares

INTRODUCTION

LTDs limited by shares are usually formed with just one or two shares issued to the company promoter(s) which are then transferred to the first shareholder(s). For a pre-CA06 company, subject to the amount of capital authorised in its MEMORANDUM and any limit on the directors' powers contained in the ARTICLES or in a SHAREHOLDERS' AGREEMENT, or by resolution of the shareholders, the directors can issue (i.e. allot) additional shares. CA06 companies do not need to have an 'authorised share capital' and, unless their powers are constrained by the Articles the directors can simply issue the capital they determine is required from time to time.

Authority

The maximum value of, as well as the denominations of, the share capital of pre-CA06 LTDs limited by shares is stated in the company's Memorandum. Shares in the defined CLASSES (ordinary, preference, deferred etc.) can be issued up to that maximum, but before any shares are to be issued in excess, the shareholders' authority is required (i.e. to increase the authorised share capital). However for CA06 companies, 'authorised share capital' as a concept (and limitation) is abolished and a company can have whatever share capital its directors determine, subject to any restrictions set out in the Articles. Thus for new companies (unless there is a restriction) the share capital can simply be increased by resolution of the board.

Under many company Articles (and/or SHAREHOLDERS' AGREEMENTS) however, shareholders may have a right of pre-emption (i.e. a requirement that when new shares are issued, they have 'first refusal' on them, in the proportion that their shares bear to the total). This means that the board is precluded, without first gaining shareholder approval, from issuing further shares. Other restrictions could include a prohibition on the issue of shares that would result in any one holder owning more than (say) 50 per cent of the total and thus having voting control. Exceptions to a pre-emption rule (i.e. those that do not need the members to waive their pre-emptive rights) are as follows:

- shares issued for employee share schemes;
- issue of non-participating preference and similar securities, or of any other non-equity securities;

- allotment of shares for a non-cash consideration;
- allotment of shares under a renounceable letter of allotment.

Administration

Shares which are not fully paid (that is the full issue price has not yet been paid for them) must be numbered and such numbers must be used in all transactions, so that the 'status' of the shares is obvious. Once all the shares are fully paid they do not need to be numbered. Before new shares are allotted, the authority of the board is required and a record of this resolution, with the effective date, must be recorded in the minutes. Entries (full details of the new shareholders or the addition of new shares to an existing shareholding) must also be made in the register of members and under s.555 CA06 a return of allotments (form SH01) must be made to CH within 28 days of the resolution. The following board minute might be appropriate:

Example	Board minute
	Board Meeting: 1st December 2XXX

It was resolved that the following shares be and they hereby are allotted as follows, amounts in respect of the subscription monies referred to having been received from each person. It was further resolved that the Secretary should issue the appropriate share certificates in accordance with the Articles, make the necessary entries in the share register and notify the Registrar.

New shareholder	Number of shares	Cash rec'd
A Bloggs	1000 Ordinary shares of £1	£1000
B Jones	2000 Ordinary shares of £1	£2000
J Smith	10000 Ordinary shares of £1	£10000

Controlling who holds the shares

Many Articles of LTDs limited by shares grant the right to their directors to prevent (by blocking a share transfer) someone unacceptable to the board becoming a shareholder (hence such companies being referred to as 'private'). Under s.771 CA06, any board wishing to block a transfer of a share must be prepared to give reasons for this no later than two months from receipt of the proposed transfer. If an LTD wishes to RE-REGISTER as a PLC, this right of the directors to prevent shares being transferred to holders unacceptable to them must be abandoned.

Payment, premiums and part payment

The original subscribers to the Memorandum of a PLC must pay for their shares in cash. LTDs' shares can be issued in exchange for the rights to property, or a patent, or a new process, etc. Where shares are issued other than for cash, the asset(s) must be passed to the company within five years of the date of the share issue. If transfer of the asset(s) does not take place, the allottee is liable to pay cash (and any premium) plus interest. If shares are to be issued in exchange for an asset, the value of the asset must be assessed by an expert (defined as a person capable of acting as an auditor) and stamp duty may need to be paid.

A PLC must have an issued share capital of at least £50,000 and cannot allot shares unless at least 25 per cent of the value of such shares (together with any premium) has been paid in cash. Most ordinary shares have a nominal value (e.g. £1, 50p, 25p) and the prospective shareholder pays the full amount for each. However, if a company wishes to issue more shares but feels they are worth more than the nominal value, they could issue the new £1 shares at (say) £1.50 each. In such a situation, in respect of each share issued, £1 will be credited to the company's Share Capital account and 50p to its 'Share Premium account'. There are restrictions on the uses of money held in a Share Premium account – it cannot, for example, be used to pay a dividend.

Shares can, however, be issued 'partly paid'. If the ordinary shares have a nominal value of £1 they (or further shares of that class) could be issued on the basis that the subscribers will pay initially (say) 50p per share. The new £1 shares are then described as *'partly paid'* and the remaining 50p per share which has not so far been paid is described as *'uncalled capital'*. There may be contractual obligations (e.g. timing) regarding the payment of the uncalled capital but subject to that the company can then *'call'* the remaining amount in whole or part and the shareholders must pay up (or sell their shares 'partly paid' – but obviously at a lower price than a fully paid share).

Should the company get into financial problems an insolvency practitioner will demand that shareholders owning partly paid shares immediately pay the *'uncalled'* amount.

Share transfer

Shareholders can transfer their shares by completing a signed (and, if required, stamped) stock transfer form (STF) and their share certificate(s). However, if a shareholder dies, is sectioned under the Mental Health Act, or is declared bankrupt, and thus lacks 'capacity to sign' an STF, control can be passed to another person under share *'transmission'* arrangements. The authority to deal with the shares is then vested in the shareholder's personal representative(s) (executor or administrator), committee or receiver, or trustee in bankruptcy. For CA06 companies, on the death of a shareholder, subject to production of Probate or Letters of Administration, the shares can be put into the name of a 'transmittee' (i.e. a person entitled to the shares because of the death, etc.) and the directors have no right to object to that person holding the shares. However a 'transmittee' is not a full member of the company and has no right to attend or vote at General Meetings. The directors do, however, have the right to refuse to accept a subsequent transfer from the 'transmittee' to an 'unacceptable' third party.

Share registration work is involved and complex, and most listed PLCs with a large number of shareholders and/or companies with active share registers tend to place such work with specialist companies. For a small LTD, particularly if family owned, share transfers may be relatively rare.

Stamp duty

Until March 2008 stamp duty had to be paid on all share transfers. Apart from some exempted transactions the amount of the duty was in proportion to the value of the shares changing hands (*ad valorem*). This meant that it was first necessary to establish the value of the shares – a relatively easy requirement for companies whose shares were listed on a stock exchange but far more difficult for non-listed companies, where usually a valuation would be sought from the auditors. Transfers in respect of shares where the value is less than £1000 are now exempt from paying duty. If a company receives an STF in respect of a transaction where the value exceeds £1000, the form should be returned to the shareholder with a request that it be sent (within one month of the date it bears) to HMRC for duty stamping. If an STF is submitted to HMRC more than a month after it is dated there may be excess charges. A non-duty paid STF which is acted upon when duty was due fails to give a good title to the transferee, and those responsible can be fined £300.

The following transfers are also exempt from stamp duty subject to confirmation (by a certificate required to be completed on the reverse of the STF) that the transaction falls within one of the categories, i.e. it is:

- of property in the name of a trustee to a new trustee;
- by way of security for a loan;
- to a beneficiary under a will;
- to a beneficiary from an intestate's estate;
- to a residuary legatee;
- on, and in consideration of, marriage and/or a civil partnership;
- by the liquidator;
- not on sale and not arising from sale where no beneficial interest passes (e.g. from one nominee to another nominee);
- by way of gift.

Record and title

The issue of a share certificate acts as both receipt for the money subscribed and evidence of title. However, some Articles stipulate that a share certificate is only valid as evidence of title if it bears the common SEAL of the company. If a company wishes to dispense with its use of the seal, either its Articles should be changed to ensure share certificates can be issued validly without being sealed, or alternatively a 'securities seal' can be retained purely for the purpose of authenticating share certificates.

Single member company (SMC)

If a transfer of shares results in the company having only one member i.e. creating an SMC (see TYPES OF COMPANIES), a note of this fact and the date must be entered in the folio in the register of members for the sole member. Should an SMC issue share(s) to an additional person(s) then the fact that that company is no longer an SMC and the date should be added to the entry in the share register. The Articles of a company that becomes an SMC should be examined for any implications – e.g. the quorum for meetings may be 'two'! The surviving shareholder of a company which becomes an SMC by default (e.g. shares are sold to one remaining shareholder) after six months will have unlimited liability for the acts of the company.

Reduction of share capital

Provided there is nothing in its Articles to prevent it, a company by special RESOLUTION can reduce its share capital. Since this could prejudice the interests of the creditors, in addition to passing the resolution, a PLC must seek the permission of the Court under a scheme of arrangement. Although, under s.643 CA06, LTDs no longer need Court permission, they can opt to use the same procedure. If not, then following the passing of the special resolution, the directors must sign a solvency statement confirming that each director has formed the opinion that:

- there is no ground on which the company could be unable to pay its creditors or discharge its debts;
- during the year ahead the company will be able to pay its debts as they fall due;
- (if it is intended to wind the company up in the following year) the company will be able to pay its debts in full within a year of the commencement of the winding up process.

Two copies of the special resolution or the solvency statement must be sent to CH within 15 days of the passing of the resolution.

Buying back shares

There are strict rules regarding share buybacks and advice should be sought from the AUDITORS. A company can buy back up to 10 per cent of its shares and hold them 'in treasury'. During their time 'in treasury' the voting power of such shares is suspended and they do not rank for dividends. They can be re-issued at any time and will then be treated in exactly the same way as other shares. Shares 'in treasury' can also be cancelled which will result in (thus requiring the authority related to) a reduction in capital. CH will have to be notified (form SH03) and if the shares are cancelled form SH06 will have to be filed.

INTRODUCTION

Every year a company must produce a report for its members and file a copy with CH. Filing makes the figures available to the public at large and also helps (at least in theory) to protect the interests of the company's creditors who can inspect the accounts to see the perceived 'safety' of their debts. An 'unlimited company' is not obliged to file its accounts (unless it is part of a group which includes other limited liability companies) since the liability of its shareholders to its creditors is unlimited and, thus, should it fail, creditors can take action against its shareholders personally.

The annual report of a high-profile listed PLC requires considerable investment in both time and money, but this may be cost effective since it can also be used a public relations document. Although the required content is similar, for most LTDs a far more modest document will suffice.

(a) The chairman's statement

Under Stock Exchange requirements listed PLCs must include a chairman's statement which is often the focal point of the whole document, not least as it looks forward whereas the rest of the report looks back. The statement usually includes comment on:

- financial and other results;
- recommended final dividend;
- significant developments and changes;
- competition and market conditions;
- political and economic developments;
- capital expenditure and requirements;
- training and managerial development;
- staff contribution;
- corporate social responsibility;
- CORPORATE GOVERNANCE obligations;
- environmental obligations;
- future expectations, and so on

and then provides a detailed review of each part of the company.

CHECKLIST   Preparation of chairman's statement

✓   Decide on theme and style.

✓   Collate background data from previous statements, media comment and interviews, results of competitors.

✓   Collate data on external factors – political, economic, environmental etc. – which have impacted/could impact business.

✓   Assess impact of results on current and future prospects.

✓   Report on capability of personnel current and anticipated and steps being taken to ensure adequate skills supply.

(b) Report of the directors

This is a legally required statement and advice from the company's AUDITORS should be sought to ensure compliance with the latest requirements. The main contents include statements regarding:

- the principal activities of the company;
- the trading results;
- transfers to and from reserves and any movements in assets in the period under review;
- the dividends paid and proposed;
- acquisitions and disposals;
- details of DIRECTORS during the year under review and, for those seeking re-election at the AGM, of any service agreements;
- the auditors and a note regarding their re-election or replacement;
- developments in employment, employee involvement, disabled employees and health and safety;
- donations made, separating political donations from others;
- major shareholdings (if any) in the company;
- the development of the business;
- any share option and/or share ownership scheme(s);
- activities of significance that have taken place since the date of the balance sheet;
- that the directors take responsibility for the financial statements and accounts.

(c) Annual accounts

The directors must provide details giving a true and fair picture of the company's financial state. In addition, unless the company is exempt, or is under the audit threshold, the accounts must be backed by an auditor's statement to that effect. The accounts package will normally comprise a profit and loss statement, funds flow statement, balance sheet, details of accounting policies and any change thereto, plus explanatory notes.

(d) Notice and agenda of the Annual General Meeting

It is customary (but not an obligation) to include the AGENDA and notice of the Annual GENERAL MEETING in the report as the accounts and balance sheet, together with a note of any dividend proposed, must be given to the members. Under CA06 an LTD is not obliged to hold an AGM, unless its Articles or the directors or shareholders require it.

(e) Auditor's statement

The accounts must be accompanied by a statement, signed by the auditors, indicating that the accounts give a true and fair view of the company's financial affairs as at the date of the balance sheet. If the auditors feel this is not so, they can qualify their statement, stating the scope of their qualification. Companies whose annual turnover does not exceed £6.5 million (unless they are charities or involved in financial services) are not required to have their accounts audited.

(f) Statement of compliance with requirements of the UK Corporate Governance Code (UKCGC)

A COPORATE GOVERNANCE statement is required of listed PLCs. A company that does not comply with the detailed requirements must provide an explanation for non-compliance.

Business review

Section 417 of CA06 requires medium and large companies (see USING THIS BOOK) to publish a business review, the purpose of which is to inform members and help them assess how the directors have performed their duty to promote the success of the company having regard also to employees, community and the environment. It must contain:

- a fair review of the company's business;
- a description of the principal risks and uncertainties facing the company;

and be a fair analysis of

- the development and performance of the company's business; and
- the position of the company's business at the end of the financial year.

For the purpose of understanding the performance, development or position of business, it must also state:

- analysis using financial key performance indicators; and
- where appropriate, analysis using other key performance indicators including information relating to environmental and employment matters.

The last two items of non-financial information are optional for medium sized companies.

Listed PLCs must also state:

- trends and factors likely to affect the company's future development;
- principal risks and uncertainties;
- information re environmental matters, employees, social and community issues;
- details re. key contracts (that is 'significant relationships with major suppliers which are likely to affect (directly or indirectly) the value and performance of the business').

Directors are personally liable for the content of the report and could be held liable to compensate anyone for any loss they suffer as a result of any untrue or misleading statement in, or any omission from, the report, if they knew (or were reckless as to whether) the statement was true – or knew the statement to be a dishonest concealment of a material fact.

Since listed PLCs are required to comply (or explain non-compliance) with UKCGC they must disclose:

- the manner of the board operation; the types of decisions taken by the board and those that are delegated to management;
- the names of the chairman, deputy chairman (if applicable), the chief executive, the senior independent director and the chairman and members of the various board committees (i.e. nomination, audit and remuneration);
- the number of board and board committees meetings; and individual attendance at both by directors;
- the names of non-executive directors that are independent (and the reasons for that assessment);
- any significant commitment(s) of the chairman outside the company;
- the manner in which the board, its committees and members are evaluated;
- the procedure by which the board (especially non-executive directors) understand the views of the company's major shareholders;
- how the board's nomination committee carries out its work in finding new board appointees and explaining whether the advice of external advisers has been sought regarding the appointment of the chairman or deputy chairman;
- how the board's remuneration committee complies with the requirements of the Directors' Remuneration Report Regulations 2002;
- whether any executive directors serve as non-executive directors of other companies and, if paid, whether the directors retain such earnings;
- statements explaining the directors' responsibility for preparing the accounts and (from the auditors) their reporting responsibilities;

- that, subject to any qualifications, and/or with assumptions used, the business is a going concern;
- that the board has conducted a review of the effectiveness of the internal controls used by the company;
- that there is a risk assessment committee which regularly assesses and reports to the board on risk across all aspects of the company' activities
- details of the work of the board's audit committee and, (if applicable) the reasons for not using an internal audit function;
- should the board have refused to accept a report and recommendations from the audit committee regarding the appointment/retention of the external auditors, the reasons for the rejection;
- details of any non-audit work the external auditor carries out for the company.

In addition, the following information is required to be disclosed either in the annual report or on the company's website:

- the terms of reference of the board's committees (nomination, remuneration and audit) explaining their roles and authority;
- the terms and conditions of appointment of the non-executive directors;
- a statement, if any remuneration consultants were appointed, of whether they had any other connections with the company.

In addition, where there is a resolution regarding the re-election of directors/auditors, the company must provide:

- biographical details that will enable shareholders to take an informed decision on their election or re-election;
- the reason(s) for someone being elected to a non-executive directorship;
- if the re-election of a non-executive director is to be considered, the chairman's confirmation that the performance of the person has been evaluated and has been found to be effective;
- if the re-election of an auditor is to be considered and the audit committee's recommendation is not accepted by the board, a statement showing both the recommendation and the reason(s) for the board opposing the recommendation.

Preparation

The preparation of an annual report is a lengthy and complex operation, particularly for a listed PLC wanting to use the document for promotional purposes. The main areas requiring attention are:

 1 Determine impression to be given (e.g. forward looking, high quality, retrenching, expansionist, etc.).
 2 Decide on theme and, if reports are written by a number of executives, ensure this theme is used consistently.
 3 Determine type of report required in relation to company and brief those invited to contribute.
 4 Calculate budget and gain approval.
 5 Prepare draft layout and content and gain approval.
 6 Gain approval for size, paper, typeface, and style, since each individually and collectively give an impression of the company.
 7 Appoint project leader.
 8 Prepare detailed timetable, allowing flexibility.
 9 Check space requirements with auditors (i.e. new or revised accounting requirements may mean a greater space being required to display financial data).
10 Prepare pro forma report and obtain quotation from typesetters and printers based on pro forma and specification.
11 Agree timetables with all involved (including accounts staff, public relations advisers, auditors, designers, typesetters and printers, registrars and despatch).
12 Agree timetable with chairman/board who will need to give final approval.
13 Publish timetable and contact names/telephone numbers to all involved.
14 Agree proofing turnround and discussion procedure with those involved. Advise printers numbers of proof copies required and destination in each case.
15 Communicate each step with all involved. Ensure those writing items for the report are chased for copy as deadlines approach.

CHECKLIST   Timetable for the production of the annual report

Item	D: Despatch Day
✓ Prepare budget and timetable (in liaison with interested parties).	D minus 100 days
✓ Prepare editor's brief, board specification and commitment to theme, style, design, concept, etc. Prepare mock-up.	
✓ Prepare pro forma and send to auditors to assess space requirements.	D minus 95
✓ Notify public relations advisors of publication and check possible clashes (e.g. are major companies or competitors likely to report around the same time?).	D minus 90
✓ Photographer/illustrator specifications drafted.	

✓ Chairman's Statement lst draft.

✓ Executives' Reports lst draft.

✓ Employee Report lst draft.

✓ Proxy and other cards lst draft.

✓ Chairman's Statement, etc. 2nd draft.   D minus 80

✓ Photographer/illustrator commissioned.*

✓ Analyse numbers of report required.   D minus 70

✓ Chairman's Statement 3rd draft and copy to typesetter/printer.   D minus 60

✓ Liaise with Registrars and provide checklist.

✓ Liaise with corporate public relations (PR).

✓ Liaise with brokers.

✓ First proof back, checked and returned to printers.   D minus 50

✓ Second proof to company/auditors.

✓ Photographs reviewed and agreed.   D minus 40

✓ Third proof (colour) to company/auditors.

✓ Preliminary announcement.   D minus 30

✓ Insert figures in third proof for printers.   (Hold period: D minus 30 to D minus 25)**

✓ Commission dividend warrants.

✓ Final proof checked by company/auditors agreed.

✓ Print order given. Printers liaise with registrars re. mailing addresses.   D minus 20

✓ Report despatched externally.   D minus I

✓ Report despatched internally.   D day

* Some companies retain a photographer to capture events during the year so that illustrations are available when the report is being created.

** The purpose of a 'hold' period is to allow time for an objective consideration of the production when no deadlines are pressing, although in practice, it tends to be used to catch up on time slippages!

Approval and filing

The board must formally approve the company's individual (and any consolidated) accounts and balance sheet and the directors' report and business review. A director must sign the balance sheet although the directors' report can be signed either by a director or the company secretary. The signatories' full names must be shown on the printed copies. The accounts and balance sheet are then presented to the members of the company in general meeting and (a black and white copy) must be filed with CH within the following time limits (as required under CA06):

- by the end of the sixth month after the financial year end or accounting reference date (ARD) for PLCs;
- by the end of the ninth month after the ARD for LTDs.

CH has announced its commitment by 2013 for all filing (including accounts) to be carried out electronically and powers are granted to CH under CA06 to insist not only that all filing be carried out electronically but also that all company formations use this format. To file electronically, the company must first apply for a password and a reference number.

Failure to file accounts within the time limits renders the company liable to a fine (currently ranging from £150 to £15,000 depending on the status of the company and the delay in filing) and, for those responsible, to prosecution and disqualification.

The accounts of a newly incorporated company must be filed not more than nine months after incorporation or not more than three months after its first ARD whichever is the later.

Despatch to owners

CA06 permits companies to communicate with their shareholders (e.g. sending reports etc.) by electronic means (email, fax, disk in post etc.). Website communication is also allowed and unless shareholders specifically opt out of 'using the website' they will be regarded as having 'received' the document if it is posted there. If they opt out then they must be sent the information in some other way. However, when a document is posted on the website, companies must notify their shareholders of this (using hard copy unless the shareholders have agreed that the notification itself can be transmitted electronically).

Under the Companies (Registrar, Languages and Trading Disclosures) Regulations 2006, companies using a website must include their name and registered number and office, country of registration and VAT number (if appropriate) on the display. The details do not have to appear on every page and there is no stipulation as to where it appears. Similar information has always been required to be displayed on external emails under s.349/351 CA85 although this was a requirement far more noted for its breach than its observance!

Wherever electronic communication is used a shareholder still has the right to a hard copy version (even if the shareholder has agreed to receive documents in electronic form) within 21 days of such a request.

Companies can:

- publish their annual reports and accounts on their website and simply advise shareholders that they are so available;
- allow shareholders to use fax and email to appoint proxies and give their proxies voting instructions;
- publish other information on their website (it should be made clear whether such information has been subject to audit or not).

The *ICSA Guidance on Electronic Communications with Shareholders 2007* can be downloaded from the ICSA website at **www.icsa.org.uk**.

CA06 requires PLCs to publish their annual reports on their websites as soon as they are available and immediately after they have been approved by the board and auditors and the report is available to the market. It is recommended that this should happen within 120 days (roughly four months) of the year end.

Over 70 per cent of the UK's FTSE 100 publish financial information on the internet. Companies adopting this option need to liaise with their auditors since they may wish to check that it is made clear what information is subject to their audit – and what is not. Suitable security of the website is essential to prevent unauthorised changes.

Summary financial statements (SFS)

Listed PLCs can produce an SFS for those shareholders not wishing to receive the full report yet wanting to see the salient points of the results. An SFS must contain:

- details of developments of the business during the year under review and since the year end;
- profit and loss account;
- balance sheet;
- comparative figures;
- details of directors;
- events since year end;
- and must state that a member has a right to apply for a copy of the full report.

The SFS must:

- state that it is a summary;
- contain an auditor's statement that it is consistent with the full report;
- state whether the auditor's report of the full report was unqualified or not; and
- be signed by a named director on behalf of the board.

A company whose Articles incorporate Table A of an earlier CA may find that its ARTICLES OF ASSOCIATION do not allow it to send an SFS in place of the full accounts, and if it wishes to do so, it must first change its Articles.

Requesting an SFS

Shareholders must be asked their preference by the passive or the active method. The passive method entails sending both SFS and annual report to the shareholders with a reply-paid card. To receive subsequent full reports the shareholder must return the card indicating this.

The active method entails canvassing the shareholders in advance as to their choice; those who do not reply should be sent the full report.

INTRODUCTION

Since '*the price of limited liability protection is disclosure of information*' each year companies must make information publicly available, which is achieved by records on every company being kept and updated at CH. Data on changes to company status, control, results and direction must be filed – mainly on forms which can be downloaded from the CH website (**www.companieshouse.gov.uk**). Making such records available to all-comers enables anyone with an interest in the company (particularly its creditors) to inspect such information.

Annual obligation

To ensure the records are up to date, each year every company must provide a return of the salient information regarding the corporate entity to CH using an annual return (AR01). AR01 costs £14 if filed electronically (£40 in hard copy – only available until 2013), must be accompanied by a declaration signed by a director or the company secretary, and must be filed within a set time limit. Failing to file the return by the 'due date' can result in the officers of the company being fined and prosecuted – and possibly even the company being struck off the register. The 'due date' is the date not more than 28 days after the 'return date'; whilst the 'return date' is any date convenient to the company no later than the anniversary of the 'return date' to which the previous return was made up. Thus, although the return date of a subsequent return can be brought forward, it cannot be postponed.

The return

Form AR01 is divided into a number of parts, with a distinction between 'traded companies' and 'non-traded companies'. For non-traded companies, addresses of their shareholders are not required to be disclosed.

Part 1

This consists of three pages requiring details regarding:

- the name of the company and its registered number;

- the date to which the return is made up (CH has powers to prevent a change of return date if the last two AR01s have been filed late);
- details of the principal business activity (in accordance with the trade classification code or a description of the main business activity if the code 'cannot be determined');
- the company type (i.e. PLC, LTD by shares, LTD by guarantee etc.);
- the address of the registered office (currently the registered office can only be situated in the country in which the company is registered. Thus a company registered in England and Wales must have its registered office in England or Wales, a company registered in Scotland, must have its registered office in Scotland, and a Northern Ireland company must have its registered office in Northern Ireland. Any change of location of the registered office must be notified to CH on form AD01);
- details of any designated office (i.e. a SAIL) where the company records can be inspected (this must have been advised using form AD02 or, if not, that form must accompany AR01);
- details of which records are held at the SAIL (however, if all the records are held at the registered office none of the boxes need to be completed).

Part 2

This requires the company to provide details of its officers, i.e:

- an individual who is the company secretary (optional for LTDs, unless their Articles require it);
- the secretary's service address (which can be the company's registered office);
- (if applicable) a corporate secretary;
- if there is a corporate secretary, where the location of the register concerning that body is kept, either within or outside the EEA;
- individual directors of the company (if these details are different from those filed at CH the appropriate form (e.g. CH01) must accompany the return);
- the service address(es) of each individual director (this can be the registered office of the company if they do not wish their private addresses to be publicly available);
- (if applicable) corporate director(s);
- if there is a corporate director, where the location of the register concerning that body is kept, either within or outside the EEA. Although corporate directors are permitted there must be at least one real person on every board unless an exemption has been granted.

Part 3

Requires details of the share capital of the company both in £ sterling and any other currency.

Part 4

Requires details of the shareholders. 'Non-traded' companies need only provide a full list of shareholders if one did not accompany the last two returns and do not need to show their shareholders' addresses. 'Traded' companies must provide a list and details of all shareholders holding five per cent or more of each share class.

Part 5

Is a signatory clause with space for the signature of the presenter, followed by a 'presenter information' completion of which is voluntary, and a number of continuation pages in case the space provided for earlier data provision was insufficient.

If paying by cheque (made payable to 'Companies House') the company number to which the return refers should be written on the reverse of the cheque (since many cheques accompanying AR01s are drawn on bank accounts other than that of the subject company, and cheque and return can become separated at CH).

Completion problems – and fining for lateness

CH states that:

- nearly 30 per cent of annual returns contain incorrect information, and have to be returned;
- a considerable number of envelopes for hard copy filings contain a cheque but without the AR01;
- a number of envelopes arrive containing AR01 but without a cheque; and
- a number of entirely empty envelopes are received!

Where problems occur, having the presenter's contact details enables speedy return of the document and may allow re-submission without infringing the time limit.

A substantial proportion of all returns are filed late which can incur a fine. In 2010 CH collected over £85 million in fines (and late filing penalties) for late filing of required documentation (mainly accounts).

If filing by hard copy, it is advisable to keep a photocopy of the return. The original should be sent to CH with a covering letter (in duplicate and with a stamped return envelope) or with CH's POST 31 form asking for a receipt. In both cases an adhesive barcode is attached to the returned document. A company's first AR01 must be made up to a date no later than the anniversary of the date of its incorporation.

Returns *must* be filed with CH within 28 days of the operative date if a penalty is to be avoided. Late or non-filing an annual return is a criminal offence. Thus if a return is late or not filed, CH can take action to require compliance, including prosecution of the directors. Those found culpable will get a criminal record and a one-off fine of up to £5,000 plus a fine of £500 for *each day* the company was in default.

Electronic filing

Companies wishing to file electronically can register via the CH website and obtain (by post) an authentication code. The payment fee can be collected by credit card transfer or via the account system (see REGISTRAR OF COMPANIES). Those responsible for filing for a number of companies can opt to have just one personal authentication code for all such companies.

Note

As this book went to print Companies House announced some minor changes to Returns filed after 1 October 2011. The company classification number will be a five digit code and there are some minor changes to the information regarding shareholders.

Articles of Association

INTRODUCTION

The Articles are the contract between the shareholders and those they appoint to run their company – the 'rules' with which the owners expect the officers to abide. Hence the board (and particularly the company secretary advising them) need to be familiar with the requirements. In respect of any question concerning the control and operation of the company, an immediate response should be '*what do the Articles say?*'

Adoption

All companies are legally required to have Articles – and under s.17 CA06 these now become the 'Constitution' of the company. Although there is no required format, previous CAs contained model sets of Articles which could be used in whole or part. Under CA06, three sets of model Articles (for PLCs and LTDs limited by either shares or guarantee) are available from DBIS. Any company feeling it can operate with such standard rules, can simply adopt these instead of drafting its own version. Indeed if a company fails to adopt Articles, the pro forma set of Articles as at the date of the company's registration apply by default as far as is possible (s.20).

Although it is administratively simple to adopt an entire pro forma set of Articles, many companies 'cherry-pick', using the pro forma sections they want, and drafting their own Articles either in substitution for those they discard, or simply devising their own versions. The 'standard' Articles are intended only to be used as a foundation to facilitate customised versions. A company can include virtually any provision in its Articles although legal advice should be sought (for example, to ensure any restrictions are feasible and not in breach of company, or any other, law). Once adopted, such provisions become binding. The original Articles are adopted by being signed by each subscriber to the MEMORANDUM (each signature needing to be witnessed) and filed with CH as part of the INCORPORATION of the company.

Notes

I   If only some regulations from the pro forma are used, it is helpful to set out their contents in full (amended as required) plus any customised articles in a full version. Unfortunately many Articles of pre-CA06 companies simply cross-refer to regulations in Table A of the relative Act, leaving the reader to source that Table before they can comprehend the full obligations. Then of course two detailed documents need to be read as one.

2 There are over 2.6 million UK companies most of whose Articles will be based on the Tables set out in CA85 which was drafted in the early 1980s. It is unlikely that operating a company with such dated Articles is entirely appropriate for many companies now. If the directors act in breach of the Articles, they can be held personally liable for such acts, so regularly reviewing the Articles (and updating them if necessary) should be regarded as essential.

Changing the Articles

To update (i.e. change) its Articles, the company must obtain the approval of its members by means of a special RESOLUTION (i.e. one that requires the approval of at least 75 per cent of the votes *cast* in person or by proxy) at a GENERAL MEETING or by written RESOLUTION (which needs approval of 75 per cent of the *total* voting strength). Such resolutions must be filed with CH within 15 days.

If the change is minor (or only affects part of the Articles), the wording of the special resolution could simply include details of such change, although pre-CA06 companies who wish to change their Articles must now incorporate their objects clauses into the Articles (either transferred directly from their Memorandum or as revised with the authority of the shareholders), so this would also have to be set out in the notice of the meeting. As a result of CA06, the availability of the new drafts, and the requirement to incorporate the objects clauses, it may be felt more appropriate to update the entire Articles. This may be particularly apposite for groups with subsidiaries registered under earlier Acts as any new subsidiary must be formed under CA06. The company secretary (or other person responsible for compliance) will then have the challenge of dealing with sets of Articles derived from different legislative enactments.

As well as the new wording, the reason for each change and its effect should be outlined in the notice to the members, with the advice that a copy of the proposed new Articles (or the whole revisions) is available to those who wish to inspect it, although it may be felt more appropriate to send a new set with the notice.

The pro forma Articles for a CA06 LTD limited by shares are much shorter (53 sections, 86 for a PLC) than, for example, Table A of CA85 which contains 118 regulations. Companies wishing to use the latest version may wish to retain some of the large number of items have been omitted. Some of those for consideration for retention are included in the following checklist.

CHECKLIST   CA85 Table A regulations (in brackets) for consideration for retention when using CA06 drafts as basis

✓   Granting the right to the company to have a lien over shares where the shareholder has not paid in full for the amount due (CA85, Table A, reg. 8). Alternatively consideration could be given to reserving the right to disenfranchise shares where calls made have not been paid.

✓   The administration by which the board can make calls on shares issued partly paid (reg. 12).

✓   How shares are to be transferred (regs. 23 and 25–31).

✓   If an LTD wishes to continue to convene AGMs the provisions concerning such meetings need to be added (regs. 36–63).

✓   If an LTD wishes to continue to operate with a company secretary it might be as well to make this clear (reg. 99).

And so on.

Companies are not allowed to:

■   make any Article unalterable;

■   increase the size of the majority required to authorise a change in its articles beyond that required for a special resolution (that is 75 per cent of the votes cast when voting in person or by proxy or, if by written resolution, 75 per cent of the total voting strength);

■   increase the financial liability of its members without their written authority, or to require members to subscribe for additional shares. However where there are different classes of shares, a company may be able to incorporate Article(s), the effect of which could be to restrict the rights of holders of those shares. Legal advice should be sought if this is required as the law gives protection where such interests might be prejudiced.

Ultra vires – *'acting beyond one's powers'*

If the board or individual directors fail to act in accordance with the require-ments of the Articles they are deemed to be acting *ultra vires* and can be held personally liable for any losses thereby incurred by the company. Thus it is vital that the company secretary either has a good working knowledge of the company's Articles or at least a summary of the principal requirements. If there is a group of companies it may be convenient if they are given, as far as possible, the same Articles – at least it is only one set demanding familiarisation!

Case study	Acting *ultra vires*

In *UK Safety Group Ltd v Hearne*, a managing director (one of six directors) decided he needed to delegate his sales responsibilities to a sales director. He met a young, ambitious, and good salesman who seemed ideal for the post. Since the managing director was concerned in case this appointee could in the future set up his own business in competition using the contacts (especially the customers) he would make from working for the company, his advisers devised a watertight contract including a 'garden leave' clause which would minimise this potential effect. When the appointee agreed and signed the contract, the managing director appointed the young man as a director.

After a short time the sales director left to start his own business in competition. Relying on the 'garden leave' clause in the contract the managing director went to Court to prevent a breach. The company lost the initial action since it was pointed out that the sales 'director' had not been properly appointed. The Articles stipulated that directors could only be appointed at a 'properly convened and constituted Board meeting' – which had not taken place.

In making the appointment, the managing director had exceeded his authority and was acting '*ultra vires*' the Articles. Accordingly the shareholders could hold him liable for any loss occasioned to the company. CA06 makes it easier for shareholders to sue directors – see DERIVATIVE CLAIMS.

(During the case the managing director stated '*but we sent the form to Companies House*', to which the judge retorted '*That's just a piece of paper*'! Whilst CH must be advised, they have no means of knowing whether an appointment has been correctly made.)

It is not only directors who could lose out because the requirements of the Articles are not known and therefore ignored.

Case study	Restriction in Articles

In *T A King (Services) Ltd & Cottrell v King*, Cottrell (C) held 75 per cent of the shares and King (K) the remaining 25 per cent. When C died the shares in his name were automatically →

Case study	Restriction in Articles – *continued*
	transmitted to his widow (Mrs C) who became the new majority shareholder. K objected because the Articles stipulated that on a member's death their shares had first to be offered to the remaining member at a price to be determined by the auditors. The dispute finished in the High Court which held that the transmission to Mrs C was void and that she had to transfer C's shares back to C's estate. The executor of the estate had then to offer the shares to K. If K agreed to buy the shares (at valuation) the proceeds would be passed to C's executor.
	Ironically, since he held 75 per cent of the shares, C could have changed the Articles by a special resolution taking out the provision – unless, of course the obligations under a SHAREHOLDERS' AGREEMENT precluded him from doing so.

Note

Since they must be filed at CH, a company's Articles are a public document and the law must be observed in framing them. However, where the shares are tightly held (e.g. by say no more than four shareholders) there would seem to be nothing to stop them entering into a shareholders' agreement to, for example, require the level of support for special resolutions to be 80 per cent rather than 75 per cent (meaning that all four shareholders – assuming they have equal holdings – would need to agree).

INTRODUCTION

Other than for dormant or exempted companies, accounts must be audited by authorised accountants. If a company subject to audit does not appoint auditors, it must notify the Secretary of State (an officer failing to do so being subject to penalty), who can make the appointment. Auditors are required to report to the members, although, particularly with smaller companies, the auditors often become virtually board nominees reporting to, working with and being overseen by the board. Within the accounts, however, it must state that it is the responsibility of the *directors* to ensure accounts are prepared in accordance with the law, and that it is directors who must answer criticisms regarding such accounts.

Qualification

An auditor must have a recognised accountancy qualification supervised by Recognised Qualifying Bodies (RQB) whose operation is regulated by Recognised Supervisory Bodies (RSB). A single body can operate as both an RSB and RQB but must be approved by the Secretary of State. Only registered auditors are eligible to audit company accounts. If accounts are audited by an unregistered auditor, CH can reject the accounts and require them to be properly audited – the cost of the 're-audit' being borne by the directors.

By virtue of their appointment by the members, auditors are required to hold an independent view of the activities of the company and the board and to report to the members. Although they may need to work closely with the board and company secretary, their first duty is to the members and should there be irregularities, these should be brought to the attention of the members. An auditor has a right to notice of, and to attend and to speak at the company's general meeting.

Appointment and term

The first auditors are appointed by the directors prior to the first ANNUAL GENERAL MEETING (AGM) (which must be held within 18 months of the date of incorporation of the company). At the first and subsequent AGMs auditors are appointed (or re-appointed) by the members and hold office (other than in the period leading to the first AGM) from the conclusion of one AGM until the conclusion of the next – or, if the company does not hold AGMs, until their appointment is terminated. If an auditor resigns the directors can appoint a replacement who holds office until the conclusion of the next following AGM. It can be administratively convenient for auditors to be replaced – for example, if a parent acquires a new subsidiary, it might be logical for the parent company's auditors to audit the new subsidiary company's accounts.

A resigning auditor is required to lodge at the company's registered office a statement of any matters that the auditor feels should be brought to the attention of the members and creditors. If the auditor has lodged such a statement, the company has 21 days to take the matter to Court to gain authority to have such a statement suppressed, and, if so, must notify the auditor that it has taken such action. If, within 21 days of lodging the statement, the auditor has not received a statement that an appeal has been made to the Court the auditor must lodge his original statement with CH. The Court has the authority either to suppress the statement or to require that copies be distributed to the members.

To ensure matters are brought to the attention of the members, a resigning auditor who feels that members should be made aware, can call upon the directors to convene an (extraordinary) General Meeting. This request must be actioned within 21 days of the request and be held within 28 days of the notice of the meeting. The auditor also has the right to have a statement distributed to members and to be heard at the meeting, although no further action can be taken, unless (a) member(s) wish(es) to press the point.

Removal

A serving auditor can only be removed from office by resolution of the members in general meeting. Special notice must be given of an ordinary RESOLUTION. If the resolution is passed, CH must be notified within 14 days – even if the change is made at the AGM at which the auditor's re-appointment would otherwise be proposed.

Any member wishing to propose that the current auditor not be re-appointed must give notice of this proposal (which can only be made once in each year) to the company's registered office. The auditor has seven days to respond, and then the request and any representations from the auditor must be sent to the members giving 21 days' special notice of the meeting to consider the proposal. If the resolution is passed, then the auditor's office terminates at the end of the current financial year. If, however, such a notice is lodged within 14 days of the issue of the accounts for the previous financial year, the auditor's appointment may cease with effect from the end of the financial year being reported upon.

Rights

In addition to the right to attend and be heard at general meetings, auditors have rights of access to all records of the company including board meetings minutes (in case there are any commitments made by the board which could affect the results) necessary for them to be able to complete their audit, and to require directors and staff of the company to provide information, and answer their questions. The auditors must also be sent a copy of every written resolution. Failure to comply attracts a £500 fine.

Payment

Fees paid to auditors must be determined by company in general meeting although it is usual for the members to delegate the responsibility for this task to the board. Auditors' fees must be disclosed in the accounts, split between charges for audit and any other work, for example, taxation advice and calculations, consultancy, etc.

Exemption from audit (and its retention)

The following companies are exempt from the requirement to have their accounts audited:

- a charity whose gross income does not exceed £250,000 (although such a company may need to have its accounts audited under charity law requirements);
- a small company (i.e. one whose turnover does not exceed £6.5 million) provided it is not a PLC, bank, insurance company or broker registered under the Financial Services Act 1986 or the Trade Union and Labour Relations (Consolidation) Act 1992.

Dispensing with an audit has been taken up by under 10 per cent of the companies entitled to do so. There are several reasons. The role of the directors is to take risks and to drive the company forward in accordance with the law. Some however can be tempted to fail to conform to legal and accounting convention practices. Knowing that such practices could be challenged by the auditors can act as a brake on such activities. Without this 'audit brake' such practices can go unchecked – and potentially unnoticed – until the company fails. Even where there is no dishonest intent, an independent view may highlight genuine mistakes. Lacking audited accounts those whose interests could be prejudiced include: trade creditors and lending banks (which might preclude the company obtaining credit); shareholders and non-executive directors (lacking an independent view); regulatory bodies and insurers (being unaware of whether such results of companies have been prepared in accordance with the requirements); as well as the directors themselves as they could find difficulty calculating the company's tax liability (and to ensure the company gains all the exemptions and allowances to which it is entitled – and complies with the latest disclosure requirements) without an auditor's advice.

The EU is proposing to exempt companies whose turnover is less than €1,000,000 and which have fewer than 10 employees from the need to file accounts at all. This could put such companies at an even worse disadvantage than companies which at least have unaudited accounts available.

Authority, control and delegation

INTRODUCTION

If a signatory lacks authority, the validity of a contract they sign may be challenged or rendered void, although if it was reasonable for the third party to believe the signatory did have authority, it may be binding. To ensure authority is delegated and granted to the appropriate level, that there is clarity of control of authority, and that only authorised persons can commit the company contractually, a delegated authority chart could be adopted. Indeed it is arguable that without one, should there be fraud and the company lose as a result, shareholders could make a DERIVATIVE CLAIM holding the directors culpable for not having taken suitable precautions. It may also be advisable to provide suppliers with such guidance so that they are aware who in the company has commitment authority. Such a control mechanism may also provide evidence of compliance with the Bribery Act 2010.

Members

A properly approved members' resolution contains the highest authority to bind the company, for example changing the rules under which the company operates which are contained in its MEMORANDUM and ARTICLES both of which, since they are filed at CH, are public documents. Such changes need the approval of a majority of the votes cast at a general meeting (either a simple or a 75 per cent majority depending on the subject matter) or over the total votes if a written RESOLUTION is utilised.

Directors

The authority of the board is derived from the members via the Articles or their resolutions and operates on the basis of collective responsibility. Decisions are taken 'by the board' in meetings and evidenced by minutes of those meetings – compiling which is a legal obligation. In dealing with third parties, it may be convenient to pass a resolution at a board meeting and, as evidence of such authority, provide the third party with a copy of the appropriate minute. Usually the extract from the minutes will need to be certified as a true copy by the chairman to evidence its authenticity.

Example	Extract from the minutes of a board meeting

Board meeting of J. Bloggs & Company Ltd

held on 29th November 2XXX at [address]

Minute 157 – Brazilian contract

It was resolved that the company enter into a contract with San Paulo Constructiones for the supply of steel [amount/brief specification] for a 10-storey office block for a contract price of [sum], on terms to be agreed in discussion and that T Smith [a director] be and he hereby is authorised to agree terms and sign the contract on behalf of the company.

Certified a true copy of Minute 157 · ....

J Bloggs, Chairman

Date ....

Under such a resolution, collective authority of the board is granted to the contract itself, whilst T Smith is granted individual authority to agree its terms and to sign it on behalf of the company. Although many commercial contracts require only a signature, possibly witnessed, some companies may find the other party insists that the document bears the common SEAL and additional attestation.

Notarial certification

If a company trades with the 'BRIC' – the acronym formed by the initial letters of Brazil, Russia, India and China – the four fastest expanding economies in the world – it may find that organisations in those countries require contracts to be attested by a Notary Public. It may be necessary to provide an 'audit trail' to prove to the satisfaction of the Notary that the person signing a document is who they say they are, holds the position stated and is authorised to sign. Retaining a local Notary and arranging for them to meet the officers may assist as the Notary can then rely on his personal knowledge of the signatories.

Officers

Directors are officers of the company and as such have authority to bind the company. However for their own protection as much as that of the company it may be advisable to delineate the levels of authority attaching to each director and manager. Like the directors, the company secretary is an officer of the company and is often referred to as its chief administrator and '*keeper of the company conscience*'. Every PLC must have a company secretary who can also be a director. An LTD may have a company secretary, although under CA06 this is not compulsory unless it is required under the company's Articles etc. The company secretary has authority to bind the company in administrative duties ('ostensible' authority) but may not be able to enter into new commercial contracts except with the authority of the board. If, however, it has been customary for the company secretary to sign particular contracts for some time, authority to continue to sign such contracts may actually be 'derived' from what has gone before and been accepted previously. Under 'actual' authority the company secretary can sign (for example) a contract of employment, the terms of which have been approved previously by the board.

Some companies prefer to enter brief details of each contract in a contracts register, entries in which, like the register of seals, are periodically approved at board meetings. Obviously there is nothing to stop these two 'registers' being combined.

Other signatories

The value of a delegated authority chart, which needs to be regularly reviewed, is that it not only sets out limits of authority for those lower down the chain of command (and can help reduce the likelihood of fraud or, at least, the exploitation of loopholes) but also grants express authority to signatories. It helps demonstrate that there is effective control regarding the delegation of authority.

Case study	Assumed authority
	In *Pharmed Medicare Private Ltd v Univar Ltd* two employees described as 'managers' of an organisation placed a number of small orders which were fulfilled by the supplier and paid for by the employees' organisation. The two employees then placed a much larger order under a pro forma invoice. There was then a dispute about paying for the goods, with the buying organisation stating the supplier should have known that the two 'managers' who placed the orders did not have authority to do so. The supplier successfully claimed that the employees concerned had ostensible authority since previous transactions entered into by them had been honoured by the buying organisation (i.e. it had paid for the goods they ordered).

Example	Authorities chart

BUSINESS NAME   AUTHORITY
                                                      LEVELS

It is essential for the proper control of the organisation that approval is granted to contracts by suitably appointed personnel, and for the allocation and disposal of money and stock assets of the organisation, that authority is granted at an appropriate level. Employees may only commit the company in accordance with the stated levels.

CONTRACTS

All contracts between the company and third parties, other than those covered by items set out below, must be channelled through the company secretary's office, to ensure correct status (i.e. whether they are to be regarded as a Deed or not) and approval.

The company secretary will arrange the passing of suitable board resolutions granting approval to specified person(s) to sign on behalf of the company. Sufficient time to obtain such a resolution should be allowed.

CASH COMMITMENT

Capital projects

Authority for all projects (no low cut off)	Board
(All items must be supported by a Capital expenditure – Capex – form)	
Repairs and renewals, purchase of furniture and fittings	
(All items must be supported by a Capex form)	
Up to £1000	Manager-level
Over £1000 and up to £5000	Director
Over £5000	Board

Vehicles

(Supported by Capex form, for new allocations, or replacement form for write-offs and replacements)	Board
All purchases to be in accordance with Policy	→

Example	**Authorities chart –** *continued*

Expense items

Up to £500	Manager-level
Over £500 and up to £1000	Senior manager
Over £1000 and up to £5000	Director
Over £5000	Board

Committed expenditure

Rent, rates, utility costs:

– where no change or increase is less than rate of inflation	Manager-level
– where change has taken place	Director

Bought ledger

Raw materials, services etc., in accordance with budgeted level of production	Purchasing manager
Not in accordance with level of production	Director

Personnel matters

Recruitment

– as per plan	Director
– additional to plan	Managing Director

Wage adjustment

– Annual review	Board
– Other than annual review, or for new staff, or replacement at other than at old rate	
Salary up to £10,000 p.a.	Manager-level
Salary over £10,000 p.a.	Board

Warnings

– written (grades ....)	Director
– written (grades ....)	Managing Director
– verbal	Manager
Dismissal	Managing Director

(No hearing which could result in dismissal will take place unless the requirements of the ACAS code – or equivalent – have been followed.)   ➡

Example	Authorities chart – *continued*

In course of business

Credits (cash or stock), samples, etc.

In accordance with policy and less than £1000	Manager-level
Over £1000	Director

Gifts, donations (cash or stock)

In accordance with policy and budget	Personnel Manager

Stock write-off and/or authority to dispose in stated area (e.g. to market trader, staff shop, by gift, etc.)

Up to £1000	Sales Manager
Over £1000	Sales Director in liaison with Finance Director

Personal expenses
(inc. telephone bills etc.)

Up to £500	By level above level submitting the expense claim (i.e. using the required company form)
Over £500	By level two levels above person submitting expense claim.

Removal expenses

In accordance with range of reimbursement agreed at time and may only be authorised by a Board member. All invoices should be submitted in the name of the company to allow recovery of VAT.

Loans

Loans to assist a new employee during the first weeks of his employment (i.e. during the working of the 'week in hand' arrangements)	Personnel Manager
All other loans	Board

Example	Authorities chart – *continued*

Tips and inducements

Other than normal business entertaining and acknowledging special service, the provision of inducements and bribes etc. in the name of the organisation is expressly forbidden, it being a criminal offence. Any instance where this is expected or required should be referred to [name] for guidance. All employees are expected to act to prevent bribery, breach of this obligation being a dismissable offence.

Price fixing

It is illegal for any organisation to conspire with another to fix the price of any product or service – indeed even discussing prices might infringe the rules. Sanctions include imprisonment. On no account is any employee permitted to discuss prices with a competitor or to enter into any arrangement regarding prices no matter how informal. Any instance where this is expected or required should be referred to [name] for guidance. Breach of this rule is gross misconduct (i.e. can generate dismissal).

Issued by finance director on (date). To be updated 6 monthly

(Next review due…)

(Figures are purely illustrative.)

Notes

1 Whilst delineating and defining levels of authority is a sound control mechanism, it may also be necessary to advise third parties that a former employee no longer has authority to bind the company. If a dispute has resulted in summary dismissal for instance, those with whom the employee dealt (particularly if the employee was responsible for buying or selling) should be advised immediately by email or fax.

2 The reference to outlawing tips and inducements is included partly because a company should wish to act ethically and partly due to the impact of the Bribery Act 2010. The Ministry of Justice has stated that, if facing an allegation of bribery, in order to successfully use the defence that *'reasonable steps were taken to prevent it'* a company must be able to show that:

a) it regularly assesses the nature of bribery risks to which it is exposed;

b) prevention of bribery is a top level consideration and the commitment to operating without bribery is clearly communicated to everyone;

c) there are adequate policies and practices that cover all parties to a business relationship;

d) it has implemented its anti-bribery policies and procedures and these are set out in practical terms (i.e. examples are provided – see GIFTS);

e) that it monitors its requirements to ensure compliance.

The guidance on the Act however states that normal business entertaining is to be exempt from prosecution under this new law. One commentator stated *'the Government has made it clear that it has no intention of seeking to prohibit corporate activities aimed at building corporate relations and promoting business'*. However, it is an offence to provide 'hospitality' if it can be proved that the intent was to persuade someone not to act 'in good faith, impartially, or in accordance with a position of trust'.

3   The reference to price-fixing is included to draw the attention to those involved in placing contracts (buying or selling) that there are criminal penalties for those that breach the Competition and Enterprise Acts. Any organisation that engages in anti-competitive practices (participating in a cartel, price-fixing, collusive tendering, bid rigging, customer allocation, etc.) can be fined up to 10 per cent of its turnover whilst individuals responsible (directors, company secretaries, senior managers etc.) can be jailed for up to five years. In addition anyone (which could be an individual) who has suffered loss because of such arrangements (i.e. paid a higher price because there was a price-fixing cartel in operation) can sue the organisation(s) involved for the loss sustained.

4   Whilst this is essentially a document aimed at enhancing internal controls mechanisms, there is little confidential about it and there may be some logic in providing a copy (and regular updates) to suppliers so that they are advised *'who can bind the company and to what level'*.

Board meetings

INTRODUCTION

Members of companies are required to appoint officers to run their company which implies that directors must meet, although there is no explicit obligation for them to do so. However, boards that fail to meet (or, at least to record formally their decisions and the decision-making process) may find it difficult, if challenged, to demonstrate that they have exercised their required duty of care and that the decisions they took were reasonable in the circumstances. Under proposed EU legislation, a board of a listed PLC would be required to meet at least four times each year in order to consider certain prescribed business, whilst CA06 places specific duties on directors (compliance with which may need to be evidenced) as well as repeating the previous requirement that MINUTES of all directors meetings must be taken and preserved. 'The board's role is to provide entrepreneurial leadership of the company within a framework of prudent and effective controls' (FRC 'Guidance on Board Effectiveness').

Attendance

Many boards meet regularly in something approaching formality and (probably more often) informally, to take both long and short term decisions. Only directors have a right to attend board meetings, and although very often others may be present to give reports, answer questions etc., they should take no part in the board's decision-making process. Although there is no explicit legal requirement for directors to attend board meetings, directors cannot abrogate their legal liability for the company's actions, so, if nothing else, attending such meetings is in their own self-interest. Indeed the internal rules may require attendance as reg. 81 of Table A of CA85 states that any director who does not attend board meetings without reason (or permission of the board) for six months can be removed from the board by the other members. Since directors have a collective responsibility for board decisions whether present or not, for their own protection if nothing else, they should regard such attendance as mandatory.

The company secretary has no right of attendance although any company secretary regularly excluded from board meetings should consider whether he is comfortable with the situation. After all the company secretary is an officer of the company and liable as such. In addition, part of the company secretary's role is to compile the record of the board's decisions. If the company secretary is not present someone else needs to do this, since compilation and retention of board minutes is a specific legal requirement.

Administration

Meeting administration starts with setting the dates of meetings – possibly looking at least six months ahead (with a larger company/board, perhaps 12 months or more) on a rolling six-month basis. Despite directors already knowing the dates well in advance, specific notice of each meeting with an AGENDA should be sent to all entitled to attend at least three to four working days prior to the meeting. Even if it is known in advance that a director will be unable to attend, an agenda plus supporting papers should still be provided – not least since directors (including non-executives) must keep themselves updated on all subject matters, reports etc. concerning the company. Directors have a legal obligation to keep themselves informed on company matters, as well as a legal right to notification of board meetings.

Case study	Keep updated
	In a hearing following the collapse of Barings Bank after the devastating losses caused by Nick Leeson's illegal trading in its Singapore office, the Court stated that '*directors* [including non-executives], *collectively and individually (have) a duty to acquire and maintain a sufficient knowledge of the company's business to enable them to discharge their responsibilities*'.

Agenda

A well-prepared AGENDA can assist the efficient execution of a meeting, although experience indicates that producing a very skeletal board agenda (often with hardly any advance notice) is widespread. Such an agenda may be adequate, but it often provides no detailed guidance regarding each item requiring a decision. A detailed agenda such as the example set out in that section may help members to prepare themselves properly for the meeting.

Composition

A meeting's length tends to be proportionate (sometimes disproportionate!) to the number of people present. If that number is swelled by persons whose contribution is unnecessary, effectiveness may be diluted and a meeting's duration extended needlessly. Effective contributions that are concise yet comprehensive should be sought. Setting a time limit for the meeting (or for each item of business) may encourage this and may minimise time being wasted on trivia. Conversely, applying such guidelines too strictly can mean sufficient thought and discussion is curtailed. Every director has a right to be heard on every subject – and of course has a vote. The chairman also has a vote and often under the Articles may have a second or casting vote in the event that there is a stalemate. The model Articles under CA06 for an LTD limited by shares grants the chairman a casting vote but companies not using these Articles should clarify the situation.

Considering the data

Reports, etc., should accompany the agenda or a note regarding late or delayed submission (with a date of expected arrival) be appended. Tabling a bulky or complex report at a meeting should be avoided – since decision-taking on its contents could be uninformed.

Case study	Acting recklessly
	In *Gwyer & Associates v London Wharf (Limehouse) Ltd*, a director of a company in financial difficulties made no effort to ascertain what were the interests of his company before voting on a board resolution. The Court held he was not only negligent but also in breach of his fiduciary duty to exercise his discretion independently and *bona fides* in the interests of the company. It went on to state that, where a company was on the brink of insolvency, the directors owed a duty '*to consider as paramount*' the interests of the creditors.

On occasion, because of time pressures it may be impossible to provide directors with enough 'reading time' before a decision is needed. In that case a brief synopsis of the main points and effects should be presented. Ideally, however, directors should avoid taking a decision on a material matter when they have not had time to consider the full implications.

Example	Summary sheet for board reports

Organisation name   Standard covering sheet

Report title .... Date of report ....

Author/sponsoring dept ....

Date to be considered by meeting ....

Subject matter...

....

Recommendations 1 ....

2 ....

3 ....

Synopsis of facts/ contentions supporting recommendations ....

....

....

....

Synopsis of facts / contentions contesting recommendations ....

....

Implications for organisation if not proceeded with ....*

....

Implications for organisation if not proceeded with NOW ....*

....

Capital expenditure implications..

....

Skill/personnel implications ....

Safety implications ....

* These questions are posed to delineate the likely impact of the recommendations of the report and a guide to those asked to make a decision when they may not have had a chance to study the report and consider such implications.

Notes

I   Where there are time constraints and the matter is material, it may be practicable, rather than holding a meeting, to obtain approval of all the directors by means of a written resolution. This entails drafting a resolution and sending it to each director asking them, if they agree, to sign and return it. The individual signed copies should be preserved in the minute book. Such a procedure needs to balance the need for urgency with the overriding principle that each director should be given as much information as possible and have the opportunity to requisition an emergency meeting of the board to *discuss* the matter prior to commitment. Alternatively, the board could conduct their business by using the telephone or teleconference facilities, although it might be best if these methods of arriving at board decisions were referred to in the Articles to avoid any challenge to the validity of decisions arrived at in this way and/or that all such decisions are subsequently recorded in writing with each director signing their agreement.

2 The term 'material' may need to be defined. This could range from 'contracts in the ordinary course of business' to 'contracts not in the ordinary course of business'. Financial limits should be set where appropriate.

The chairman

The role of the chairman is key to the success of the board and of the company. A chairman needs to have attributes that 'make things happen', such as:

- Vision, to move the meeting towards the attainment of its aims.
- Perception so that almost by instinct and certainly from a process of sound leadership and active listening the chairman is aware of the aspirations and preferences of each member.
- Good communication skills so that this vision is easily communicated to board members.
- Enthusiasm to motivate members so that they believe in plans and in their own ability to perform and achieve them.
- The ability to delegate, to force decision making and accountability down the chain of command, not so that someone at a low level is left 'carrying the can' but to widen their horizons, make them aware of the issues and encourage them to make suggestions.

Good chairmanship:

(i)   sets the aims, values and ethos of the board and the company;
(ii)   (with the company secretary) sets the agenda for each meeting, ensures relevant data is prepared and provided to directors in sufficient time in advance of each meeting so that content and possible effects can be considered;
(iii)   demonstrates genuine and effective leadership and is always available for guidance;
(iv)   inspires and motivates directors and employees;
(v)   interfaces with owners, authorities and the media to promote the company's interests;
(vi)   ensures new directors undergo meaningful induction and all directors performance is regularly evaluated;

(vii) oversees the work of sub-committees of the board and ensures committee chairmen mirror the board chairman's performance and approach;

(viii) ensures all directors contribute, their ideas are heard and there is rapport between them in sharing common goals;

(ix) encourages all directors to speak their mind and to listen to any objective criticism;

(x) ensures risks facing the company and its progress are identified and suitable controls are set up (and regularly reviewed) to minimise adverse effects;

(xi) implements a reliable information and reporting flow;

(xii) plans for managerial and directorial succession;

(xi) acts as the spokesperson for the company

and so on.

(See FRC 'Guidance on Board Effectiveness'.)

Aims

To be effective all meetings should have targets. As Sir John Harvey Jones stated in his best-selling management book *Making it Happen*: *'you've got to have a clear idea of where you want to take whatever it is you've got'*. In order to focus the attention (individual and collective) of members on the subject matter, and to try to avoid a meeting descending into what can otherwise become a meandering discussion, targets should be identified. An agenda for a regular meeting can provide additional short-term aims, even though longer term, strategic aims may be set out elsewhere. In convening and running a routine meeting, longer-term aims may, to some extent, be taken for granted. An agenda can act as a directing force on the meeting, creating latent pressure on its members to work towards target attainment. Thus, although a board of directors might have adopted as the overall targets of the company:

- maximising profit to at least £X million in the current financial year whilst not utilising any additional capital;
- keeping employment costs to no more than 25 per cent of gross margin;
- earning Y per cent return on capital employed;
- achieving output of Z per cent over previous financial period;
- maintaining quality and service, to levels as defined; and so on,

these are statistical guidelines or long term strategies, within which it is possible to implement a number of shorter-term alternative actions or tactics. The horizon and timetable of actions of the board are essentially long-term but there will understandably be deviations in the short term. Section 172 of CA06 explicitly requires boards to consider (and balance) not only the long-term consequences of their decisions, but also the interests of what have been called the company's 'stakeholders' – e.g. the company itself, its shareholders, employees, customers, creditors and suppliers, society and the environment.

Procedural guidelines

The level of formality of the meeting will differ widely according to company custom. For example, it was once fairly common (though not a legal requirement) for board members of many companies (particularly charities) to sign a book of attendance, and to address and speak only through the chairman, and some boards still operate a system whereby a director is only allowed to speak once on a subject. Whilst this latter restriction may assist in forcing members to marshal their thoughts and arguments it may prevent subsequent constructive thoughts. Ideally a board should operate as a dynamic – ideas from one person creating reactions and new ideas from others. Restricting a director's input to just one opportunity to make a point can stultify creativity.

Decisions reflect the 'collective responsibility' doctrine of board work and once everyone has had their say (every director has a right to be heard on each subject), the chairman should summarise arguments, before taking the 'sense' or decision of the meeting – usually by consensus, but if necessary by vote. The following guidelines may be helpful, although boards operate in different ways and they need to be customised to fit specific requirements.

Example	Guidelines aimed at improving meeting efficiency
	Requirements to be issued to all meeting members and those submitting information to be considered at the meeting.

A Timetable

1   A timetable for all required to attend and to submit data to and draw information from the meeting will be prepared on a rolling six-month basis and issued by the company secretary.

2   Other than in the most exceptional instances, the timing of meetings will not be changed and any member unable to attend a meeting must inform the chairman/company secretary as soon as possible.

3   An agenda with supporting data must be issued at least four working days prior to a meeting.   ➔

Example	Guidelines aimed at improving meeting efficiency – *continued*

B Data required

1. All information and reports for consideration must be made available to the company secretary at least seven working days before the meeting.

2. All data should be submitted with the stated number of copies required. (The 'stated number' should be the number of persons entitled to receive the agenda plus any required to be sent out for information, plus, say, one spare for each five persons on the distribution list. Where it is usual for a number of documents to accompany the agenda, colour coding such documentation for ease of reference could be considered.)

3. If data is not available to meet the submission deadline an indication of the availability date must be given, the chairman/company secretary should be informed and a note of the expected date of receipt/issue entered on the agenda. Those submitting data late must make every effort to convey it directly to meeting members prior to the meeting with the required number of spares to the company secretary. Asking for data to be allowed to be tabled at the meeting, particularly if it consists of detailed, involved or lengthy reports, is best avoided. It may result in the item being 'left on the table' for consideration at a later meeting.

4. Documentation will be presented in agenda order.

C Presentation

1. Every item prepared for the [board / committee] will be required to prepare a standard covering sheet (see example above).

2. Subsequent sheets may be presented in the most suitable format.

3. The utmost brevity, commensurate with the subject matter, should be employed. Commentary should be avoided and facts and suppositions, and opposing data, suitably differentiated must be presented clearly.

4. Source(s) of data should be referenced, and a summary used, rather than including such data as part of the submission.

5. The conclusions and recommendations, as required to be set out on the first page of the report, must be clearly evidenced within it.   ➜

Example	Guidelines aimed at improving meeting efficiency – *continued*
	6 Plain English should be used with jargon avoided. Where jargon is unavoidable, a glossary accurately defining the terms used should be included. ***D Supporting commentary*** 1 At the meeting, the report's originator or person responsible for the subject matter should be prepared to speak to the report, to answer questions from other members and generally to assist the meeting to come to a suitable decision regarding its content and/or recommendations. 2 Should the meeting require amplifying documentation this must be provided in the same format as that used in the original report and submitted for the next following meeting. 3 Proposers should endeavour to cover all salient facts in one short presentation. This will entail marshalling all facts, data, comments and so on, balancing brevity against comprehensiveness, highlighting only the most important aspects and avoiding repetition, other than when necessary as a result of other members' questions. 4 After such proposal and counter-comments, if the subject is of such import the chairman may wish to encourage a short general discussion on the subject, otherwise the next move will be to summarise the content and take the sense of the meeting. ***E Decisions*** Board decisions will be communicated externally by the meeting convener and/or the sponsoring member. If approved or referred back for reconsideration the decision will be supported by a copy of the appropriate minute including any conditions, timing, capital expenditure, and so on.

The ICSA code on Good Boardroom Practice suggests:

1   The board should establish written procedures for the conduct of its business which should include the matters covered in this code. A copy of these written procedures should be given to every director. Compliance should be monitored, preferably by an audit committee of the board, and breaches of this procedure should be reported to the board.

2 The board should ensure that each director is given on appointment sufficient information to enable him to perform his duties. In particular, guidance for non-executive directors should cover the procedures:

- for obtaining information concerning the company;
- for requisitioning a meeting of the board.

3 In the conduct of board business, two fundamental concepts should be observed:

- each director should receive the same information at the same time; and
- each director should be given sufficient time in which to consider any such information.

4 The board should identify matters which require the prior approval of the board and lay down procedures to be followed when, exceptionally, a decision is required before its next meeting on any matter not required by law to be considered at board level.

5 As a basic principle, all material contracts and especially not those in the ordinary course of business, should be referred to the board for decision prior to the commitment of the company.

6 The board should approve definitions of the terms *'material'* and *'not in the ordinary course of business'* and these definitions should be brought to the attention of all relevant persons.

7 When there is any uncertainty regarding the materiality or nature of a contract, it should normally be assumed that the contract should be brought to the board.

8 Decisions regarding the content of the agenda for individual meetings of the board and concerning the presentation of agenda items should be taken by the chairman in consultation with the company secretary.

9 The company secretary should be responsible to the chairman for the proper administration of the meetings of the company, the board and any committees thereof. To carry out this responsibility the company secretary should be entitled to be present at (or represented at) all board meetings and prepare (or arrange for the preparation of) minutes of the proceedings.

10 The minutes of meetings should record the decisions taken and provide sufficient background to those decisions. All papers presented at the meeting should be clearly identified in the minutes and retained for reference. Procedures for the approval and circulation of minutes should be established.

11 Where the Articles of Association allow the board to delegate any of its powers to a committee, the board should give its prior approval to:

- the membership and quorum of any such committee;
- its terms of reference; and
- the extent of any powers delegated to it.

12 The minutes of all meetings of committees of the board (or a written summary thereof) should be circulated to the board prior to its next meeting and the opportunity should be given at that meeting for any member of the board to ask questions thereon.

13 Notwithstanding the absence of a formal agenda item, the chairman should permit any director or the company secretary to raise at any board meeting any matter concerning the company's compliance with this Code of Practice, with the company's Memorandum and Articles of Association and with any other legal or regulatory requirement (e.g. for listed PLCs, CORPORATE GOVERNANCE requirements).

Sub-committees of the board

Many boards have the right to appoint sub-committees either for specific purposes or for ongoing considerations (e.g. a remuneration sub-committee). The terms of reference of such appointment together with initial appointees should be set out both in the board minutes and the minutes of each sub-committee meeting.

Example	Board sub-committee appointment resolution
	That [names] be appointed a committee to consider and report on [subject] by [date]. The quorum for the committee shall be [number, normally two] and the committee shall have all the powers of the board necessary for the purpose of carrying out their enquiry, subject to the rules, resolutions or restrictions that the board may impose on them from time to time. The sub-committee will have the power to co-opt such further persons that it feels will contribute to the consideration of the matter. Minutes will be prepared and submitted to the board within seven days from each sub-committee meeting.

Briefing the chairman

INTRODUCTION

Whilst most chairmen will be experienced and well able to deal effectively with meeting administration, inevitably some are not and they, as well as anyone required to 'chair' a meeting (particularly a general meeting) for the first time, may welcome being provided with briefing notes, even if these are used more as back-up rather than as a 'word for word' script or crib.

Annual General Meeting

Whilst handling a board or advisers' meeting (whether formal or not) should be well within the average person's capabilities, the legalistic overtones of statutorily required meetings, with certain forms of wording to be used regarding proposed resolutions, may cause concern. The company secretary could provide guidance – or even a complete crib.

Example	Chairman's crib for AGM
	Crib for XXth annual general meeting to be held on (date) At (time) call meeting to order with a few introductory remarks such as ...
	'Ladies and Gentlemen I welcome you to the Xth AGM of .... LTD/PLC. I will now start the formal proceedings, following the conclusion of which you will be able to meet members of the board and other executives informally over some refreshments. We have provided displays of our products and services and I hope you will find these of interest.
	The notice of this meeting was despatched to all members of the company on (date) and I will ask the secretary to read it.' *(Secretary reads notice)*
	'The first item on the agenda concerns the consideration of the directors' report with the report and accounts for the (12) months ended (date). Those accounts and the balance sheet ➡

Example	Chairman's crib for AGM – *continued*

as at that date have been audited by your auditors Messrs (Name) and I request Mr/Ms (name) a partner of that firm of registered auditors to deliver their audit report.'
(Auditor reads report)

'May I propose that the Report of the Directors, together with the annexed statement of the company's accounts for the (12) months ended and the balance sheet as at that date duly audited be received.

Has anyone any questions or comment?' *(Pause)*
(If questions are raised it will be necessary to deal with them and/or if they are of a technical/financial nature pass them to the finance director to answer)

'Following on from your consideration of the report and accounts may I also propose that a final dividend of (amount) per cent, or (amount) pence per share on the ordinary shares of the company payable on (date) be now declared for the (twelve) months ended (date). I call upon (name) to second these proposals.'
'All those in favour please raise your hands *(pause)*. Anyone against? *(pause)*' *(Assess and declare result.)*
'I therefore declare the motion carried.'

'Item 2 concerns the re-election of the retiring director(s). The director(s) retiring by rotation is/are (name) and I have much pleasure in proposing that (name) be and he hereby is re-elected a director of the company. I will ask (name) to second that proposal.
All those in favour *(pause)* and against *(pause)*'
(Declare result.)
'I declare Mr (name) duly re-elected a director of the company.'

'Item 3 concerns the re-election of Messrs (auditors) as auditors of the company and I call upon Mr (name) to propose that resolution and Mr (name) to second it.
All those in favour *(pause)*. Anyone against *(pause)*?'
(Declare result.)

'Item 4 authorises the directors to fix the remuneration of the auditors and I will ask Mr (name) to propose that resolution and Mr (name) to second it.   ➔

Example	Chairman's crib for AGM – *continued*
	All those in favour *(pause)*. Anyone against *(pause)?'* *(Declare result.)* 'Is there any other ordinary business for consideration?' 'I therefore declare this Xth AGM closed. Thank you.'

Notes

1   Reading the notice of the meeting or the audit report is unnecessary – and doing so is rare. However, reading the notice should cover the arrival of latecomers; whilst reading the audit report identifies the auditor to the shareholders.

2   Legally the shareholders only *receive* the report of the directors and the accounts both of which are approved by the board. Even if the shareholders purport to reject both, their status is unchanged and they must be filed with CH within the required time limits.

3   Only if the dividend proposed by the directors is 'final' do the shareholders have any control; they can either approve, reject or reduce it. Shareholders cannot increase the dividend above the amount recommended by the directors. If the directors feel that a recommended final dividend is likely to be reduced (or rejected) then it may be preferable to consider paying a second interim dividend (which does not need shareholder approval), and not recommend a final dividend in respect of that year's results at all.

4   If more than one director retires by rotation, separate proposals are required for each unless a proposal to deal with all such re-elections as a single resolution is first passed by the meeting. Proposals may also be needed to re-elect any directors who have been appointed since the previous AGM. Re-elected directors may wish to express their thanks to the meeting.

5   Other than the proposal of a vote of thanks to the chairman/board it is unlikely that anything else can be discussed by the meeting since notice of such business will not have been given. However, if every shareholder entitled to be present, is present and everyone agrees to waive notice the meeting could consider other matters.

General Meetings

For CA06 companies, the word 'extraordinary' in relation to any meeting of the shareholders other than the AGM has been dropped, such meetings being simply referred to as GENERAL MEETINGS. However pre-CA06 companies using pro forma Articles from a previous Act (e.g. Table A of CA85) may find reference to an EGM. This will continue unless and until their Articles are changed. By its very nature (that is, not being 'ordinary' and non-controversial) it is more likely that business at such a meeting can provoke greater attention and even disagreement and dissent. This is more likely to be the case should the company be experiencing financial difficulties, and unpalatable measures need to be considered. There follows a condensed version of a chairman's brief for an EGM, developed jointly by the chairman and company secretary of a company in serious financial trouble, where the former chairman/managing director had been forced by the board to resign to facilitate a capital restructuring to be put in place in an attempt to save the company. Notice of the EGM having been given, the ex-chairman (who held shares) submitted an item he wanted considered at the meeting. Rather than risk the need to convene a further EGM (and the inherent costs and dilution of effort) the new chairman requested the meeting to allow consideration of the matter (which it did) although the proposal was then voted down. It was fortunate that all members were present, as, had fewer than the holders of 95 per cent of the shares been present and thus able to waive notice of the item, it is unlikely if it could have been properly put to the meeting at all.

Example	Chairman's crib for EGM

The commentary and advice to the chairman is shown within square brackets.

[Mr Chairman – I have assumed that voting will be by show of hands in which case a simple majority of hands carries the resolution – i.e. each shareholder has one vote. It is, however, possible under the Articles for any shareholder to demand a poll, in which case the meeting must be adjourned whilst we conduct a poll where the votes in accordance with number of shares held will decide the outcome. If a poll is demanded we also need to appoint tellers. I have prepared three sets of voting slips in case polls are required.

I have also primed several shareholders so that each time you ask for a seconder you should always find someone prepared to do so.

I have prepared a handout which details all the resolutions and proposals to be placed before the meeting (including a synopsis of the additional matter put forward for consideration by Mr K) and will give one to each member as they arrive. This should make it easy for them to follow the business as it proceeds.

Call meeting to order at 12 noon.]

Example	Chairman's crib for EGM – *continued*

Chairman: 'Ladies and gentlemen, my name is [x]. At a meeting held on 4th February, the board elected me its chairman. This extraordinary general meeting was convened by the board by a notice issued on 28th January which I propose we take as read – does anyone object to that?'

[*Pause – then, assuming no objection ...*]

'Subsequently a shareholder holding in excess of 10 per cent of the shares, as is required by the Articles, requested that a further item of business be considered at this meeting. We will deal with that request later.

Since the first item on the official Agenda concerns myself I shall vacate the chair and ask Mr Y to deal with it.'

RESOLUTION 1 – Confirmation of appointment of 'chairman'

Y: 'Thank you Mr Chairman. Ladies and gentlemen, as you will see the first item on the agenda concerns the proposal to confirm the appointment as chairman of Mr X. Neither this nor items 2 and 3 need shareholder approval nor are they required to be dealt with at a general meeting, but in view of the financial situation of the company and the dissent that has prefaced this meeting, it was thought this would be advisable. Accordingly I would like to propose that Mr X's appointment as chairman of the board be and it hereby is confirmed. Do I have a seconder?

All those in favour? Anyone against?

I declare the motion carried and hand the meeting back to the Chairman.'

RESOLUTION No 2 – Confirmation of appointment of managing director

CHAIRMAN: 'Thank you. At the meeting which appointed myself as chairman, a majority of the directors also appointed Z as managing director. I would now like to propose that Z's appointment as managing director be and it hereby is confirmed. Do I have a seconder?

All those in favour? Anyone against?

I declare the motion carried.'

Example	Chairman's crib for EGM – *continued*

RESOLUTION No 3 – Confirmation of appointment of secretary

CHAIRMAN: 'The directors also requested Mr Y to assume the role of company secretary in addition to acting as a non-executive director and I would like to propose that Mr Y's appointment as company secretary be and it is hereby confirmed. Do I have a seconder?

All those in favour? Anyone against?

I declare the motion carried.'

RESOLUTION No 4 – Creation of additional share capital, alteration of memorandum

'The next two items on the agenda concern the creation of additional share capital which is necessary so that the major restructuring of the company on which we have been urgently working for some weeks can take place. Copies of the formal resolution which must be filed with the Registrar of Companies have been given to you and I would now like to propose

THAT the share capital of the company be increased from £10,000 to £2,000,000 by the creation of:

a) 990,000 new ordinary shares of £1 each ranking in all respects pari passu with the 10,000 existing ordinary shares of £1 of the company,

AND

b) the creation of 1,000,000 Cumulative Redeemable Convertible Preference Shares of £1.

The notice refers to a coupon rate of 10 per cent but on reflection the board feels that the rate needs to be left for individual negotiation. Does anyone object to this?'

[*Assuming no one objects (and having canvassed all the shareholders and found that no-one currently does), the motion itself can then be put to the meeting.*]

'Do I have a seconder?

All those in favour? Anyone against?

I therefore declare that resolution carried.'

Example	Chairman's crib for EGM – *continued*

RESOLUTION No 5 – Change of auditors

[I have checked with the retiring auditors who have no objection to making way for the new auditors. They have confirmed that with the steps currently being taken by the board, including the matters that are to be dealt with later in the meeting, they have no intention of lodging any statement requesting that any matters be brought to the attention of the shareholders.]

'Your Board originally requested ABC to act as auditors, a role they carried out until the end of 2XXX, when it was felt more advisable to appoint auditors located nearer to the company. Messrs ABC have indicated their willingness to resign. As part of the investigation carried out by Mr Z, an audit-type investigation on the activities of the company to 31st December 2XXX was completed by Messrs DEF, and I now propose that Messrs DEF be and they hereby are appointed auditors of the company until the conclusion of the first Annual General meeting which must be held within the next few weeks. Do I have a seconder?

All those in favour? Anyone against?

I declare that resolution carried.'

RESOLUTION No 6 – Company strategy

'The next item concerns the restructuring of the company and the strategy for the next two years, details of which are included in a report from Mr Z, copies of which have been sent to you. The restructuring report, and the "audit" report contained within it were prepared very urgently and within a very short time span. Inevitably, some shortcuts have needed to be taken and the board is aware of a number of errors in the report which need to be rectified. We are asking today for shareholder approval in principle to the plan which entails amongst other things, the conversion of shareholder loans with which I will deal later.

I would like you to confirm your acceptance of this plan with those comments in mind, and without discussion since the matter is so urgent we need to move to the next item. However if any shareholder does wish to make any comments …'

[You will have to play this by ear. Since all the shareholders have already received a copy and we have spoken to several and dealt with a number of their queries, this may go through 'on the nod' →

Example	**Chairman's crib for EGM** – *continued*

– which is hardly surprising bearing in mind the pressure evinced by the shareholders to nominate Mr Z as the replacement MD. You can expect Mr K to object of course but unless he can be specific and concise I suggest you request him to put his comments in writing for the attention of the board when it comes to implement the plan. In any event, and as I am sure Mr K knows, the voting strength is overwhelmingly in favour of acceptance.]

PROPOSAL No 7 – Conversion of loans made by shareholders into share capital

'The next item concerns the conversion of loans made by us all to the company as part of our shareholding investment. Although it may be arguable that it is permissible for such loans to be counted as shareholders' investments, the advice the board now has, including that from its new auditors, is that these loans do not constitute part of the shareholders' investment and that if their total is excluded from that category, the company is insolvent and should not continue trading. We need everyone to agree today to convert these loans into ordinary shares, and unless this is done, we cannot see that new money can flow into the company which is the only way the company can survive. Thus the directors view this matter as a question for shareholders of *"convert your loans into shares or the Board will have to recommend that the company be put into receivership"*. If the loans are not converted your investment is lost, whereas if they are converted, there is a chance of saving the company and thus your investment. This is not something on which we can vote since it must be an individual decision, although the protection of everyone's investment depends on everyone agreeing to convert. I must stress that as one of the largest investors and, in terms of my shareholder loan, one of the largest creditors of the company I am prepared to convert my loan into shares immediately after this meeting. Any comments?'

[Again you will have to play it by ear. I have forms that will enable shareholders to either a) convert loans into ordinary shares, or b) convert some loan into shares and some into Cumulative Redeemable Convertible Preference Shares (CRCPS) or c) invest new money in Ordinary shares and/or CRCPS. You will need to try to 'insist' that before people leave they sign a form.]

Example	Chairman's crib for EGM – *continued*

PROPOSAL No 8 – Item put forward by Mr K

'The last item concerns a request made by Mr K for an alteration to the Articles. Before we can consider the item itself (which we have set out on the handout) you will note that the short notice given in respect of this item needs to be agreed. The board think it would be advisable for everyone to agree to consider the item and thus I would propose that proposal (8) be considered by the meeting notwithstanding that short notice was given – those in favour? Any against? I declare the motion carried in which case we may now deal with the proposal put forward by Mr K that the articles of association be changed as set out in the wording of the resolution. Mr K do you wish to make any comments regarding this resolution?'

[Again you will have to play it by ear but at the end of any discussion, you may like to comment – the board's view being entirely against the proposal – and need to put it to the vote (in favour, against, declare result). I suppose it is just possible that we might have a demand for a poll here, although my canvassing indicates little support for a proposal that really could have the effect of restricting the actions of the board in its efforts to save the company.

If there is any argument, you could make the point that the chance of saving the company is slim, and it may be the only way forward is to transfer ownership of part or all of the company which would almost certainly mean the offer of additional shares. Since no existing shareholder is willing to put more money into the company it is difficult to see the point of the proposal.]

'That concludes the business of this extraordinary general meeting. May I thank you for attending.'

Notes

1   The confirmation of the appointments of chairman of the board, managing director and company secretary are not matters for the shareholders and this was only adopted to test support for the actions of the newly constituted board in a difficult situation. Had such support not been forthcoming, attempts to save the company would probably have been abandoned immediately by the board.

2   The question of issuing convertible preference shares with a variable coupon rate requires legal advice. In fact here, against the advice of a

number of people involved (including the author who was the newly appointed company secretary), it was put to and approved by the meeting, although the issue was never actually implemented as the board (failing to obtain additional finance) had to invite the lending bank to put the company into administrative receivership (see WRONGFUL TRADING) within a few weeks of the meeting.

3   The value of canvassing support, particularly in difficult situations like these, cannot be over emphasised. Whilst not wishing to stifle fair criticism and comment, the will of the majority needs to prevail (subject to there being no oppression of minority rights) so the company can make progress.

4   Using a handout, particularly as here where there was an extra item of contentious business, aids attention, and thus the flow of the meeting.

5   The preparation of such a script/crib (providing advice on each item), and the canvassing of support, took several hours but, since the meeting went without a hitch, the aim was achieved. The concept was to try to pre-empt every alternative, or to provide an answer for every possibility and or concern.

Charging assets

INTRODUCTION

The company secretary often has responsibility for company assets (effecting insurance and protecting them from theft and damage), and keeping and providing records of transactions concerning them for production to the AUDITORS. There may also be a need to record the acquisition and disposal of certain assets in the board minutes, and, for a listed PLC, obtaining shareholders approval for major or material acquisitions and disposals. Assets may not only be used for business purposes but can also be used as security for loans to generate working capital for business use. Lenders may wish to protect their position by requiring the company to create a charge (or mortgage) over an asset in their favour. The company cannot then dispose of the asset without first repaying the lender (or gaining their explicit permission); whilst should the company fail, the person in whose favour the charge exists has control over that asset to the exclusion of the powers of the insolvency practitioner.

Borrowing on asset value

The creation of a charge, or the acquisition of property on which a charge exists, may entail the company registering details within a set time limit with CH. The purpose of this is to *put into the public arena* details of the charge so that the company's creditors are put on notice that company assets appearing in the accounts, which might otherwise support their debt, have actually been taken out of the 'pool of assets' available for that purpose. The assets over which the creation of a charge requires registration are:

- the securing of debentures;
- a charge on uncalled capital;
- a charge evidenced by an instrument which, if executed by an individual would require registration as a bill of sale;
- a charge on land or any interest in land;
- a floating charge on the undertaking of the business or its property;
- a charge on calls on share capital made but not paid;
- a charge on a ship (or a share in a ship) or aircraft;
- a charge on goodwill or intellectual property (including any patent or trade mark, registered design, unregistered design right, copyright or any licence in respect of any such rights);
- a charge on book debts.

Administration

In order to register a charge a company must file with CH:

- particulars of the charge;
- the instrument of charge;
- form MG01 (see s.860 CA06);
- a fee (currently £13).

These items must be filed within 21 days of the creation of the charge. If the company attempts to file details after the 21-day period the documents will be rejected by CH stating that before the items can be registered the company needs to obtain clearance from the Court (which will require an explanation for the delay). Assuming the Court accepts the reason, it provides clearance which is then submitted to CH. When CH accepts the documents, a certificate of filing is issued which confirms that the charge has been entered on the records at CH and is available to anyone inspecting the company's records. Those inspecting the register of charges are however warned that they should not rely on the certificate in terms of the accuracy of the charge itself.

Legally it is the responsibility of an officer of the company to register the charge, and under CA06 the officers are liable if they do not do so. However very often, in practice it is the lender who files the charge as it is in its best interests to ensure the item is registered properly.

Effect of late and/or faulty registration

In the event of late registration (i.e. one filed more than 21 days after creation), the charge is voidable against a liquidator or a person who acquires an interest in the property subject to the charge until it is registered, although the charge remains valid between the company and the creditor. Late registration may be caused (for example) by documents needing execution and transmission from overseas.

If incorrect details have been registered the company can submit a corrected version.

Register of charges

Every company (even one that has no charges) must keep a register of charges at its registered office or SAIL and make it available to shareholders and creditors on request. If a request is not met within 14 days the company and an officer are in default (s.877(5) CA06).

Release of charge

Subject to receipt of a statutory declaration (before a commissioner of oaths who will make a charge) by an officer of the company with a form in accordance with s.872 CA06, that the debt for which the charge was given has been paid or satisfied, and/or that the property charged has been released from the charge or has been sold or otherwise disposed of, CH accepts the form and places the detail on the record. The charge itself however remains as part of the record – with the discharge effectively cancelling it out. Under CA06 a discharge will only be accepted as forming part of the Register if, in addition to the above, there is confirmation from the lender that the money has been repaid and therefore that the charge can be lifted.

Discharging a charge in respect of a loan that has been repaid is often overlooked and it has been estimated that as many as a third of all the charges registered at CH are in respect of loans that have been repaid. Obviously failing to notify CH that the money has been repaid and the charge discharged could damage the company's perceived credit worthiness in the eyes of anyone conducting a company search.

Development of concept

Since 1989, there have been three major consultation processes leading to recommendations for changes to the existing situation. The Law Commission's most recent set of proposals suggested:

- filing of details of charges with CH (which would not – as at present – issue a confirmation) would be carried out online by companies filing a 'financing statement' (this would include details of the debtor and the secured creditor, the security itself and whether the statement is for a set time or is to continue indefinitely);
- precedence would be decided by date order of filing;
- the online register would be called the Companies Security Register;
- filing could be carried out by either the company or the secured creditor;
- failure to file would result in the charge being ineffective against an administrator or liquidator of the company;
- a floating charge registered at certain times prior to the onset of insolvency proceedings would be void;
- the current rule whereby a fixed charge ranks before a floating charge would be changed so that the precedence would be in accordance with the dates of filing (meaning that floating charge holders could rank in precedence to preferential creditors);
- the list of assets which are covered by the existing registration rules would be replaced by an assumption that all security interests are registrable unless excepted;

- fixed charges over registered land which are required to be lodged with the Land Registry would not also need to be notified to CH;
- charges over unregistered land (regardless of whether they are lodged at the Land Registry) and all floating charges would need to be filed;
- factoring or invoice discounting facilities would need to be registered.

These matters are still under consideration but in the meantime the most recent consultation process also asked for comments on:

- which charges should be registrable;
- whether there should be a time limit on registration and the penalties for failure to comply;
- how should the procedure for registration be formulated (particularly electronic registration);
- how disclosure to third parties could be effected;
- whether the rules should apply to overseas companies; and
- whether charges registered in a specialist register might count as being registered at CH.

At time of writing it has been announced that the proposals have been 'adapted', and there will be a single UK-wide scheme that will not only apply to all companies but also to unregistered companies and limited liability partnerships. It is not expected however that any new arrangements will be operative until 2013.

Classes of shares and class meetings

INTRODUCTION

The authorised share capital of a pre-CA06 company is specified in its Memorandum which sets out all the classes of shares, with wording such as: *'The share capital of the company will be £1,000,000 divided into 500,000 ordinary shares of £1 and 500,000 preference shares of £1'*. For CA06 companies the requirement to have a stated authorised share capital in the Memorandum is abolished, and, if a set amount is required, it must be stated in the Articles. If the Articles do not curtail the directors' powers, they can issue the number and value of shares that they feel is appropriate without referral to the members. There are many classes of shares – ranging from ordinary shares whose holders assume the greatest risk (i.e. losing their investment) should the company fail, to those with more protection – and consequently smaller return.

Ordinary shares

Ordinary shareholders have no right to any payment (dividend) in respect of their shareholding – or any repayment of capital if the company is insolvent and fails. If the company is successful and profitable their returns could be considerable. Where a company is profitable and yet the directors do not wish to pay a dividend (without good reason), the ultimate recourse of the ordinary shareholders would be to remove the directors (see DIRECTORS – REMOVAL) or to apply to the Court (see DIVIDENDS).

If the board of a listed PLC feels the market price of the company's shares is too high, subject to shareholder approval or to authority given to the board in the Articles, it can increase the number of shares by issuing additional shares (i.e. making a *bonus issue*) in proportion to the shareholders' original holding e.g. one bonus share for every five shares held. The number of shares increases by 20 per cent although (in the absence of any other action) the proportion held by each holder to the total number of shares in issue remains unchanged. The total value of the original holding plus the bonus shares should be the same as the total value of the existing shares before the bonus – each share is simply worth less.

If the board wishes to increase the number of shares in issue and, at the same time, raise more capital, provided it has or obtains authority from the existing shareholders, it can make a *rights issue*. This gives the existing shareholders the right to subscribe more capital for additional shares at a price which is often set at a discount to the market price to encourage subscription for the new shares. Shareholders wishing to subscribe, pay the price required and the new shares are added to their original holding. Alternatively the rights to subscribe for the new shares (or some of them) may be able to be sold since they could have a value of their own (since they entitle the subscriber to obtain shares at less than the market value). Some holders of large numbers of shares adopt the policy of selling sufficient of their rights to generate enough cash to subscribe for the remainder (known as 'swallowing the tail').

Preference shares

As the name implies, holders of these shares take precedence (re. annual dividend and repayment in a winding up) over ordinary shareholders. Preference shares usually have a stated rate of interest e.g. '7 per cent preference shares of £1' indicating that each year the holders must be paid a dividend of 7p in respect of each share held. Some company Articles specify that if the dividend on their shares is in arrears, preference shareholders have the right to attend the AGM and vote in respect of the number of preference shares they own. They may have similar voting rights should there be a proposal to wind up the company.

Cumulative preference shares

If a year passes without payment of a dividend on their shares, shareholders have no right to recoup a 'missed dividend' later. Holders of cumulative shares, however, do have a right to recovery of missed dividend(s).

Convertible preference shares

Holders of such shares have the right (usually at specified times in the future and sometimes at specified rates of exchange) to convert their preference shares into ordinary shares.

Redeemable preference shares

Such shares can be given a redemption date requiring the company to return the nominal value of the shares at that date (or within a specified period). Thus someone holding 7 per cent Cumulative Redeemable Preference shares 2012/13 would have the right to have the shares redeemed (usually at par) between 2012 and 2013.

Non-redeemable preference shares

These shares can neither be redeemed nor converted into redeemable preference shares since this could be deemed to be preferential treatment to the detriment of the creditors. They normally have a stated 'coupon rate' which must be paid, but only if they were also cumulative shares would holders be entitled to any missed dividends.

Deferred and/or Founder shares

Usually holders of such shares surrender immediate income from dividends on their shares in the hope or expectation that at some set or unspecific time in the future they will share in profits, usually at a very advantageous rate – or see the value of their shares increase.

Debenture or Loan stock

These are not shares but forms of guaranteed or secured borrowing. Debentures (with a set annual rate of interest) are issued under a trust deed which enables the appointed trustee for the debenture holders, to protect their interests and to take action if interest is not paid or there is a breach of any other covenants in the trust deed. Debentures are usually backed by a CHARGE over all the assets and undertaking of the business (a floating charge) or some specified assets e.g. a freehold property (a fixed charge).

Pre-emption

Generally (unless the Articles declare otherwise) if new shares are to be issued, they must first be offered to existing shareholders in the proportion that each individual holding bears to the total in issue. This is called a right of pre-emption (or 'first refusal') and is very pertinent if the proportions of shares held are important – e.g. a holder of 75 per cent of the ordinary shares has considerable power since with that proportion of votes they can change the Articles. If shares are not to be issued in accordance with this right, the existing members must first consent to waive their pre-emptive rights by resolution in General Meeting (or by a written resolution) and, if this varies the Articles, it needs a special resolution (i.e. one requiring 75 per cent approval of those voting either in person or proxy or, if passed by written resolution by 75 per cent of the total voting strength).

Pre-emption rights do not need to be waived for:

- shares for employee share schemes;
- non-participating preference and similar securities;
- any other non-equity securities;
- allotment of shares for a non-cash consideration, and
- allotment of shares under a renounceable letter of allotment.

Payment

The original subscribers to the Memorandum of a PLC must pay for their shares in cash. But shares in LTDs can be issued instead in exchange for the rights to property or a patent or a new process, or other intellectual property rights etc. If shares are issued for a consideration other than cash (i.e. assets) then such assets must be handed over within five years of the shares being issued. If such a transfer does not take place, then the allottee is liable to pay cash for the shares (and any premium) plus interest for the period from the issue to the date of the transfer.

If shares are to be issued in exchange for an asset, the value of the asset must be assessed by an expert (i.e. a person qualified to act as an auditor).

A PLC cannot allot shares unless at least 25 per cent of the value of such shares (together with any premium) has been paid in cash.

Record and title

The issue of a share certificate acts as both receipt for the money subscribed and evidence of title to, or ownership of, the shares. Some Articles state that share certificates are only valid as evidence of title if they bear the common seal of the company, and if a company with such Articles, wishes to dispense with its use of the SEAL, either the Articles need to be changed or a 'securities seal' purely for use on share certificates should be retained.

Each time new shares are allotted the secretary must:

- enter the name of the allottee in the register of members;
- issue a share certificate;
- send (within 28 days) notice of the allotment to CH using form SH01 in accordance with s.555 CA06.

Single member company (SMC)

If a transfer of shares results in the company having only one shareholder or member (i.e. the transfer creates an SMC), this fact and the date of the event must be stated on the account for the remaining member (e.g. 'From [date] this is a single member company'). Conversely should a single member transfer some of his shares to someone else, or (a) new share(s) be issued to a second shareholder, then the message 'From [date] this is no longer a single member company' must be written in the shareholder's account.

Meetings

Normally only holders of ordinary shares have the right to attend general meetings of the company. However when there are matters which may affect the interests of holders of various type of shares or loans they may have the right to convene and attend a meeting of their own 'class' of shares. The Articles will normally provide a protection to holders of such shares by stipulating that nothing affect their interests without their agreement.

If agreement is needed to such a proposal the holders of the shares affected by the proposal have the right to meet to consider the matter. The detailed procedure for convening such a meeting will usually be set out in the Articles but, if not, CA06 states that two or more holders owning 10 per cent or more of the shares of that class may convene a meeting. Legal advice should be taken to ensure the correct procedure and wording is followed so that there is no prejudicial effect.

Example	Notice of class meeting
	To: The holders of the [specify] shares of [company name]
	NOTICE OF CLASS MEETING
	Notice is hereby given that a meeting of the holders of the [specify] shares in the company will be held at [time] on [date] at [place] for the purpose of considering and, if thought fit, passing the following resolution
	'THAT this class meeting of the holders of the [specify] of the [company] by this extraordinary resolution hereby consent to the variation of their rights by [specify]'
	By order of the board
	Secretary 17th October 2XXX
	A member entitled to attend and unable to do so may appoint a proxy to vote in his/her place. Such proxies should be sent to the Registered Office of the company to arrive not later than 48 hours before the commencement of the meeting.

Section 334 of CA06 stipulates that the quorum for a class meeting is *'two persons … holding at least one third … of the issued shares … in question'*. If 15 per cent or more of the affected members feel their interests have been prejudiced by the resolution or action they have the right to apply to the Court and the resolution (if passed) cannot be implemented until the Court sanctions it. Legal advice should always be sought if class rights are to be varied.

Company secretary

INTRODUCTION

Under CA06 the appointment of a company secretary continues to be mandatory for PLCs (and there are required levels of expertise), however somewhat ironically the same Act, whilst increasing legal compliance and requiring greater attention in this area makes the appointment optional for LTDs (unless the Articles of the company, or the members or directors require it). CA06 also creates dilutions available to LTDs which need to be checked out before they can be used – thus requiring the attention of exactly the appointee performing the role and undertaking the duties of the company secretary! If there is no company secretary someone else (ideally a director in view of the importance of compliance) must carry out these duties. The company secretary is an officer of the company and the appointment (which must be notified to CH) is the responsibility of the board.

The role

Sir John Harvey Jones (former chief executive of ICI when that company was one of the largest UK companies) put the role of the company secretary into perspective when he said *'in many ways the appointment and role of the company secretary is key for the company – more vital than that of many directors – not least because of the increasing weight and scope of legislation and the increasing criminalisation of the activities of officers of the company… the company secretary needs to be dynamic'*.

Such an appointee is:

- a *guardian*, ensuring fulfilment of the company's obligation to comply with an ever-increasing range of legislation as well as protecting its books, registers, assets, reputation etc.;
- a *facilitator*, easing communication between board and management;
- a *recorder* taking and protecting the legally required minutes of board and general meetings;
- a *confidante*, supporting all members of the board and particularly the chairman; and
- the *chief administrative officer* of the company (i.e. being a legal 'officer' of the company with all the attendant responsibilities and liabilities that description entails).

Master of the Rolls, Lord Denning who coined that definition of 'chief administrative officer' of the company, went on to state '*he regularly makes representations on behalf of the company and enters into contracts on its behalf. He is entitled to sign contracts – all such matters come within the ostensible authority of the company secretary*'. Since then the role has gained an increasing prominence – not least regarding obligations under CORPORATE GOVERNANCE. The company secretary must be fully aware of all legal requirements affecting the company, its officers, its employees and its agents. Quoting Sir John again: '*I always work with a positive board system, by which I mean I don't allow silence. After discussing each subject I ask each member of the board what their opinion is and why – this includes the company secretary as I have always believed that his view should be heard.*'

The importance of the role is determined by the fact that unlike directors, there are restrictions on those who are able to be appointed company secretary (at least in theory) for PLCs. Effectively, unless there are very strong reasons for the board ignoring the requirements, the company secretary of a PLC should hold one or more of several stated professional qualifications. Indeed the views of the company secretary may be more objective than that of directors, some of whom may, despite their board responsibilities, be more interested in '*fighting the corner*' for their own executive responsibilities.

A prime responsibility is to 'keep the company legal' – and the directors out of jail! Although the ultimate responsibility for all the acts of the company rests with the directors, the company secretary is an officer of the company and should never be in a position where he has a conflict of interests. Like the other officers, the company secretary has a fiduciary duty to put the company's interests before his own.

The above encapsulates the challenge for those companies that decide not to appoint a company secretary. The role is very different to that of a director – who must take risks and drive the company forward. Companies need both 'risk taker and driver' and '*keeper of the company's conscience and compliance officer*'.

Responsibilities

There are over 2.6 million UK companies and no doubt around 2.6 million different job descriptions for company secretaries. The following checklist sets out the main responsibilities which the board should ensure are carried out.

CHECKLIST   Company secretary's duties

✓ **Understand and interpret the requirements and obligations contained in the Articles** (and a pre-CA06 company's Memorandum) and guide the board on these, recommending when and how the Articles should be updated or revised.

✓ **Maintain statutory registers.** This entails keeping updated the various statutory books including the register of members and dealing with share registration work.

✓ **Update the company file with CH.** Although the board is ultimately responsible, it is normally the company secretary who advises CH within specified time limits of changes in directorate, charges over assets, changes in shareholders etc., at least once a year, and of any other matters affecting the corporate nature of the company.

✓ **Ensure compliance with company law.** The company secretary must have a good working knowledge of the requirements placed upon the officers under company law and ensure that the company complies.

✓ **Liaise with shareholders.** The extent of this responsibility will depend on individual companies – in some, the directors take on this role, however, in most the secretary is responsible for the documentary contact with shareholders – i.e. notice of general meetings, preparation and despatch of annual report etc.

✓ **Ensure legally required documentation is prepared.** This is a very wide-ranging responsibility since much of what is required is derived from obligations under commercial, employment and other laws and familiarity with such laws and obligations is essential.

✓ **Convene company and board meetings.** The company secretary can only do this at the direction of the board, but to ensure the board fulfils its legal duties the company secretary needs to ensure that board meetings are held regularly. It is in his own interests as an officer of the company that he attends board meetings.

✓ **Compile minutes of board meetings and sub-committees** – not only to preserve the record of control, but also to have available documentary evidence which might be needed as a defence in any actions against directors (e.g. to be able to prove they exercised their duty of care and took account of the interests of the company stakeholders as is now specifically required).

✓ **File accounts and annual returns and other forms etc. on time.** Increasingly the obligation to file such items within specified time limits is being backed by rigorously enforced fines. Repeated failure to file on time can lead to disqualification of the director(s) under the Company Directors Disqualification Act.

✓ **Carry out instructions of board.** As the chief administrative officer the company secretary may have the prime role for interfacing with management. Alternatively executive directors may take this role – whoever takes it needs to comply with the exact requirements of the board.

✓ **(For listed PLCs only)** Liaise with the Stock Exchange and ensure the requirements of the Listing Agreement are complied with.

✓ **Act as board/chairman's confidante.** This is often one of the roles played by the company secretary particularly where he is not also a director as he can bring an objective view to the work of the board. It is also often possible for the company secretary to be aware of internal developments of which directors are not aware and thus provide a valuable communication conduit to the chairman / board.

✓ **Act as chief administrative officer.** This responsibility will vary depending on individual organisations, nevertheless the company secretary is often the source from which management first learn of and are required to implement decisions.

✓ **Protect the company's assets.** It is the company secretary's duty to protect the statutory books and records and the confidentiality of the board's work. It may be logical to make the company secretary responsible for other aspects of corporate security.

✓ **Oversee legal matters.** Often the company secretary is legally qualified or will be the only executive with some experience of the law. Increasingly, the law is intruding on all company activities and someone must assume this responsibility.

✓ **Oversee the arrangements to allow shareholders and others to inspect certain records of the company** and to provide access to statutory and other bodies to inspect other records.

✓ **Ensure compliance generally** – with all contractual and commercial law, health and safety law, environmental law, employment law, and so on.

Many company secretaries also take responsibility for insurance, pensions, property, security, employment and/or financial matters. This is a vast obligation – particularly legal compliance given the amount of legislation enacted (around 3,000 items a year) that has been the case recently. With such a background, allowing LTDs to dispense with the appointment seems evidence on the part of the lawmakers of ignorance of, and a lack of understanding of, the responsibilities of the role particularly since companies where there is no company secretary are still required to comply with all the legislation but without the appointee who was the focal point for ensuring such compliance. During the consultation period for CA06 this proposal received almost unanimous criticism from people at the sharp end (not least on the basis that the proposal gained little but had much to lose).

Board meeting duties

Much of the company secretary's basic work may revolve around convening, servicing and supporting the work of board meetings. His responsibilities in this work are summarised below although inevitably companies will have specific requirements. Directors have an obligation to ensure that this work is carried out appropriately bearing in mind that board meetings (and the legally required minutes thereof) provide evidence of the reasons for and the decisions taken by the board – which could provide valuable evidence should there be a DERIVATIVE claim.

Comments made by the DBIS inspectors following their investigation of the Phoenix/MG Rover collapse put this into perspective. The report highlights the following breaches by that company, most of which one would have expected to be avoided by an effective company secretary, and the dangers of other companies doing without someone with that role. The Phoenix/ MG Rover board:

- convened board meetings without notifying all directors entitled to be there;
- did not take minutes of Board meetings at which important matters were '*decided*';
- created false minutes (e.g. directors were shown to be present when they had no knowledge of the meeting and, in some cases, were out of the country);
- allowed directors to vote on matters in which they had an interest;
- allowed directors to benefit from decisions in which they had an interest;
- did not approve minutes at subsequent meetings, and so on.

One commentator stated that '*it would seem to offer an open and shut case for the directors of MG Rover Group to be disqualified for life*'.

The company secretary should:

1 Ensure the composition of the board is in accordance with the Articles, that members have been properly appointed, have declared interests etc.

2 Generate an AGENDA and notice of meetings in liaison with the chairman.

3 Ensure all data for consideration by the board accompanies the agenda or there is a date by which it will be ready and distributed. Accompanying data should be presented in the order in which it will be considered on the agenda.

4 Convene the meeting in good time. There is no legal requirement regarding the amount of notice due to be given of a board meeting but to allow the directors to be properly briefed at least seven days' notice with required data should be given. It would also be logical for the company secretary to take responsibility for compiling and updating a timetable of future meetings.

5 Ensure, if a QUORUM is required to be present before the meeting can commence, that at least members satisfying that requirement will be present to avoid wasting the time of others attending. Checks would also need to be made to ensure that, if required, there is a disinterested quorum, i.e. that any directors with interests in third parties are excluded from discussions affecting those third parties (see 8).

6 Record apologies for absence and note any late arrivals or early departures so that it can be shown who was present when any decision was taken.

7 Have available any statutory and other registers that need to be inspected and/or signed (e.g. the registers of seals, director's interests, etc.).

8 Ensure that any notifiable interests of directors (where these might affect the capacity of the director to vote or form part of the quorum) are updated.

9 Check members have all the documents required (and having available spare documents in case members have mislaid or forgotten them).

10 Ensure the meeting's supports – provision of refreshments, note-taking aids, protection against interruption, and so on, are in operation.

11 Ensure the chairman adheres to and does not overlook any item on the agenda.

12 Ensure those who speak and vote are entitled to do so (see 8 above regarding those with potential conflicts of interest).

13 Ensure the meeting does take required decisions and that these are clear and clearly understood by all present.

14 Ensure the appropriate voting power is reflected when votes are taken. In some joint venture companies, in the event of an equality of votes, directors nominated by one of the partners to the joint venture have enhanced voting rights.

15 Record the sense of the meeting in notes that will become the first draft of the minutes.

16 Prepare minutes, have them approved in draft by the chairman, and distribute to the members for approval by them at their next following meeting.

17 Keep the minutes secure. (The legal minimum is 10 years but many commentators feel it should be 'life of the company'.)

18 Make the minutes available to members of the board and the auditors.

19 Ensure action is effected as required by the meeting and reported on at the appropriate time.

20 Anticipate the level of support available, and any antipathy or opposition to, matters due to be considered by the board and briefing the chairman accordingly.

21 Be proactive in all respects.

And so on.

Authority

The company secretary is an officer of the company and, in the event of culpable non-compliance, is liable with the directors for fines and other penalties. In the event of default, there is no way such responsibility can be evaded.

The secretary has several types of authority:

■ *Actual* – by delegation from the board (via specific requirements set out in the board minutes etc.).

- *Ostensible* – since many documents require the signature of the person holding the post of company secretary at that time.
- *Derived* – from what has gone before and been accepted both internally and externally.
- *Express* – in that the secretary is appointed to hold office by law and the shareholders.

Unfortunately, it is not always the case that legislative and contractual requirements have been complied with and a newly appointed secretary should never assume that everything required to be done has been done by their precedessor. On appointment, checking the following may be advisable.

CHECKLIST   On appointment

✓ **Check authority of appointment.** A note of the appointment should be made in the board minutes, recorded in the register of secretaries and notified to CH using form AP03 within 14 days of the operative date.

✓ **Check the Articles (and, for pre-CA06 companies, the Memorandum), any changes thereto and compliance therewith.** Articles of LTDs should be reviewed at least every three years to ensure they reflect changed circumstances. Within a group it may be helpful to give all subsidiaries the same articles to aid ease of recall of requirements.

✓ **Check statutory books entries** (change of directors, secretary, shareholders etc.). Buying a pro forma combined register is advisable (alternatively a computer package can be utilised although this may not be cost-effective for a group of less than, say, 15 companies).

✓ **Locate the Certificate of Incorporation.** This Certificate records the exact name and number of the company which must be used where required, as well as its date of incorporation. If the company's name (or its type of registration – e.g. LTD to PLC) is changed, a fresh Certificate is issued by CH confirming the new name – but the number remains unchanged. The Certificate should be kept safely but no longer needs to be displayed.

✓ **Check disclosure of corporate details including NAME.** A company's name is the embodiment of what it is and does – and may have a value in its own right. As such it needs to be protected and used. The way in which it is used is subject to controls and the company secretary needs to be aware of these controls and requirements.

✓ **ANNUAL RETURN.** Check the return's filing is up-to-date and note the due date of the next return.

✓ **Ensure the accounts are filed within the time limits.**

✓ **Check the register of CHARGES is up-to-date.** Every company must have a register of charges (whether it has any charges or not).

✓ **Locate and secure the minute books.** Minutes of general meetings of the shareholders must be held at the registered office and made available for inspection and copying by such shareholders only. Minutes of board meetings can be kept anywhere and can be inspected by directors and auditors only (i.e. not by shareholders or guarantors).

✓ **Locate and secure any SEAL.** The (optional) seal is the binding signature of the company. It should be kept safely and its use recorded.

✓ **Ensure directors with interests with third parties have declared these** and brought/bring their declaration(s) up to date.

Maintaining a 'Registrar's' file

When filing items with CH, not only should a copy of every form filed be kept, but also a receipt for every document filed should be obtained. With the (still relatively few forms) that can be filed electronically this is automatic, but for companies filing hard copy, a receipt can be obtained by sending in duplicate a covering letter referring to the item enclosed (see example in REGISTRAR OF COMPANIES). Alternatively, a duplicate of the item itself or form POST 31 could be sent for stamping and return. Provided a reply paid envelope is also enclosed, CH affix an adhesive bar code to the item as a receipt. Recently CH acknowledged that over an 18-month period around 200 accounts submitted had been lost internally so a receipt may be essential evidence that at least the item was received by CH. Both a copy of the item sent and of the receipt should be added to the CH file as a permanent record of what was sent and when.

Joint and deputy company secretaries

Joint company secretaries can be appointed with each having joint responsibility and liability. Unless the company's Articles allow, all so appointed will have to sign documents requiring the company secretary's signature. Details of the appointees must be filed at CH in the normal way. A company's Articles may also permit there to be a deputy or assistant secretary. In such a case, should the company secretary be unable to act (or the position falls vacant) the role can be filled by a deputy or assistant.

Qualification

Anyone can be the company secretary of an LTD. For a PLC, CA06 requires the person appointed to hold one of several professional qualifications, although this requirement is somewhat negated by the clause also allowing the directors to appoint someone who '*appears to the directors to be capable of discharging [the] functions [of the company secretary].*'

A corporate body can act as a company secretary as can a partnership. If a partnership is used:

- in an English or Welsh company all the partners are joint secretaries of the company;
- in a Scottish company the partnership itself is the secretary.

Corporate governance

INTRODUCTION

The development of the global market has led to the formation of mega-corporations – over 50 per cent of the 100 largest 'economic entities' in the world are corporations not countries. Whilst the economic rationale for such conglomerates may be unarguable, big business means big influence and big power – it also means when one part of the global market is adversely affected this can infect the whole. This has led to widespread (and renewed) unease and to demonstrations against globalisation, particularly against meetings of the government representatives of the largest economies (the G8 and G20 meetings). The concern has been exacerbated by the fact that in some cases (particularly in companies featuring in a number of recent scandals) those who control such organisations have seemed to be virtually unaccountable and unrepentant; whilst the level of cavalier risk taking at senior levels in some financial services organisations seen prior to the banking crisis in 2007–8 is breathtaking.

Size equates to power

Paralleling the above there had also been for some time concern that many boards of large boards were and are virtually self-perpetuating. A common theme was that shareholders should be encouraged to exercise in practice the control they had in theory. Although the principles and practice of the movement that became known as 'corporate governance' (CG) may be sound, they must have been called into question by the recently exposed activities – which in some cases it is not too extreme to describe as crass stupidity at the most senior level of management – of some banking and finance houses albeit encouraged in the USA by governmental edicts and in the UK by sound regulations being watered down by the then Government. The problem with the concept is that it assumes reasonable and responsible behaviour and decisions and a common sense (commercial 'nous') approach to business – if that base is lacking then no amount of words and checklists and governance guidance that have been developed over nearly two decades can truly be effective.

Putting morality into capitalism – 'corporate governance'

In 1991 the Cadbury Committee reported on the *Financial Aspects of Corporate Governance* and its conclusions became known as the 'Cadbury Code'. The aim was to make boards of companies more accountable. In the decade following the setting up of the Cadbury committee (which published its report '*A Code of Best Practice*' in 1992), five further committees – Greenbury, Hampel, Higgs, Smith and Turnbull – gave further consideration to the topic. The amalgamation of the advice of these committees was encapsulated into what is now known as the UK Corporate Governance Code (UKCGC) with which the Stock Exchange expects all listed PLCs to comply – or, if they do not, to explain their reasons. Although non-listed companies are not required to observe these requirements, many corporate entities may either be forced to do so by public and employee opinion or will wish to subscribe to the principles, or at least the recommendations of the original committee. CG in terms of a constant examination of the way in which companies operate, relates to the environment, produce and sell goods, employ and cease to employ people, including their social responsibility (which is also required to be reported on in the annual reports of listed PLCs and large LTDs), is a matter of considerable and widespread concern which is unlikely to do anything other than grow.

The Code

UKCGC's main principles are:

1 Every company should be headed by an effective board collectively responsible for the success of the company.
2 There should be a clear division at the top for the running of the board and the running of the business. No one individual should have unfettered powers.
3 The board should contain balance of executives and (in particular) independent non-executives so that no one group can dominate.
4 The board must identify in the annual report those non-executives that it considers to be independent.
5 There should be a formal rigorous and transparent procedure for appointing new directors.
6 The board should be provided with timely information in a form and of the quality necessary for it to do its job. All directors should receive induction upon appointment and should regularly update and refresh their skills and knowledge.
7 The board should annually review formally and rigorously its own performance, that of its committees and that of its individual directors.

8   Remuneration should be sufficient and adequate to attract, retain and motivate directors of the right quality but not to be more than necessary. A significant proportion should be linked to corporate and personal performance.

9   There should be a formal and transparent procedure for developing policy on executive pay and perks and for fixing the amounts for individual directors. No director should be involved in setting their own remuneration.

10 The board should present a balanced and understandable assessment of the company's position and prospects.

11 The board should maintain a sound system of internal control; to safeguard shareholder's investments and the company's assets.

12 The board should establish formal and transparent arrangements for considering how they shall apply the financial and internal control principles and for maintaining appropriate auditor relations.

13 The board has a duty to ensure that a satisfactory dialogue takes place with shareholders based upon a mutual understanding of objectives.

14 The AGM should be used to communicate with investors and encourage their participation.

15 Institutional shareholders should enter into a dialogue with companies based upon a mutual understanding of objectives.

16 All relevant factors should be weighed and examined when evaluating governance disclosures (particularly board structure and composition).

17 Institutional shareholders have a duty to make considered use of their votes.

There are supporting principles for each of the above general principles explaining how the general principles are to be implemented.

Updating the Code

Revised Code

In 2008 the Financial Reporting Council published a revised Code. The main changes were:

- removal of the restriction that an individual should be chairman of only one FTSE100 company, and
- permitting the chairman of a listed PLC (of companies below the FTSE 350) to be a member of (but not the chairman) of the audit committee as long as he was considered independent when appointed.

In addition companies are required to include in their annual report, statements:

- so that its shareholders could evaluate how the company has applied the main principles in the Code;
- showing whether the company has complied or not complied with the Code. If there is non-compliance, details of the provisions broken and . reasons for such must be stated.

There are specific requirements for disclosures as follows:

- how the board operates; the types of decisions taken by the board and those that are delegated to management;
- the names of the chairman, deputy chairman (if applicable), the chief executive, the senior independent director and the chairman and members of the various board committees (i.e. nomination, audit and remuneration);
- the number of board and board committees meetings; and individual attendance at both by directors (many companies include a chart showing how many were attended by each director during the period under review);
- the names of non-executive directors that are independent (and the reasons for that assessment);
- any significant commitment(s) of the chairman outside the company;
- the manner in which the board, its committees and members are evaluated;
- the procedure by which the board (especially non-executive directors) understand the views of the company's major shareholders.

Companies must also state:

- how the board's nomination committee carries out its work in finding new board appointees and explaining whether the advice of external advisers has been sought regarding the appointment of the chairman or deputy chairman;
- how the board's remuneration committee complies with the requirements of the Directors' Remuneration Report Regulations 2002;
- whether any executive directors serve as non-executive directors of other companies and, if paid, whether the directors retain such earnings;
- statements explaining the directors' responsibility for preparing the accounts and (from the auditors) their reporting responsibilities;
- that, subject to any qualifications, and/or with assumptions used, the business is a going concern;
- that the board has conducted a review of the effectiveness of the internal controls used by the company;
- details of the work of the board's audit committee and, (if applicable) the reasons for not using an internal audit function;
- should the board have refused to accept a report and recommendations from the audit committee regarding the appointment/retention of the external auditors, the reasons for the rejection;

- details of any non-audit work the external auditor carries out for the company.

Information required to be disclosed either in the annual report or on the company's website, include:

- the terms of reference of the board's committees (nomination, remuneration and audit) explaining their roles and authority;
- the terms and conditions of appointment of the non-executive directors;
- a statement, if any remuneration consultants were appointed, of whether they had any other connections with the company.

In addition, where there is a resolution regarding the re-election of directors/auditors, the company must provide:

- such biographical details that will enable shareholders to take an informed decision on their election or re-election;
- the reason(s) for someone being elected to a non-executive directorship;
- if the re-election of a non-executive director is to be considered, the chairman's confirmation that the performance of the person has been evaluated and has been found to be effective;
- if the re-election of an auditor is to be considered and the audit committee's recommendation is not accepted by the board, a statement showing both the recommendation and the reasons for the board opposing such recommendation.

Current accounting periods

For all current accounting periods traded companies are also required:

- To stress the chairmanship's leadership role on the board and explain how directors are given adequate, accurate and timely information. The (annually elected) chairman should agree individual director's development requirements.
- To ensure directors rigorously challenge substantive issues with strength of character. Non-executives should have dedicated information flows. The board should have a balance of skills, experience and independence. Board evaluation should be carried out at least every three years.
- To ensure there is a link between remuneration and risk policy. Non-financial metrics should be used to measure performance. Non-executives should not be paid on performance-related criteria.
- To set up RISK committees at board level with the board's responsibility clearly demonstrated. Business models and financial strategies should be stated in the annual report.

As well as a committee focusing on the control of risk, there should be separate committees dealing with audit matters, the nomination and induction of new directors and remuneration matters.

Alternative Investment Market (AIM) company obligations

Compliance assistance for smaller quoted companies is provided in the Quoted Companies Alliance (QCA) 'Guidelines'. The recommendations include:

- a schedule of matters for board attention/decision should be compiled;
- the roles of chairman and chief executive should not be exercised by the same person;
- the company should have at least two independent non-executive directors;
- all directors should seek re-election regularly;
- audit, remuneration and nomination committees should be established;
- there should be a regular supply of management information in a timely manner to enable the board to discharge its duties;
- the board should regularly review the effectiveness of the internal controls and report this fact to the shareholders;
- the board as a whole has responsibility for ensuring that a satisfactory dialogue takes place with shareholders, based on a mutual understanding of objectives.

Evaluation

To assist with the process of checking how effective a company's commitment to the principles and practice of effective corporate governance is, ICSA (in conjunction with Kingfisher plc) developed an evaluation process which entails a three-year cycle, to assess the framework within which the board operates. The evaluation involves each board member, not only in identifying the procedures and processes of the board, but also in deciding the action to take where there is a need for improvement. The board can decide whether or not to publicise the review, but if progress on areas have not been made in the second and third years of the process, ICSA will not allow its name to be used in conjunction with the process. Such is the concern that boards should be made accountable in this way that it may be advisable for boards to prepare for the possibility of this being a requirement that could be imposed on them. Details of the ICSA process which include:

- assessing the balance of skills within each board;

- identifying attributes required for any new appointments;
- reviewing practices and procedures to improve efficiency and effectiveness;
- considering the effectiveness of each board's decision-making process; and
- recognising the board's outputs and achievements

are available from ICSA Corporate Services Policy Unit, 16 Park Crescent, London W1B 1AH.

Meaning for and effect on LTDs?

The main thrust of the foregoing affects listed PLCs which must either comply or explain why not. However, corporate governance principles could be argued to be applicable to all companies – listed or not. Indeed many large charities have voluntarily adopted at least some of such principles. Most LTDs will feel that even the shorter AIM company code or QCA guidelines are too complex for them although some of the principles and practice could be valuable, particularly where there are shareholders not on the board. However, it could be argued that such boards could adopt a much 'slimmed down' code including (for example):

- recognition that the board is responsible for the success of the company and must organise itself to provide skills and experience suitable to achieve that end;
- board decisions as well as decisions of the owners should be transparent to all;
- board decisions must be taken in the best interests of the entity as a whole recognising the interests of the various stakeholders in the company (see DIRECTORS – DUTIES AND LIABILITIES), sublimating their personal interests if necessary;
- it is the board's direct responsibility for obtaining and providing accurate and reliable financial and supporting information;
- ongoing RISK assessment.

These items should form a base to which other aspects of the combined code could be added as required.

The Institute of Directors (IoD) CG Guidance and Principles for unlisted companies (**www.iod.com**) suggests that the foundations of good governance include:

- Acceptance that delegation of authority should be approached systematically with clear demarcations of where responsibility lies.
- Setting up a system of checks and balances so that no single person has 'unfettered power over decision-making'. It is recognised that this may be difficult in smaller companies where often there may be autocratic

control. Whilst this may be inevitable where the founder continues to run an expanding organisation, this may not be a sustainable model for the longer term.

- Recognition that professional decision-making is essential. This should emanate in general from the board and in particular from the chairman (see BOARD MEETINGS) who needs to create an effective team at the top – with open discussion encouraged. There needs to be clear documentation of all decisions with promulgation to all involved.
- Delineating clearly the chain of command with meaningful accountability at all levels.
- Ensuring transparency of the company's activities and ethos to encourage the highest standards of behaviour.
- Avoiding conflicts of interest where ever possible; but, if impossible, declaring these so that there is complete transparency of activities.
- Ensuring incentives are related to genuine personal and team performance.

The challenge for the company secretary

The person ideally suited to monitor CG issues may be the company secretary, since that person fields legal compliance issues and CG requirements are simply an extension of legal obligations. Particularly if he is not also a director, the company secretary should be able to have an objective view of activities and control of all the items listed and be able to advise when there is deviation from the principles and practice. If a system of 'checks and balances' is required it is the company secretary who should be ideally placed to provide impartial input. (Of course the secretary is envisaged as the person who would provide secretarial support for committees required to be appointed by fully listed PLCs.)

Postscript

In the light of recent history it seems extremely unlikely that however detailed and complex legislation or codes become, they are powerless to prevent imprudent decisions being made at very senior levels, particularly where the incentive of large bonuses can lead to a suppression of objective risk assessment. One argument is that, where organisations become 'too big to fail', there seems little need for them to assess risks – if the risky investment works, the perpetrators gain exorbitant bonuses, whilst if they fail the Government is forced to step in. This is surely untenable. The exorbitant bonuses that banks, bailed out by the UK taxpayer, are paying post collapse belie belief and raise the question 'have they learned nothing?' Indeed an onlooker can be excused for wondering what so-clever activities generated such payments? Those in receipt are unlikely to seek alternative employment elsewhere were the bonuses scrapped – although given their record this might be best – at least for the UK taxpayer. As the under Secretary of State for Trade stated '*(these) bonuses contributed to excessive risk taking*'.

Cupidity can lead to and encourage stupidity unless adequate controls and checks are in place – this is the real challenge for corporate governance. As the former head of risk at the (but for State and Lloyds Bank Plc intervention) failed HBOS bank said '*I strongly believe that the real underlying cause of all the problems was … a total failure of all key aspects of Corporate Governance.*' It was even more of a failure in his case since, having warned directors in the bank of the '*too high level of risk the bank was taking on*', they fired him. HBOS was a listed PLC required to have a whistle-blowers policy and to protect people who made comments such as these. It is all very well those formerly in charge apologising to their shareholders and employees later – talk is cheap and does nothing to repay the debts incurred. It seems that the kind of attitude of senior managers and directors referred to above is not an isolated incident. Post-crash, a City firm of headhunters surveyed 50 managers involved in compliance and internal audit working for FTSE 100 companies and discovered that half of them did not believe that they had sufficient influence to manage risk properly in their organisations; indeed 13 per cent stated that '*they were not influential at all*'. If this is so it would seem that a substantial proportion of some of the UK's largest companies are paying little more than lip service to corporate governance or risk assessment, which was not the idea behind the movement at all. Indeed as Hector Sands, head of the Financial Services Authority stated: '*Corporate governance activists may be able to hold their heads high – but they are few and far between*'.

Derivative claims

INTRODUCTION

CA06 (s.260/9) enhances shareholders' rights against directors. If a shareholder believes that a director has failed to act in the best interests of the company and/or that the company has suffered loss because of a director's *'actual or proposed act or omission involving negligence, default, breach of duty or breach of trust'*, he can initiate legal action against the director *on the company's behalf* (hence it being termed 'derivative').

Taking action

Shareholders have always been able to sue directors for failing to act in accordance with the provisions of their company's Memorandum and/or Articles. Since the Articles are the rules under which the company is to be directed any breach means that those responsible are acting *'ultra vires'* (beyond their powers), and can be held liable for any losses. If directors allowed the company to act outside its objects clauses (set out in pre-CA06 companies' Memorandums) this was also acting *ultra vires*. However, this last 'offence' was diluted by CA89 which allowed the shareholders retrospectively to authorise acts outside a company's objects clause – although directors who breached the requirements could still be held liable. Prosecuting an action against directors acting *ultra vires*, was not an easy process but CA06 makes it easier for a shareholder to take such action on behalf of the company. If the claim is successful, it is the company (not the shareholder initiating the action) that benefits, at the director's expense.

This right to initiate such claims has changed the previous situation that a director was not normally held liable for making a 'wrong' decision provided it was made in good faith, to one where a director can be held liable for an act (or omission) even if it is made in good faith and the person taking the decision does not benefit from that decision. With hindsight everyone can always make impeccable and correct judgements, but directors have to take decisions on what is known at the time – responding to many (sometimes conflicting) pressures – not least, under CA06, taking account of the interests of a number of *'stakeholders'*. If it is easier for members to take legal action, making a contemporaneous record (i.e. detailed MINUTES) available as a defence may assume an even more important facet of company administration and record, showing what were the parameters within which the decision was made *at that time*.

Obviously in companies where all the members are directors, the possibility of facing a derivative claim is minimal (although there can be dissent and enmity in family-owned companies!). However, where there are 'outside' members (i.e. shareholders not on, or represented on, the board) the possibility of a derivative claim could be far more likely, as the number of instances where a director could be accused of failing to act in the best interests of the company/shareholders could be considerable.

Disgruntled shareholders' actions

It is not impossible to imagine a scenario where an individual shareholder, angry at some action (or perceived action) or inaction of the director, decides to initiate a claim; or simply a situation where a shareholder thinks he might benefit from a 'payment to desist' as a result of threatening such action. However, to bring a derivative action, a shareholder must firstly apply to the Court for the right to initiate it. Only with Court sanction can the action proceed. Traditionally, Courts have always been loath to interfere in the internal activities of companies and if this precedent is followed perhaps the number of such actions may not be as large as was initially contemplated by some commentators.

A claim will not be allowed to proceed if:

- the act (or omission) complained of has since been ratified by the company; or
- it is unreasonable (e.g. the act complained of is such that a person trying to promote the success of the company would not make such a claim).

The Court has discretion taking into account the views of independent shareholders and:

- whether the person bringing the claim is acting in good faith;
- the relevant importance of the claim to a person trying to promote the success of the company;
- whether the matter that is the subject of the claim is likely to be authorised by the company;
- whether the member could bring the claim in their own right and/or whether the company itself had already decided not to bring such a claim.

Notes

1   Unless they are charities, banks etc., companies whose turnover is less than £6.5 million do not need to have their accounts audited. Directors of such companies might find it prudent to consider whether retaining the independent view of their figures might help dissuade potential derivative claimants. Indeed, the very fact that there are independent persons reviewing company and board actions may deter even disgruntled shareholders from taking such action.

2   The EU has proposed that companies with turnover of less than €1,000,000 would not need to file accounts. This could be dangerous for directors of companies with shareholders not on the board.

3   In the event of a claim being prosecuted and the Court finding it to be unreasonable, costs can be awarded against the claimant. Conversely if the Court feels it was a reasonable case, the Court could award costs even to an unsuccessful claimant.

Directors: appointment, induction and evaluation

INTRODUCTION

One of the COMPANY SECRETARY'S prime responsibilities should be to support the directors and provide them with guidance to their duties, responsibilities, obligations and expectations. Such guidance could be essential on the appointment of a new director – particularly a promotion from within. Most managers will appropriately 'fight their own corner' to obtain investment and the best deal etc. for 'their' department. As a director, however, such 'vested interests' must be sublimated to the 'collective responsibility' concept of board work. This requires directors to take decisions which are in the best interests of the company as a whole (even if those decisions are diametrically opposed to the interests of a particular director's department) and to support such decisions when taken – even if they argued and voted against it. Under their fiduciary duty to the company, directors must put its interests before any other interest, including their own.

Numbers of directors

Articles very often state that there will be a minimum number of directors, for example, two – which is compulsory for PLCs. Some Articles also specify a maximum number and care needs to be taken that either such a maximum is not exceeded or, before directors additional to the maximum are appointed, the Articles are changed to permit this. Any 'directors' appointed in excess of a specified maximum could find themselves personally liable for their actions on behalf of the company.

Eligibility for directorship

1   Both real and corporate persons can be directors. However, there must be at least one real person on every board.
2   The minimum age for a UK director is 16.
3   There is no upper legal age limit. Any stated maximum age could be subject to challenge under age discrimination legislation.
4   A person cannot be a director during a period of disqualification – either in the UK or in an overseas jurisdiction.
5   A person cannot be a director during any period he is sectioned under

the Mental Health Act or is an undischarged bankrupt (unless the Court permits).

6   The company's auditor cannot be a director.

7   Neither a beneficed clergyman nor a convict can be a director.

8   Individual Articles may prohibit other persons from being directors.

Aspects of directorship

All directors are of equal status with no distinction between executive and non-executive directors, or between a director properly appointed in accordance with the Articles and company law and a shadow director. The board is usually given the right under the company's ARTICLES to make a 'casual' appointment to the board (i.e. the appointment by the board of an additional director) normally only at a properly constituted and convened board meeting. Since ultimately directors are appointed by shareholders, the Articles usually require that all those so appointed must retire at the next meeting of the members to seek confirmation of their appointment.

The specific requirements of the ARTICLES must be complied with. Thus there should be a minuted Board resolution, for example:

'It was unanimously agreed that Mr J Bloggs be appointed a director of the Company with effect from [date]'

or, if the appointment is required to be made immediately,

'It was unanimously agreed that Mr J Bloggs be and he hereby is appointed a director of the Company.'

Registering the appointment

Form AP01 (AP02 for corporate directors) must be sent to CH within 14 days. This form must be signed by a serving officer of the company, and the newly appointed director must sign the 'consent to act' section of the form. Personal details of the director must be recorded in the statutory books of the company as follows.

Register of directors

The director's name, date of birth, private address and (if the director does not want his private address made public) a service address (for public disclosure) must be inserted in this register. Copies of this information are included on form AP01, where as well as signing to indicate their consent to act (to ensure that the director knows of the appointment), full details (including any former name) must be given. Failure to provide and file such personal data is an offence subject to both initial and daily fines. Whilst the director's private address must be disclosed to CH in case official notice (e.g. for failure to file accounts, annual return, etc.) has to be served, a 'service address' can be supplied to be treated as the address available for public scrutiny.

All changes to the details (e.g. names, nationality, address, etc.) must also be entered in the register and advised on form CH01. Although the residential address will not be available publicly, CH is obliged to disclose residential addresses if required by the Court, and to specified authorities and credit reference agencies.

Similarly on termination of the appointment the effective date must be entered in the register and filed with CH (using form TM01) within 14 days.

Notes

1 The protection of personal addresses may be of limited protection, since some older CH records are not yet 'screened'. If someone asks for an annual return prior to say 1995, the private address of a person who was then a director (unless he has since moved) will be available.
2 Married female directors (and company secretaries) are required to disclose their maiden name and any previous married surnames.

Register of directors' share interests

For PLCs, details of each director's interests in the shares of the company and any subsidiary, fellow subsidiary or holding company must also be notified to the company within five days of the person's appointment and all changes thereafter must be separately notified within five days of their occurrence. This obligation not only relates to shares held personally by the director, but also to shares held by a director's spouse or partner and any infant children – what are known as 'connected persons' (see s.809 CA06).

In addition, any share options (and changes including their exercise) issued by the company to a director or his connected persons must also be recorded.

The only exceptions to this rule are:

■ if the director holds the shares only as trustee (i.e. he has no personal interest in them);
■ if the director is also a director of the company's holding company which already holds all such details; or
■ if the holding is in a company incorporated overseas.

LTDs are no longer required to keep this register although it may be useful to retain it (deleting the word 'share' from its title) to serve as a record of any interests the director has in or with third parties etc.

Register of directors' interests in contracts/third parties

Under ss.175–185 CA06, directors are obliged to notify their company of any interest they may have in contracts (or proposed contracts) being made by the company with a third party. Interests are defined as either general or specific.

- *General* – the director has an interest in all matters concerning a named third party. Such a statement could be made upon the director's appointment and/or when it occurs.
- *Specific* – a director has an interest in a particular contract. Such a declaration must be made at the first board meeting which considers the proposed contract, or on the director acquiring or becoming aware of the interest. There is no explicit requirement for the company to keep a register of such interests but directors themselves may feel it prudent that it should be kept as evidence that they have informed the company, not least since failure to notify an interest is an offence punishable by initial and daily fines. In addition it may be a valuable defence should there be an investigation under the Bribery Act (see AUTHORITY CONTROL). As well as using this register as a document of record it may be advisable for it to be brought to every board meeting so that the members of the board can see if any director has an interest (or new interest) in any matter under discussion (see MINUTES).

To compile such a register directors could be asked to state on appointment as well as annually thereafter (whether or not there have been any changes) whether they have any interests in third parties that could conflict with those of the company. At the same time directors could be asked to confirm that they have not been disqualified both in the UK and overseas.

Example	Confirmation of interests and non-disqualification
	To [Board of company – name]
	Name [of director]...................... Date....................
	I confirm that
	* I am not disqualified from acting as a director under either UK law or the legislative process of another country.
	* I nor any connected person have any interests with third parties with which the company may do business
	* I and/or a connected person have the following interests in third parties with which the company does or may do business [give details]
	* Delete as applicable
	Signed...............................

Notes

- *'Connected persons'* are defined in ss.252–4 CA06 as spouse, civil partner, (and any person with whom the director lives as partner in an enduring family relationship), child or stepchild (up to age 18), parents and any company or body corporate in which the director has a voting interest of 20 per cent or more.
- Obviously circumstances change and it may be prudent to ask for such disclosure on occurrence (when it could be entered in the register of directors' interests) and by completion of an updated form, annually (say at the first board meeting each new financial year).
- Some organisations (as a result of the implications of the Bribery Act) also require a statement of all instances of providing entertainment and being entertained in an annual declaration. Alternatively this could be achieved by entries being made in the register of directors' interests.
- Not all directors involved in failed companies are disqualified and to provide such 'track record' information, business information/credit agency Experian (**www.experian.com/bi**) maintains a database showing the names of directors who have previously been involved in such companies.

Induction

Ideally there should be a structured process by which new directors are made familiar with the company and the board activities. Under CORPORATE GOVERNANCE requirements the company must be proactive in this and consider a programme by which a director is provided with the information and support so that he can swiftly become an effective board member. This can be considered in two parts – firstly from the 'relationships' viewpoint, and secondly from the personal familiarisation viewpoint. The FRC 'Guidance on Board Effectiveness' defines an effective board as one that:

- provides direction for management;
- demonstrates ethical leadership;
- creates a performance culture;
- makes well-informed and high-quality decisions;
- is accountable;
- thinks carefully about its governance arrangements;
- and creates the right framework for helping directors meet their statutory duties.

Experience indicates that whilst most of these are, almost instinctively, addressed by most boards (and the companies of those that don't tend to fail) that last item is often overlooked. Guiding directors regarding their obligations may be a task for the company secretary.

CHECKLIST   Board induction – I

Preparation
✓ Set up a budget to cover board appointment induction.
✓ Appoint a senior director to oversee the process.
✓ List shareholders and provide this to the new director possibly arranging meetings with major holders.
✓ List all advisers and scope and areas of work.

Provide
✓ Details of any shareholders' agreement.
✓ Commentary to and copy of strategy of company.
✓ Copies of minutes and supporting papers.
✓ Copies of accounts.
✓ Summary of key factors and suggested methods of achieving.
✓ Current budget (and performance to date with commentary explaining variations).
✓ Banking arrangements, charges, covenants etc.
✓ Details of current products/services and developments.
✓ Promotional and advertising plans.
✓ Details of all locations and status (freehold, leasehold etc.).
✓ Details of any outstanding legal actions.
✓ Staff details, newsletters, works council minutes etc.
✓ Organisation chart(s).
✓ Ethical and/or corporate social responsibility statement.
✓ Relationship with non-executives/executives/company secretary.
✓ Personal details of such directors and guidance to areas of operation.
✓ Monitoring of the performance of both the board and individual members.
✓ Name and personal details of board member appointed to mentor the newcomer.

Many directors are appointed 'from within' – that is, promoted from management. However, accepting a directorship requires a quantum leap from operating as a manager and it is important that those undertaking the job realise what is required of them. Companies must discover the range of knowledge of their directors, and supply means by which gaps in that knowledge are filled. Directors have personal legal liability for their companies' activities. Literally *'the buck stops in the boardroom'* and thus those in the boardroom need to know for what they have responsibility. If any answers to the questions in the following checklist are 'no' – research may be necessary to fill the gap. Almost certainly this will be on-going since many aspects are constantly changing. It might be helpful for a brief précis of legislative and other changes to be presented at each board meeting.

CHECKLIST   Directors induction – 1

Legal obligations

Does the director understand the legislative environment under which the company operates e.g.:

✓   the basis and outline of company law?
✓   the latest commercial legislation, including competition law?
✓   outline requirements of employment law?
✓   general requirements of other legislation specifically affecting the company?
✓   the internal operating rules of the company (e.g. the Articles)?
✓   has the chairman checked the scope of such knowledge?
✓   that the board are responsible for the information required to be regularly filed at CH?
✓   (if a listed PLC) the latest requirements under CORPORATE GOVERNANCE?

Finance

Does the director understand:

✓   the management and published accounts and ancillary data?
✓   that he has joint personal responsibility for the figures?
✓   the method by which queries should be raised?
✓   that, since he must always be confident of the future solvency of the company, he should not allow credit to be taken on when it might not be paid on the due date or within a reasonable time thereof?
✓   that commitment to expenditure on behalf of the company should only be in accordance with the regularly reviewed authority / risk chart?

Board work

Does the director realise:

✓   that he has a fiduciary duty to the company and must always put its interests first and foremost (sublimating his own and, if applicable, his departments' interests)?
✓   that for the company's success, its aims and the means to attain those aims must be delineated (and updated regularly)?
✓   that he has an implied obligation to attend board meetings – and to contribute to the discussion (which infers that he is satisfactorily briefed on all matters)?
✓   that he should always declare an interest in any third party with which the company is dealing?
✓   that he should always exercise his decision-making process independently of other directors (even if this means being in a minority of one)?
✓   that minutes should be read and agreed (or objected to and corrected) and not passed without consideration?
✓   that his role is proactive not reactive – he must make things happen?
✓   that the performance of every board member should be regularly and formally assessed?

✓   that he should insist (except in emergency) that at least two working days are allowed between the receipt of items (other than routine matters) and a decision time?

✓   that he should insist decisions are properly minuted and that any requested dissent is included?

✓   that if there are matters of which he is unaware (both in and outside the board room) that this should be made clear and he must take steps to obtain the information?

Morality

Has the director:

✓   been given a copy of the code of gifts, ethics, corporate governance and/or any other similar requirements?

✓   shown that his knowledge of such items is adequate?

✓   been told that bribes inducements etc. must not be offered or made by any person on behalf of the company (and that he could be personally criminally liable if this occurs)?

✓   if he becomes aware of wrongdoing, been told that he should take immediate steps to ensure it ceases and the errors are, if at all possible, rectified?

Accountability

Does the director realise:

✓   that he is answerable to the shareholders for the activities and actions of the company and its results?

✓   that he is expected to take risks but only after a proper assessment of those risks and their potential outcome? (Note: This may not be applicable for charitable companies since, under Charity law, risks must not be taken.)

✓   that contingency and disaster recovery plans should be prepared and updated covering all major eventualities?

✓   that he is answerable to the various regulatory authorities for the activities of the company and its employees?

The value of this kind of checklist is that unless the director can truthfully answer 'yes' to each question, it demonstrates an area where knowledge is incomplete.

Listed PLCs are required to ensure those appointed to the board undergo a process of induction. The above checklist is a non-authoritative (and non-exhaustive) checklist which can act as a base to try to comply with this requirement. Whilst it may be tempting for directors of non-listed PLCs and LTDs to feel they can ignore the above, since under company law there is no differentiation between the types of companies or the obligations of their directors, they too are assumed to be able to answer 'yes'. Ignorance of the law is no excuse.

Responsibility

A board of directors acts as an entity with shared (collective) responsibility for all the company activities. Irrespective of his executive responsibilities for a particular discipline, a director must take decisions, and share in the overall decision-making process in the interests of the company. This could mean that the director must support a board decision which is detrimental to the interests of the discipline he heads. Once the decision has been made, even a dissenting director must accept it and work to make it happen. If a director finds a material decision impossible, and cannot persuade the other directors to change their views, his only recourse may be to resign.

Evaluating directors

Listed PLCs are required to ensure that the performance of each director is evaluated each year and the recommendation for boards of FTSE350 companies is that such evaluation should be sourced externally. The effectiveness of the board as a whole as well as that of individual members should be monitored. This could include examining:

- the skills within the board available to deal with the challenges facing the company;
- the validity and quality of board discussions and decisions dealing with such challenges;
- the means by which, as well as quality of, information is made available to the board to enable it to make informed decisions;
- the procedures by which board decisions are communicated and promulgated;
- the effectiveness of each individual and the way in which they inter-relate to one another;
- (for companies subject to the UK Corporate Governance Code) the relationship between chairman and senior independent director, chairman and company secretary, and executive and non-executive directors etc.

The FRC 'Guidance on Board Effectiveness' recommends that boards should commission an outside body to judge the effectiveness. For boards not wishing to use (and pay for) such external facility, determining the answers to the following might be applicable:

CHECKLIST   Evaluation

In the past year has the director:

✓   contributed to (and to what extent *) and worked towards implementing the decisions arrived at by the board?
✓   contributed (*) effectively and validly to the corporate strategy decision making?
✓   assisted (*) in the formulation of the aims and purposes of the company and board and worked to the implementation of these?
✓   helped (*) ensure that short term decisions have not been made which impede the progress to the long term strategy?
✓   helped (*) formulate/update, promulgate and ensured adherence to an internal code of ethics, as well as its own Constitution (i.e. the Memorandum and Articles) and, if a listed PLC, the listing agreement?
✓   promoted (*) the corporate entity and developed products/services for the future?
✓   updated his own skills and knowledge and made them available at board level (and through board members and management at all levels)?
✓   motivated (*) the team to perform well and monitored results?
✓   applied controls over the commitment of the company to contracts, etc., ensured adequate authority control over all purchases?
✓   displayed a comprehensive understanding of the financial records and reports of the company?
✓   assisted (*) effectively in the expansion of the company based on well-researched, well-prepared, and well-considered, plans?
✓   developed contingency plans to protect the company's earning capacity in the event of a downturn or change in demand, and the effects of possible disasters affecting operations?
✓   helped protect the corporate entity and the products/services from criticism, attack and loss as far as possible?
✓   ensured there is adequate comprehension of all new legislative enactments affecting the organisation?
✓   made effective contributions (*) but properly independent attitude at all Board meetings?
✓   applied the corporate governance principles and ensured such principles (as applicable) have been adopted by the board?

and so on.

Note

ICSA provides a service enabling boards to comply with the requirement under the corporate governance code to assess the effectiveness of their directors by:

■   assessing the balance of skills within each board;

- identifying attributes required for any new appointments;
- reviewing practices and procedures to improve efficiency and effectiveness;
- considering the effectiveness of each board's decision-making process; and
- recognising the board's outputs and achievements.

New developments

The EU wants PLC boards to be 30 per cent female by 2015 and 40 per cent by 2020. The statistics regarding female directors of listed companies are depressing – there are only 130 (around 12.5 per cent of the total) female directors serving on the boards of the top 100 listed PLCs whilst the statistics for the FTSE 250 boards are worse – under 8 per cent are female. The UK Government's strategy is to encourage the voluntary appointment of more women to such boards to achieve 25 per cent by 2015. However, if the voluntary approach fails listed PLCs may be obliged to appoint a female quota. This was accomplished fairly successfully by Norway some years ago and France and Spain have similar initiatives. The Government is also committed to ensuring that half the appointees to the boards of public bodies are female by 2015.

Directors: employment status

INTRODUCTION

CA06 S.250 repeats the earlier 'definition' of a director as *'any person occupying the position of director by whatever name called'*. Generally, anyone who controls, or contributes to the control of, a company is regarded (even if they do not use the title 'director') as a director, and as such, having a fiduciary duty and obligation to the company, i.e. they must act in the utmost good faith putting the interests of the company first. Directors are 'officers' of the company but what is unclear is whether they are also employees.

Employment test

Although directors may be paid via the company's payroll, with PAYE and NI contributions deducted, this, of itself, does not make them employees. However, given their considerable potential liabilities, it is arguable that executive directors should have the protection of employment legislation. But the evidence must support that relationship.

Case study	Judged to be an employee/director
	In *Pemberton v Claimstart t/a Parkin Westbury & Co*, Mrs Pemberton owned a third of the shares of the company of which she was a director and company secretary. The company was put into receivership, and following her dismissal by the Receiver, she claimed unfair dismissal. The tribunal decided she was not an employee and thus they had no jurisdiction to hear her claim. This was perhaps unsurprising since the decisions in the *Fleming* and *Bottrill* cases (see below) had not been promulgated at the time. However, the EAT held that being a shareholder did *not* preclude her from also being an employee.

The EAT suggested companies should ask the following questions:

- Is the employment salary determined by the board?
- Is the salary commensurate with responsibilities?

- How much remuneration does the director receive via dividends (i.e. do they draw the bulk of remuneration via dividends or salary)?
- Are directors listed as employees in the company's 'wages book'?
- Have their earnings increased in the last three years (if so it would suggest employment)?
- How are directors' salaries assessed?
- Did the board meet in the ordinary course of business or not? If not then that would suggest there was no genuine employment relationship between the parties.

To avoid disputes, the dual or triple (i.e. shareholder, director and employee) relationship with the company should be clearly evidenced in writing. If an executive director has virtually the same relationship with their company as that of an employee (probably the case for executive directors of the vast majority of LTDs and many PLCs) it should be evidenced.

Keeping separate records of the decisions of what could be loosely said to be those exercising strategical control (shareholders), tactical control and fiduciary duty (directors and other officers) and administrative control and duty of fidelity (employees) might aid the identification of the true (and possibly multi-faceted) relationship.

Service contract

The duties to be undertaken by directors for the company are customarily controlled by and set out in a document termed a 'service contract' negotiated between the director and the company on an individual basis. Whilst this will specify most of the normal details to be enjoyed by the average employee – pay, holiday, title and duties, sickness benefit, notice and termination and so on – it will not necessarily contain all the items required to be included in a contract of employment. It will often contain restrictions on the work that can be undertaken immediately after its termination which may be more restrictive than those for an ordinary employee and even a 'garden leave' (i.e. enforced idleness) clause. The service contract is itself governed by company law in that it must be made available for inspection by shareholders for two hours each working day. If it is required that the director should also be regarded as an employee, then the service contract must also address the requirements to be stated under employment law.

Clarify the relationship

Ideally a contract seeking to evidence a dual relationship of officer and employee should specify:

- that the subject of the contract is an employee as well as a director, and

- that it is the 'principal statement' required under the Employment Rights Act 1996 as well as being the service contract required to be displayed under company law.

An example of wording is given below, but legal advice should be taken to ensure proper drafting of the appropriate clauses – and their relationship to the subject company and director.

Many Articles require a proportion (very often, a third) of the board to retire, 'by rotation', at the company's Annual GENERAL MEETING and to offer themselves for re-election. If rotation is required, directors who have been in office longest must put themselves forward for re-election. Should the shareholders either refuse to re-elect or simply dismiss the director, this will almost certainly entail an action for breach of the director's service contract, but the situation regarding his employment rights may remain unclear. Indeed, if the person has duties other than his duties as a director, it could be argued that these (and thus employment) continue, regardless of the cessation of the appointment as director.

Legal precedents

Although there have been a number of cases which found that shareholding directors were not also employees in the main these have now been overtaken by the following decisions:

Case studies	Determining twin/triple relationships
	In *Secretary of State for Trade & Industry v Bottrill* and *Secretary of State v Fleming* the Courts commented that '*the fact of majority shareholding* [of a director] *was no more than a relevant factor in determining whether* [he] *was also an employee … there was no rule of law which said that a majority (controlling) director could not* [also] *be an employee*'.
	In *Heffer v Secretary of State for Trade & Industry* the EAT stated:
	• a limited company is a distinct legal entity from its shareholders and directors;
	• a director of a limited company may enter into and work under a contract of employment with that company;
	• a shareholder of a limited company may enter into and work under a contract of employment with that company.
	In *Nesbitt & Nesbitt v Secretary of State for Trade and Industry* it was held that even though the Nesbitts between them held ➔

Case studies	Determining twin/triple relationships – *continued*

99.9 per cent of the shares they were also employees of their failed company and thus could claim redundancy payments from the State. Neither of the Nesbitts had received dividends or directors fees.

In *Clark v Clark Const. Initiative Ltd* the EAT set out guidelines about the twin relationship:

- if there is an ostensible contract of employment, the onus is on the other party to prove that it is not what it appears to be (for example, if such a contract has not been set out in writing, that could be an argument against employment);
- whether the director works in accordance with what would normally be expected of an employee (if so that could be a strong argument in favour of him being employed);
- the mere fact that the director has a controlling shareholding does not prevent him also having a contract of employment (although it may raise doubts about it);
- taking a salary rather than dividends is an argument in favour of employment;
- the fact that the person founded and built the company will not prevent there also being an employment relationship;
- the fact that the person had financial arrangements with the company (e.g. had loans from it or made loans to it, or gives guarantees will not normally be of assistance in determining whether there is an employment relationship).

In *Neufeld v A&N Communications in Print Ltd (in Liquidation)* Neufeld was originally an employee. He started work in 1982 but became a shareholder and a director in 1988. He was then made managing director with 90 per cent of the shares. He gave guarantees in respect of the company's liabilities. Although there were no written contracts between the three directors and the company, Neufeld, despite his large shareholding, continued as part of the sales team – working as a salesman. When the company went into liquidation, the EAT found (confirmed on appeal) that he was an employee and entitled to redundancy and other payments in the same way as other employees.

Administration

Some companies not only set out the relationships in a joint service/employment contract, as mentioned above, but also insert a clause which, in the event of its termination, grants to the company a power of attorney giving it the right to act as if it were the director. Thus, the company would then be able to sign a resignation letter and any other documents which, in the event of a dispute, the director would no doubt refuse to sign to retain greater bargaining power (see NOMINEE SHAREHOLDINGS). Granting such power could not restrict the right of the director to take action under the service contract, for breach, and possibly, under the 'contract of employment', for unfair dismissal. Alternatively the situation could be clarified in the Articles, with authority by which directorships can be 'resigned' being included. Again, legal advice should be taken.

Example	Sample draft contract

This Agreement is made this   day of   2XXX, between [the company] and .... (the executive).

It is hereby agreed that

1   The company shall employ the executive as [title, list of duties, etc.] and the executive shall serve the company commencing the   day of   2XXX (the commencement date) for a rolling period of a maximum of three years so that (unless either party shall have given written notice of termination of this contract) the period shall be extended by a further one year on each anniversary of the commencement date.

The appointment of the executive as director and employment of the executive shall otherwise continue until the occurrence of

(a) three months from the date on which either party shall give to the other three months notice of termination in writing. For the purposes of employment legislation the date continuous employment commenced was [date],
or
(b) the passing by the shareholders of a resolution removing the executive as a director,
or
(c) summary dismissal as a result of gross misconduct committed either as a director or as an employee.

The executive hereby grants a power of attorney in favour of the company authorising it to sign the required forms evidencing such removal as resignation from the post of director, and all ancillary matters, notwithstanding any rights the director may have under this agreement.   ➜

Example	Sample draft contract – *continued*

2 The executive shall during the continuance of this agreement well and faithfully serve the company and use his utmost endeavours to promote the interests of the company and its shareholders, giving it at all times the full benefit of his knowledge, skill and ingenuity, and shall perform all his duties as may from time to time be assigned or vested in him by the board of directors of the company (the board).

3 The executive shall during the continuance of this agreement devote the whole of his time and attention to the duties of the appointment (unless prevented from so doing by illness). He shall not, and shall cause his spouse and immediate family not to, directly or indirectly enter into, or be concerned in any manner (other than with the consent in writing of the board or as a minority shareholder in a company quoted on a public stock exchange or bourse) with any company or organisation deemed to be (at the discretion of the board) a competitor of the company.

4 The duties covered by this agreement shall be mainly carried out at the head office for the time being of the company, but the director will be expected to travel to all company locations and elsewhere on company business and may be required to relocate within a [250 mile] radius of [London].

5 During the continuance of this agreement the company shall pay the executive (monthly) at the rate of £XXXXXX per annum or such other rate as may from time to time be agreed by the Board and will provide (at the cost of the company) a private motor car to the equivalent of   [*exact terms of allocation and use could be inserted here*].

6 In addition to remuneration, the director will be entitled to reimbursement of all travelling, hotel and other expenses properly and reasonably incurred in the exercise of these duties and supported, as far as possible, by VAT receipts (if possible made out in the name of the employer) and invoices.

7 The director will be entitled to [ ] paid days holiday in each year (plus public or Bank holidays) at such times as may be agreed by the board. At least 20 days each year must be taken within the holiday year.

8 In the event of the director falling sick and being unable to perform the duties, the company will continue to pay the ➜

Example	Sample draft contract – *continued*

normal salary (for the time being) for a maximum of [ ] days in any one year. Should incapacity exceed such a period, further payment(s) will be at the discretion of the board. [*It may be advisable to specify the relationship between Statutory Sick Pay and salary – e.g. whether the company will pay only SSP or top it up to the normal pay.*]

9 Should the director become unable (by reason of ill-health, imprisonment) to perform the duties adequately, or fail or neglect to perform the duties, or breach any of the provisions of this Agreement, then the company may forthwith determine this Agreement without notice as previously stipulated.

10 The director shall not, without the consent in writing of the company, divulge to any other person, firm or company, and shall use his best endeavours to prevent the publication to any other person, firm or company of any information concerning the business or its finances or any of the secrets, dealings, transactions or affairs of or relating to the company.

11 The director acknowledges receipt of the company's code of gifts, ethics and anti-bribery and undertakes to abide by the requirements thereof.

12 The director undertakes to notify the company immediately of interest he may have in a third party with which the company does business, and of any change to such interest(s) and to advise the company immediately of any disqualification order made against him either in the UK or elsewhere.

[13 The director acknowledges receipt of the company's Stock Exchange listing agreement and undertakes to abide by the requirements thereof.]

14 The whole interest of the director in any inventions emanating as a result of his employment shall become the absolute property of the company without any payment being due to him.

15 Upon the termination of this Agreement (whether by effluxion of time or otherwise) the director shall not (without the express written permission of the company) for a period of six months thereafter be connected with, or take part in the management of, or advise or direct, another business whose activities could conflict with the activities of the company. ➡

Example	Sample draft contract – *continued*

In addition the director will not for a period of six months from such termination, solicit or take away any staff, custom, or business under the control of the company at the time of the termination

16 If the director resigns in order to join a competitor or to set up in competition with the company, the company stipulates (and it is specifically agreed by the executive) that for a period of six months from the date of such resignation he will not work for that competitor and will remain on 'garden leave'.

For the purposes of clarity it is stipulated that the principle behind this clause is to provide protection for the company in respect of up-to-date knowledge gained by the executive during employment. As such the company requires that, should a period of 'garden leave' be implemented it is expressly understood that during such leave, the director will:

- take any accrued holiday to which he is entitled
- have no right to carry out any work for the employer
- not approach or enter the premises of the employer (other than at the specific and previous request of the employer)
- not contact any employee or customer of the employer by any means whatever
- during the whole duration of the contract and during any period of garden leave, not work for or advise a competitor, or set up as a competitor of, this organisation
- not represent himself to any third party as being or still being an employee of the employer.

The provisions of the Contracts (Rights of Third Parties) Act 1999 are specifically excluded from this clause.

17 The Company's disciplinary policy (a copy of which is attached) applies.

18 Any notice or other document required to be given under this agreement shall be deemed to be served if it is sent by recorded delivery:

- by the company to the director at his last recorded home address, or
- by the director to the company via the chairman or company secretary at his last recorded home address.

Signatures of parties

Witness

Notes

1 This draft should be customised and legal advice should be taken.
2 It should be treated as a deed and sealed (or signed as a deed).
3 Unless there is no alternative, it would be preferable that the subject director did not sign on behalf of the company.
4 The requirement for the subject not to work for a competitor for a set period after termination of employment (so that personal knowledge and/or contacts become outdated and of less relevance) means the company has to continue payment for this 'garden leave' (i.e. enforced inactivity) period.
5 'Payment' in respect of garden leave periods must include all non-cash benefits in respect of the period (e.g. car, health cover, etc.) whilst holiday entitlement should be taken. Only the cash equivalent of any pre-leave accrued holiday should need to be paid.
6 The exclusion of the Contracts (Rights of Third Parties) Act attempts to prevent someone not immediately involved in the contract being able to circumvent its clauses.

Case study	Third party negates garden leave
	In a case when a husband, with a contract with a six-month 'garden leave' clause, resigned to join a competitor, his employer enforced a garden leave clause. However, his wife successfully exercised *her* rights under the Contract (Rights of Third Parties) Act to insist that his employer gave him work to do (thus at least in part negating the effect of the garden leave clause) because she didn't want him 'getting under her feet' with nothing to do at home!

Protecting the company

In a survey regarding breaches of company security, over 60 per cent of employees admitted that they had stolen confidential documents, customer databases, details of contacts and/or potential sales leads from their employers. Of those who made such an admission, half said they believed that sales leads and contacts belonged to them and not to the company. A separate survey revealed that 33 per cent of directors admitted stealing corporate information from their companies (one has to wonder how many others did so but did not admit it!) The onus is very much on the company to ensure that employees including directors realise that such theft is unacceptable. Thus a clause such as the following might be incorporated in the above contract:

Example	Company secrets clause
	'It is a fundamental term of this contract that all data, inventions, research and/or customer contracts is and always remains the property of the company. Any person during or after employment, using for personal or another party's gain, or passing to another party any such details (without previous specific authority signed by two directors on behalf of the company) is in serious breach of this clause and renders any such person (and any other party involved) liable to legal action.' Note: Such disclosure might also breach the Data Protection Act – maximum fine for breach now £500,000.

Although such a clause may be effective in terms of employees and directors the situation regarding Agents of the company is somewhat different.

Case study	Agents rights
	In *Cureton v Mark Insulations Ltd* an agent worked on behalf of the company and built up a customer database. Because the EU Database directive stipulates that whoever builds a database is its owner, he did not have to return it to the company. (It might be wise to insert in the Agency agreement that any database built by the agent reverts to the principal on termination of the agreement.)

Directors: duties and liabilities

INTRODUCTION

Directors have a fiduciary duty to their company, i.e. they must act with the *'utmost good faith"* putting the company's interests first whilst sublimating their own. They are trustees of the company's assets, giving account of their stewardship of those assets each year through the annual report and at the AGM. Such appointments not only carry prestige but also considerable personal liabilities. Breaching legal requirements (even in ignorance) can lead to fines, disqualification, personal liability and imprisonment for up to 10 years.

The seven new explicit duties

CA06 for the first time lays down explicit duties for directors. Although many will be recognisable since previously they have been implied, and they might be thought to not pose too many challenges to directors, they set criteria against which directors can be judged particularly by shareholders who may wish to initiate a DERIVATIVE CLAIM.

(a) Directors must act within their powers (s.171)

Many directors (particularly in smaller companies) are not familiar with their company's Articles which set out the owners' rules concerning directors' powers and requirements. For CA06 companies the Articles are the company's Constitution and thus all actions must be in accordance with it, whilst for a pre-CA06 company its 'Constitution' is formed by its Articles to which the objects clauses (in its Memorandum) are deemed to be transferred. Directors of LTDs that decide to operate without a company secretary must ensure at least one of them knows the Articles and the company's objects to ensure the directors do not breach them. Failing to act in accordance with the requirements under law and within the Articles can render the director personally liable for his actions.

Case study	Twin breach
	In *Smith v Henniker-Major* a director acting on his own purported to pass a board resolution at a board meeting of which he had deliberately failed to give his colleagues notice. That breached the law since all directors have a right to receive notice of all board meetings unless they are outside the UK. However, the Articles stipulated that the quorum for valid board meetings was two directors, whereas he acted on his own. The Court stated that his 'resolution' was a worthless piece of paper. Further, since he had acted '*ultra vires*' (beyond his powers) under the Articles, if the 'resolution' was effected and the company lost money as a result, he would be personally liable.

(b) Directors must promote the success of the company (s.172)

Directors must act in good faith to promote the success of the company for the benefit of and in the interests of the company's members whilst taking into account the interests of others (now collectively called 'stakeholders'). The directors also need to be aware of the consequences of their decisions and the desirability of the company maintaining a reputation for high standards of business conduct. Thus directors need to consider the:

- long term consequences of all decisions;
- interests of employees as a result of the decisions;
- need to foster the business relationships with suppliers, customers and others;
- impact of the company's operations (and thus their decisions concerning those operations) on the community and the environment;
- desirability of the company maintaining a reputation for high standards of business conduct;
- need to act fairly as between members of the company.

Additionally, directors may need to be able to prove that they did take account of these statutory duties when taking decisions. The difficulty is that some of the interests to be taken into account are diametrically opposed.

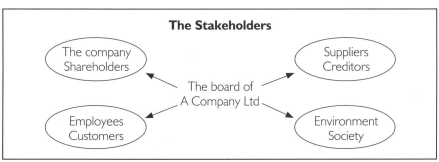

The Stakeholders

It may be that (perhaps at the first board meeting after the start of *every* financial year – and the first meeting after a new appointment to the board) there is a minute such as

'The board reminded themselves of the seven duties of directors set out in the Companies Act 2006 and confirmed that in taking all decisions they would continue to take account of these duties and bear in mind the disparate interests of the company's stakeholders.'

(c) Directors must exercise independent judgement (s.173)

A director must vote according to his own personal views – even if this results in him being in a minority of one. If a director finds himself in such a position, it might be advisable for the director to require that his dissent is noted in the minutes in case the decision is ever challenged. If including the objection in the minutes is resisted the director should write a note to the chairman (and keep a copy) objecting to his dissent not being recorded.

Case study	Investigation required before decision
	In *Gwyer & Associates v London Wharf (Limehouse) Ltd*, a director made no effort to ascertain what were the interests of his company (which was approaching insolvency) before voting on a board resolution.
	The Court held he was not only negligent but also in breach of his fiduciary duty to exercise his discretion independently and *bona fides* in the interests of the company; and went on that, where a company was on the brink of insolvency, the directors owed a duty *'to consider as paramount'* the interests of the creditors (see WRONGFUL TRADING).

(d) Directors must exercise reasonable care, skill and diligence (s.174)

The test here is that the director should act with the degree of care, skill and diligence that would be exercised by a reasonably diligent person with the general knowledge, skill and experience reasonably expected of a person carrying out the functions carried out by the director.

Case studies	Duties cannot be delegated
	In *Dorchester Finance Co Ltd v Stebbing*, there were three directors of the company of whom two, X and Y, were effectively non-executive and left the running of the company to Z. ➜

Case studies	Duties cannot be delegated – *continued*

X and Y often signed blank cheques for use by Z, and made no enquiry of how company funds were used. The company failed, owing a considerable sum to the creditors.

The Court found that both X and Y had not only failed to apply the necessary skill and care in the performance of their duties but also had failed to perform *any* duties as directors. In addition, Z (who, like X was a qualified accountant) had failed to exercise any skill or care as a director and had misapplied the assets. All three directors were held to be liable for damages.

The Court ruled that a director in carrying out his duties must:

- Exercise '*the degree of skill that may reasonably be expected*' from a person of his knowledge and experience. Thus in considering liability for wrongful trading a Court might consider a director who is a qualified accountant to be more culpable because of his professional training and expected knowledge in the corporate field.
- Take such care that a man might be expected to take on his own account. The question that could be asked is '*Would I be so cavalier concerning these funds, was this my own cash/bank account rather than it being that of my company?*'
- Exercise the powers granted to him in good faith and in the interests of the company of which he is a director.

In the *D'Jan of London* case (where a director signed an insurance proposal form that contained an erroneous statement about him) the Court stated that directors must be '*diligent person(s) having … the general knowledge, skill and experience that may reasonably be expected of a person carrying out the same functions as are carried out by that director in relation to the company*'.

The Court held that, although the director could be excused some liability as the mistake was '*not gross. It was the kind of thing that could happen to a busy man, although that is not enough to excuse it*', he would still be required to contribute £20,000 to the loss suffered by the creditors of his failed company since he had not shown the degree of care expected of him.

The judge stated that it was unrealistic to expect a director to read everything he had to sign but he had to exercise some judgment; here the proposal consisted of only a few sentences.

(e) Directors must avoid conflicts of interest (s.175)

However, a director will not breach this rule if:

- the conflict has been authorised by the directors at a meeting where there is a disinterested quorum, and
- for an LTD, it is not specifically prohibited by the Articles, or
- for a PLC, the directors are given specific power to allow it.

In addition s.182 requires that a director must declare an interest (direct or indirect) which is already in existence.

Obviously in allowing a colleague to retain a conflicting interest, the other directors would have to take the decision bearing in mind their own fiduciary duty to the company.

Since under s.184 interests are required to be brought to the attention of the directors, it might be as well for a company to maintain a register of directors' interests to be available for inspection on every occasion when board decisions are made.

Secondary legislation under CA06 stipulates that all companies formed before 1 October 2008 must obtain shareholders' consent giving the directors permission to authorise such conflicts. Although it is not stipulated that this needs to be a special resolution (thus amending the Articles) this might be safest.

Case study	'A house divided among itself must fail'
	In *British Midland Tools* (BM) *v Midland International Tooling* (MIT) four directors of BM secretly decided to leave it and set up another in competition. Three remained in office, but their colleague resigned and set up MIT to compete with BM. The three who remained in office with BM then enticed employees to join MIT and poached customers for it. The Court held that the three directors who remained in office had a duty to the original company to stop the enticement and poaching and were thus liable for not taking such action.

(f) Directors must not accept benefits from third parties (s.176)

However, the benefit could be allowed if it cannot reasonably be regarded as one that gives rise to a conflict of interest. It might be prudent to request that any benefit received from a third party – even if not giving rise to a conflict – should be entered into a register of directors' interests which could be available at each board meeting so that other board members are advised of the interest.

(g) Directors must declare any interest in proposed transactions with the company (s.177)

Such declaration can be either a specific (s.184) or general (s.185) notice but a director does not have to make a declaration if the interest cannot reasonably be regarded as likely to give rise to a conflict.

The fiduciary duty

A director owes a fiduciary duty to his company. If, as well as being a director, he is an employee he also has a duty of fidelity. Directors are required:

■ *To act at all times in the best interests of the company.* Defining what are a company's 'best interests' can be a matter of opinion but nevertheless this is an obligation and a balance or choice may need to be made between the short term and long term. As well as the interests of the company (i.e. those of the members or shareholders), under CA06 directors must also consider the interests of the employees (an obligation first imposed under CA85), the creditors (an obligation first required by the Insolvency Act 1986), its customers (originally under various trading laws particularly the Sale of Goods Acts as well as the Competition and Enterprise Acts), its visitors and trespassers (under the Occupiers Liability Act and various Health and Safety regulations), and the environment (under CA06 as well as environment protection legislation).

Directors must act fairly between members of the company and must not unfairly prejudice the interests of a minority shareholder. Their decisions must be for the benefit of the company and in the interests of the shareholders as a whole (from the decision in *Re Smith & Fawcett*).

■ *To act as a trustee in respect of the company's assets.* A director must act without any additional purpose which would affect the main and overriding interests of the company (even if this means sublimating his own interests). Directors have powers under the company's Constitution but must use those powers for the proper purposes of the company (guidance also derived from the *Smith & Fawcett* decision). A director should not make a secret profit without the consent or permission of the company members under the company's Constitution (as stated in the *Regal Hastings Ltd v Gulliver* case).

■ *To exercise the best degree of skill and care depending upon his personal knowledge and experience.* Historically a director could not be made liable for a judgmental error. He was expected to 'give of his best' and be judged in this respect on his level of experience. Obviously he could be penalised if he was found to have acted negligently. However, under CA06, it is possible for a shareholder who believes that the company has suffered loss because of the activity(ies) of a director (defined as *'an actual or proposed act or omission involving negligence, default, breach of duty or breach of trust'*) to initiate a DERIVATIVE CLAIM against the director. If the claim is successful it is the company itself (not the shareholder) that benefits.

■ *To declare all and any interests and to act honestly and reasonably, particularly where his own interests may be in conflict with the interests of the company.* Only if not proscribed by the Articles and agreed by a disinterested quorum of the board (for LTDs) and only if specifically permitted by the Articles and agreed by a disinterested quorum of the board (for PLCs) may any personal profit made by a director by virtue of the appointment, be retained by him. On appointment and on later occurrence a director must immediately declare any and all interests to the board. Failure to disclose an interest can result in personal penalties – on summary trial to a £5000 fine, whilst on trial on indictment the fine is unlimited. In addition the Court could find the director in breach of his fiduciary duty which could in turn lead to further penalties. (See a suggested form of declaration/updating of interests in DIRECTORS – APPOINTMENT.)

Case studies	Must act in company's (not one's own) best interests

In *Item Software (UK) Ltd v Fassihi*, a director sabotaged negotiations between the company of which he was a director and a third party, so that he could divert the contract to a new company he was setting up. The director was held to have:

● breached his fiduciary duty by sabotaging the negotiations for his own benefit; and
● failed to tell the company of his breach.

Obviously employees should not defraud their employing company (if they do, they breach their duty of fidelity) but they have no obligation to tell their employer of their wrongdoing. However, because they have a fiduciary duty, officers do have such an obligation.

The Court described the director's actions as *fraudulent concealment* and stated that if a director appropriates business for himself then he has a duty to account to the company for any profit. The director was ordered to pay damages for the sabotage and his failure to disclose the breach.

In *Tesco Stores Ltd v Pook*, a senior manager fraudulently arranged for payments on false invoices and received a 'bribe' for doing so from the 'supplier'. The Court held that directors and senior ➡

Case studies	Must act in company's (not one's own) best interests – *continued*
	managers (i.e. officers), because of their fiduciary duty, have an obligation to disclose their breach to the employer and advise them of secret profits. Pook was in breach of this requirement and therefore had to pass the 'bribe' to Tesco as well as the fraudulent receipts. Since he had a fiduciary duty to the company he also had a duty to tell the company what he was doing.
	In *Co-op Wholesale Society v Meyer*, the Court said a director must maintain independence of judgement and not fetter his decision, whilst in *Blaikie Brothers v Aberdeen Railway Co*, it was said that directors must not have a conflict of interests without the members consent (as CA06 now stipulates).
	● *To ensure the company acts in accordance with the requirements of laws affecting the company*: The Accounting Practices Board suggested that boards should compile a register of all the laws and regulations with which their companies are required to comply. Compiling such a register is of course merely an administrative chore – the underlying purpose is for a complete set of the company's obligations to be generated, promulgated (to encourage compliance) and policed (to deal with non-compliance).

Directors' fraudulent activities

Corporate fraud is on the increase. It has been stated that 60 per cent of all UK companies are losing as much as 5 per cent of their turnover to fraud and theft. The impact is of course felt directly on the bottom line. For a company earning 10 per cent profit, sales of 10 times any amount lost to thieves will have to be generated simply to 'mark time' (i.e. to regain the pre-theft 'profit-position'). Under the Fraud Act the offences include:

■ making a false representation (e.g. lying on a job application);
■ failing to disclose information where there is a legal duty to do so; and
■ abusing one's position.

Since a director must by virtue of his position safeguard and protect the shareholders' assets, any dereliction of this duty is fraud. Similarly if he makes a gain by abusing his position (or causes the company loss by so doing) that is also fraudulent. CA06, s.176 allows a director to seek authorisation from the board to exploit personally some property or opportunity even though there may be a conflict between his interests and those of the company. In an LTD, this can be done provided there is nothing in the Articles banning it. However, directors of PLCs can only do so with specific authorisation allowing it in the Articles – if not, the Articles would need to be changed for it to be permitted (i.e. the authority of the shareholders would have to be obtained). (See DIRECTORS – EMPLOYMENT STATUS re non-disclosure and protection of company assets etc.)

General aims/responsibilities of the board

Collective

A board must act as an entity with shared responsibility for all the activities of the company. Thus, irrespective of whether a director 'heads up' a particular discipline, he must take decisions, and share in the decision making process, in respect of all matters concerning the company as a whole, even if that means supporting a board decision detrimental to the interests of the discipline he heads – or to him. Once the decision is taken – even if he voted against it – any director not in favour of the proposal must sublimate his personal preferences and work to implement the decision with his best endeavours. If he cannot accept the decision, he should resign.

Individual

The items of a corporate nature expected of a director could include:

- ensuring company strategy is formulated, known widely and adhered to;
- formulating the aims and purposes of the company and ensuring that these are both promulgated internally and externally (e.g. to the media, shareholders, advisers, etc.);
- ensuring tactical decisions and actions take the same general direction as the strategy of the company (i.e. ensuring that short term decisions do not hamper or impede long term strategy);
- formulating, promulgating and ensuring adherence to an internal code of ethics covering GIFTS etc.;
- ensuring the company complies with its own Constitution (i.e. the Articles) and, if a listed PLC, the listing agreement and CORPORATE GOVERNANCE, and custom and practice for the industry;
- acting as company spokesperson, promoting the corporate entity and its products/ services at all times;
- ensuring the appropriate blend of skills is available at board level (and through board members and management at all other levels), that people at all levels know what is expected of them, are motivated to perform well, and warned and disciplined (in accordance with pre-set

rules) when performance or actions are not in accordance with requirements;

■ ensuring there are adequate controls over the commitment of the company to contracts, etc., and adequate authority control over all other purchases;

■ ensuring the financial records and reports of the company are prepared in accordance with legal and accounting requirements, and that such reports are filed with authorities within time limits;

■ ensuring the products and services of the company are developed so that continuity of earning power of the organisation is ongoing;

■ expanding the company based on well-researched, well-prepared and well-considered planning;

■ ensuring the company has formulated contingency (disaster recovery) plans to protect its earning capacity in the event of a downturn or change in demand, and the effects of possible disasters affecting operations (see RISK);

■ protecting the corporate entity and the products/services from criticism, attack and loss as far as possible.

Liability to employees

Directors can be held responsible for everything that goes on in the workplace.

Case studies	Employer held liable
	● A director and his company were both found guilty of a breach of safety law by using an unguarded machine, which resulted in an employee losing an arm. Rainham Waste Recycling Ltd was fined £25,000 plus £4,000 costs whilst the director was fined £5,000 and disqualified from acting as a director for five years.
	● In the Lyme Bay canoe tragedy case both company and director were found guilty of manslaughter – the director was jailed for three years whilst the company was fined £60,000.
	● In *R v F Howe & Son (Engineers) Ltd*, where the company was held responsible for the electrocution of an employee and initially fined £48,000 plus £7,500 costs, the Court of Appeal stated '*some safety offences could be so serious that they could lead to fines being levied at a rate that would bankrupt the company*'.
	The Court stated that the fines for health and safety offences were too low and, where death was involved, this should →

Case studies	Employer held liable – *continued*
	be reflected in the fine. It urged lower Courts to judge how far defendants fell short of the *'reasonably practical'* test. In doing so Courts should ignore the size of employers – i.e. the standard of care expected is the same irrespective of size.

CA06 does not specifically require the board to consider their obligations regarding 'safety' – although it could be argued that it is covered by the requirement to take account of the *'interests of employees'* in taking every decision. In a recent survey, 63 per cent of company secretaries felt *'a duty to consider safety'* should be a specific requirement. The Health and Safety Executive has recommended that safety should be a regular item on the board agenda and obviously any and all decisions regarding safety matters should be properly minuted (see MINUTES).

Taking precautions

As the corporate environment becomes more and more dangerous for those charged with running corporate bodies, an obvious question is *'how can directors negate their liability'*? The short answer is that they cannot, but they may be able to minimise or restrict their exposure by taking action.

(a) By keeping aware

In an increasingly litigious society, boards need to be aware of the liabilities they have and how this scenario is changing. Company secretaries should make themselves aware of developments, keep up to date on the law, its interpretation, the range of liability – and the level of compensation awards being made, and advise the board accordingly.

(b) By formulating rules and procedures

Adequate and effective rules, procedures etc. can provide some measure of defence in that the company can be shown to have recognised the problem and to have taken reasonable steps to try and eradicate it. Thus the company should try to ensure that:

■ all rules regarding trading, outlawing price-fixing and bribery, safety, recruitment and relationships as well as attitudes and actions towards employees during employment are clear regarding fair treatment and complete observance at all times;

- all employees have read and understood the rules and that all procedures etc., are regularly checked, reviewed and policed and always adhered to;
- immediate action is taken once there is any question of an accusation or suspicion that there is a breach of such rules and sanctions are applied against everyone in breach;
- all safety rules are adhered to, specifications regarding maintenance are compiled and inspections carried out in accordance therewith; adequate protective measures are in place and observed; and risk assessments are prepared and updated;
- all reports of problems potentially affecting safety, as well as concerning bullying, discrimination, harassment, stress etc. are immediately investigated and policed;
- all employees are advised of their responsibilities for their own, their colleagues' etc., and their employer's assets', safety;
- everyone is constantly reminded of the need to adhere to rules, procedures etc., to think before acting or speaking and to consider the implications of liability claims, etc.

(c) By obtaining an indemnity

Many directors already have an indemnity. If a pre-CA06 company used Table A of CA85 as part or whole of its Articles, it will almost certainly have retained reg. 118. This provides a standard indemnity clause for company officers. It can only be utilised by persons acting legally of course, and such an indemnity only has value whilst the company is solvent.

(d) By effecting insurance cover

Directors and officers (D&O) insurance cover could be effected. Care must be taken to check the extent of such cover – i.e. to read the small print. It is against public interest to insure an illegal act so if the matter itself is illegal even with the cover there may be no payout. Before D&O cover is purchased the board should check they have authority – it would be prudent to insert the right in the Articles.

Further guidance to the expectations of directors can be found on the ICSA website (**www.icsa.org.uk**).

The penalties?

Obviously some of the potential breaches referred to above are fraudulent in which case the offenders could be prosecuted under the Insolvency, Fraud and Bribery Acts and those found guilty could receive a prison sentence of up to seven years or 10 years where there is fraudulent trading (see

WRONGFUL TRADING). Almost certainly, guilty directors would be dis-qualified under the Company Directors Disqualification Act. As well as disqualifying the person from acting as a director of a UK company for up to 15 years this could also lead to a fine.

Case study	Disqualified and fined
	In *R v Owide*, the director was disqualified for seven years in 2000. However, he continued to run a number of businesses. In January 2004 he was disqualified for a further five years and fined £200,000. The Court also stated that unless the fine was paid within 18 months he would go to prison for 18 months.

Directors: payments, loans and interests

INTRODUCTION

Directors occupy positions of considerable power, controlling the assets of their company on behalf of their shareholders. As such their personal transactions with their company should be highly transparent. Directors subject themselves to potential considerable personal liabilities and would be prudent to consider whether there are ways in which these liabilities can be minimised – it being unlikely that they can be insured or indemnified. All obligations apply equally to all directors – there is no difference between a non-executive and an executive or between a director whose details are lodged at CH and a 'de facto' or shadow director.

Payments

All 'value' given to directors must be disclosed in the company's ANNUAL REPORT. 'Value' includes all benefits in kind, and all payments, goods or benefits given to the director and persons 'connected' to him. It also includes any sums (etc.) paid to a person as an inducement to them becoming a director as well as any such items paid to them following cessation of a directorship. Any sums given to a third party for the benefit of the director must also be disclosed.

Connected persons include:

(a) husband, wife or civil partner of a director;
(b) a partner in an enduring family relationship with a director;
(c) a director's children or step-children(from the relationships set out in (a) or (b) up to age 18;
(d) the parents of a director;
(e) bodies in which the director has a 20 per cent or more holding.

Payments to a body to which any director has been seconded must be disclosed.

Requirements re. pay

The latest disclosure rules regarding directors' pay require listed PLCs to provide explanations of:

- performance criteria for long-term incentive and share-option schemes;
- comparator groups of companies used to determine 'appropriate' pay levels;
- the balance between the elements of a package that are/are not related to performance;
- the company's policy on contracts and notice periods

as well as details of:

- membership of the remuneration committee;
- whether the recommendations of that committee were accepted without amendment;
- any remuneration consultants that advised the committee.

Companies are required to disclose the details in a set tabular format so that inter-company comparisons can be facilitated, and performance graphs must be provided to facilitate comparison of reward with an individual's pay. Boards should seek to obtain shareholder approval to directors pay, although they can implement their recommendations even without shareholders' agreement.

The Institute of Directors (IoD) welcomed the transparency required by the above but the reaction of many corporate investors was disappointment since although they have more (and comparable) information, their ability to influence rates etc. is unchanged. The 'big 8' investors who between them hold 5 per cent of the UK Stock Market combined to request a vote on pay policy at the AGMs of the largest 750 companies. In the light of recent company quasi-failures (i.e. insolvency but for injections of public money) despite massive salaries and bonuses being paid to directors, on-going attention is likely to be paid to this subject.

In 'Having their cake ... how the City and big bosses are consuming UK business' (Young and Scott, Kogan Page), the authors pointed out that the highest paid FTSE 100 directors were receiving around 70 times the pay of the average employee – a bigger differential than any other country apart from the USA; and commented 'top managers tend to be rewarded for creating a high share price, not a good company'.

This assumes they do create a 'high share price', which must be questionable. Directors' efforts are certainly one of a number of factors affecting the share price but simply basing rewards on increases in share price is overgenerous. Some share price movement is a reflection of general market trends as well as trends specific to the sector in which a company operates. Further, if rewards are to be linked to share price should they not be reduced if the share price dips?

Perhaps one benefit of the current recession may be more realism in the matter of boardroom pay – a link to a realistic multiple of the average shop floor wage should be considered. After all when the board get it wrong it is those on the shop floor that suffer most whilst those actually taking the faulty decisions are usually protected. As J K Galbraith said *'the salary of the chief executive is not a market award for achievement. It is frequently in the nature of a warm personal gesture by the individual to himself.'*

Loans

CA06 changed the requirements regarding loans being made to directors. The wording remains complex and reference should be made to ss.197–214. Subject to a £50,000 limit a company can make a loan to a director:

- to carry out the work of the company; and/or
- to incur costs in defending himself in civil or criminal proceedings or in an investigation re. negligence etc. (where if he is found guilty the loan must be repaid and, if he is innocent, presumably the loan should become a grant).

Other than loans for the above purposes, a company is only allowed to make loans to its directors and/or connected persons up to the following limits (larger amounts need the permission of the members):

- a loan or quasi loan up to £10,000;
- a credit transaction £15,000;
- a loan in the ordinary course of the company's business (e.g. part of the company's business is to lend money to allow the purchase of an individual's main residence) – no limit (previously £100,000).

If a director borrows money in breach of the Act (e.g. to the detriment of the creditors) he can be required to repay the amount. Thus in *Currencies Direct Ltd v Ellis*, a former director of a company was required to repay a loan made to him whilst he was a director.

Indemnities

Although a company may not indemnify its directors (or anyone else) against an illegal act, under ss.232/237/238 CA06 indemnities can be granted but must be recorded and kept in a register at the registered office or SAIL. Any such indemnity must be retained for at least one year from termination or expiry of contract. Companies must make the records available for free inspection by its members within seven days of a request. Directors and officers liability insurance can be effected provided this is disclosed in the directors' report (s.236).

If director(s) have been negligent, or have defaulted on required actions or breached their duties, such acts can be ratified by a majority of the members (disregarding any votes of the subject director, s.239).

Interests

Under CA06, the obligations of directors regarding matters concerning their company in which they have a personal interest are considerably expanded. Section 175 states that directors (and connected persons) must avoid conflicts of interest. However, a director will not breach this requirement if:

a) the conflict has been authorised by the directors (at a meeting where there was a disinterested quorum); and
b) (for an LTD) it is not specifically prohibited by the Articles; or
c) (for a PLC) the directors are given specific power to allow it.

When a disinterested quorum is asked to permit an interest to subsist, they should ensure in agreeing that they do not breach their own fiduciary duty to the company.

Section 182 requires that a director must declare an existing interest (direct or indirect).

Since under s.184 interests are required to be brought to the attention of the directors, it might be as well for a company to maintain a register of directors' interests to be available for inspection on every occasion when board decisions are made. Obviously there should be an element of realism concerning interests – being entertained at this level is very commonplace, so the difficulty may be in deciding what is 'run of the mill' entertaining as an opportunity to discuss business and a situation where the value of the benefit is such that to a reasonable outsider it could suggest that a 'bribe' is being offered. Bribery Act guidance indicates that unless entertaining is intended to persuade someone not to act 'in good faith, impartially, or in accordance with a position of trust' business entertaining does not breach the Act. (See GIFTS and also the draft form for declaring interests in DIRECTORS – APPOINTMENT.)

WARNING

 The Companies Act 2006 (Commencement No 5 Transitional Provisions and Savings) Order 2007 stipulates that all companies formed before 1 October 2008 must obtain shareholders' consent giving the directors permission to authorise such conflicts. Although it is not stipulated that this needs to be a special resolution (thus amending the Articles) this course might be safest.

The General Counsel of the London Stock Exchange FTSE 100 Companies has a guidance paper for those companies that wish to amend their Articles by way of a general power for directors to authorise conflicts of interests. The paper gives guidance to the wording of an amendment, best practice on directors authorising conflicts, and how to review previous authorisations.

- Under s.176 a director must not accept benefits from third parties. However, if the benefit cannot reasonably be regarded as giving rise to a conflict of interest, it can be allowed to subsist. It might be prudent to request that any benefit received from a third party – even if not giving rise to a conflict – should be entered into a register of directors' interests.
- Under s.177 a director must declare any interest in proposed transactions with the company. Such declaration can be either a specific (s.184) or general (s.185) notice but a director does not have to make a declaration if the interest cannot reasonably be regarded as likely to give rise to a conflict.

The Articles should be checked for action to be taken if and when a director notifies an interest. There is no general rule and the Articles might stipulate:

- the interest (or the directorship) cannot continue;
- the director cannot take part in any vote concerned with the third party;
- the director cannot be counted as part of the quorum for that part of the meeting (and may even be required to leave the meeting during that business item);
- the director can vote providing the interest has been previously declared (or does not exceed a stated value);
- any profit made by him as a result of such interest must be given to the company;
- any profit made by him must be declared and the board can decide the outcome;
- any profit made can be kept by him.

Directors: removal

INTRODUCTION

Directors can cease to hold office by resignation, removal, disqualification or death. Resignation infers a mutual agreement often with goodwill on both sides and the administrative requirements are likely to be completed swiftly, i.e. signed letter of resignation, entry made in the register of directors, filing of form TM01 as required under s.167 CA06, within 14 days with CH. Difficulties can arise, however, when the removal is involuntary.

Disqualification – external removal

A person will be disqualified from acting as a director, if he:

- has been declared bankrupt (unless the Court permits him continuing to act). Under the Enterprise Act 2002, a director who becomes bankrupt through no fault of his own (i.e. he is not deemed to have been irresponsible) can retain personal assets up to £20,000 and regain eligibility to act as a director in one, rather than three, years;
- has been convicted of WRONGFUL or FRAUDULENT TRADING under the Insolvency Act 1986;
- is sectioned under the Mental Health legislation. He should be removed from the board whilst sectioned. The model Articles accompanying CA06 state that a director can be removed if a registered medical practitioner gives a written opinion that the director has become physically or mentally incapable of acting as a director and the condition is likely to last for at least three months;
- has been disqualified under the Company Directors Disqualification Act 1986;
- has been responsible for the persistent late filing of documents at CH, or because his conduct makes him unfit to act and the Court has made a disqualification order.

Disqualification means that he cannot act as a director of *any* UK company during the disqualification period. Following a disqualification order, CH sends form(s) TM01 (under s.167 CA06) to each company of which he is a director, requesting him to resign his directorship(s). If the director does not act CH may seek the aid of the other directors of those companies to effect his removal.

Case studies	Mismanagement = disqualification

In *Secretary of State for DBIS v Aaron* directors of an investment services company were disqualified for misselling SCARPS (Structured Capital at Risk Products). They were in breach of the FSA Code of Business Principles and Rules in not bringing the level of risk to the attention of potential customers.

Thus as well as being liable for mismanaging a company, directors can be disqualified if they are not sufficiently concerned with regulatory requirements i.e. *'conduct as a director makes [him] unfit to be concerned with the management of a company'* (s.6 of the Company Directors Disqualification Act 1986).

A number of directors of Surety Guarantee Consultants were involved and found guilty of fraud, but one, Williams (W) claiming ignorance, was not found guilty. Subsequently it was disclosed that W did know of the fraud but did nothing to stop it. He was fined £25,000.

Forcible removal – internal

Under disqualification provisions a director ceases to hold office by the action of external requirements. However, he can also be removed by his company taking the initiative. Since the forced removal of a director can result in publicity which the company may wish to avoid, it is common for there to be a negotiated settlement contingent on the director tendering his resignation. If not, the process of compulsive removal must be followed.

CHECKLIST   Compulsory removal of a director

✓   Check the Articles to see if the board have any powers of removal. Some Articles grant the board powers to remove a director without recourse to the shareholders.

✓   Check the director's attendance record. Under reg. 81 of Table A of CA85 a director can be removed if he is absent without permission of the rest of the board for six months from board meetings held in that period, and the directors so resolve.

✓   Check the provisions of the director's service contract, some of the more recent contracts cover this point (see below and DIRECTORS – EMPLOYMENT STATUS).

✓   If the director is due to retire by rotation at a forthcoming AGM, voting against his re-election may be arranged. In this case the director would probably have a right of action for breach of contract, whilst the legality of such a move needs to be checked.

If none of the above is available, the removal will need to be effected under the following company law provisions:

- Give notice to the director of the intention to remove him at a general meeting at least seven days before the date on which notice of the meeting must be despatched.
- The director may within those seven days lodge with the company any representations (i.e. arguments against his removal).
- Called 'special notice', the reasons for the intention to remove and the director's representations against must be given to all shareholders entitled to attend the general meeting with the meeting notice.
- At the meeting, the director must be allowed to put any representations to the meeting (even if he is not a shareholder) before any vote is taken.
- Although it needs special notice, the resolution to remove is an ordinary resolution, requiring only a simple majority of those casting their votes in person or by proxy.
- Removing a director in this way does not necessarily prejudice any subsequent action for breach of contract.

On a director ceasing to hold office, CH must be advised on form TM01 (s.167 CA06) and entries must be made in the register of directors. Listed PLCs must also advise the Stock Exchange. The written RESOLUTION process cannot be used to remove a director – removal can only be effected at a meeting.

Removal powers

The company can retain to itself a power of attorney in directors' service contracts, with the sole purpose of enabling it to 'resign' the director in the event of a disagreement. The legality of such a power should be checked and the Articles' requirements reviewed. Such a device – even though it may be quite legitimate – would not prejudice any action the director may have for breach of contract.

Directors: types

INTRODUCTION

Although there are many descriptive terms used of directors, few are referred to in company law – indeed the word 'director' itself is hardly used since often the reference is to 'officers' (which includes the company secretary and senior managers as well as board members). The legal definition of a director is '*any person acting as a director by whatever name called*' so that anyone acting as a director whether recognised by such a title or not is subject to the law.

Executive

All directors are either executive or non-executive, not that there is any legal distinction between them. An executive director is a board member authorised to carry out certain day-to-day functions including entering into contracts, managing staff and assets and generally executing the decisions of the board made collectively by both executive and (if any) non-executive directors. An executive director may be an employee as well as an officer and, if so, the paperwork concerning their appointment should reflect this (see DIRECTORS – EMPLOYMENT STATUS). Although an executive director usually has specific managerial duties (e.g. a sales director heads up the selling side of the business) all departmental issues and priorities must be sublimated to the interests of the company as a whole.

Executive directors need intimate knowledge of the organisation and its employees and capabilities when pressing for initiatives and exercising judgement on strategy and tactics. They need to be aware that, if their company is to prosper, the development of tomorrow's products and services may be almost as important as the delivery of the current products and services. Whilst successes are obviously to be sought and welcomed, analysis of failures can be important as a guide to avoid repeating mistakes.

'Promotion to the board' (i.e. from internal management) should not be seen as a reward but as a challenge to help the company prosper and to drive it forward as part of the top team. As the FRC 'Guidance to Board Effectiveness' states '*an effective board should not necessarily be a comfortable place*'. Company law expects directors to take risks to drive the company forward. RISKS must be taken but one of the important roles for executive directors is to ensure all risks are identified and there is action and planning to ensure rapid and positive response should any risk occur.

Non-executive

Most company boards consist predominantly – very often for LTDs exclusively – of persons working full-time in the company, i.e. executive directors. Since it can be difficult for them to retain an objective view of the company at all times, it has become increasingly common to appoint to boards, additional directors who have no executive responsibilities in the company. Drawn from senior management (and often retired former directors) from the same or different industries as the subject company, their purpose is to provide executive directors with advice and input drawn from their experience. Since they do not depend for their living on their work for the company as do most executive directors, the theory is that such non-executive directors can be (and should be) far more objective regarding the progress (or lack of progress) of the company, and, in essence, require answers to questions the executive directors may least want asked. It may also be easier for non-executive directors to question the appropriateness of certain actions. For example, in the Guinness affair, the 'wrongdoing' of certain of the executive directors, was eventually challenged by the non-executive directors. Should the actions complained of continue, non-executive directors should find it easier to resign in protest, with possible attendant publicity (the so-called *'noisy exit'*). However, non-executives have exactly the same responsibilities – and liabilities – as executives. Both the Institute of Directors and the Stock Exchange are in favour of the extension of the non-executive director concept, whilst draft legislation from the EU requires a majority of non-executive directors on listed PLCs boards. The Non-Executive Directors Association (NEDA) promotes the concept – details available at **www.neda global.com**.

Any marked extension of the numbers of non-executive directors (for example as required by proposed new EU directives and/or envisaged by the corporate governance movement) seems unlikely in the light of recent cases where prosecutors have attempted to make non-executive directors liable for actions or inactions of the board equally with executive directors. The non-executive directors of Equitable Life (who were each being paid on average less than £20,000 a year) were collectively to be sued for £3.2 billion since it was alleged they failed to exercise due care when their company granted too-generous guarantees to policy holders. Ultimately the action was dropped, but it epitomises the potential liability of the non-executive. It would hardly be surprising if few are willing to risk personal liability for such relatively low rewards – particularly as a non-executive director is likely to know far less of the detail of what is going on in the company than their executive colleagues.

A recent survey by the Audit Committee Institute disclosed that:

(a) only one company (out of more than 700 in the FTSE All-share index) did not have a non-executive director;

(b) six had fewer than three non-executives (including a FTSE 100 company).

Case study	Executive and non-executive directors' identical liabilities
	The imminent collapse of hotel group Queens Moat Houses PLC was avoided by the creditor banks providing ongoing financial support to avoid its liquidation mainly since they could not afford to let the company fail as the massive bad debts would have affected their own balance sheets. All board members (which included three qualified accountants) were disqualified as directors for a variety of periods – ten, eight and seven years – whilst the former deputy chairman, Martin Marcus was also fined £250,000. Finally the chairman, John Bairstow, who founded the company and originally built it into a major hotel chain, was disqualified for six years.
	The judge stated '*had Mr Bairstow performed his duty as director and chairman of QMH properly, he would have been aware from the information available to him that the profit figures given to the banks were seriously unrealistic*'.
	John Bairstow commented '*It seems that all directors, including non-executives, are deemed liable for any accounts whether they had any involvement or not.*'
	Exactly so.

Note

Company law is in conflict with charity law. In running a charity, unpaid and non-executive trustees often form the entire board. Since someone must execute the decisions of the board, this would seem to pose a dilemma. Even if the person ultimately executing the board's decisions is not recognised as a director, they may be so regarded under company law (in any event they are almost certainly an 'officer'). Very often of course it is the General Manager or Chief Executive of the charity who acts in this way and recommends actions to the (non-executive) board who, by following his recommendations, so resolve. This can put such persons in a position of power vis-à-vis the board. The advice given to the Association of Chief Executives of Voluntary Organisations was that if such persons acted in this way they were almost certainly *de facto* or shadow directors. Such charities may wish to reconstitute themselves as a Charitable Incorporated Organisation (CIO) (see TYPES OF COMPANIES).

The FRC 'Guidance on Board Effectiveness' urges non-executive directors to *'devote time to developing and refreshing their knowledge and skills … to ensure they make a positive contribution to the board.'*

Chairman

Most boards can only operate if there is a person who is 'first among equals' and thus Articles usually require members of a board to elect one of their number to be chairman. Although often described as such in the media, the chairman is not chairman of the 'company' but of the 'board' and, indeed, depending on the wording of the ARTICLES OF ASSOCIATION, may be appointed only *'for the time being'* and may not necessarily be the person that takes the chair at members' meetings. It would be embarrassing if the board chairman goes to take the chair at a members meeting only to be required to vacate since, quoting the Articles, a shareholder points out that the members present may elect one of their number as chairman!

Whether the chairman has a second or casting vote needs to be determined. In the draft articles for an LTD company accompanying CA06, it is stipulated that before any person is given a casting vote all the directors must approve the suggestion – i.e. it should be decided at the first board meeting. (See BOARD MEETINGS.)

Managing director

In many organisations the functions of chairman and managing director are combined and vested in one person. In the past there has been criticism of listed PLCs that combined those posts, critics inferring that the concentration of power in one person's hands could be detrimental to the overall control of the company.

However, research suggests that the financial results of companies where the two roles are performed by one person are better than companies where the functions are split. Where there is a separate managing director function, it may be more usual for the chairman to be non-executive and to interface with external parties, leaving the managing director to ensure other board members and management who report to him carry out the requirements of the board and their own responsibilities – i.e. essentially an internal role. However, it is difficult to be precise about this since companies operate in different ways and it may ultimately depend on the personalities of those involved.

Legally the managing director may be in a different position to other directors and his powers, responsibilities and the provisions of his re-election need to be checked in the ARTICLES. Under some Articles, a proportion (often a third) of the directors must retire at each annual general meeting of the company shareholders and seek re-election by the shareholders at that meeting. A managing director, however, is often excluded from this requirement – indeed under reg. 84 of Table A CA85 only non-executive directors are required to retire by rotation. Where the chairman is non-executive, the MD is the senior executive officer (CEO) and is usually responsible for developing strategy for approval by the board, communicating it down the chain of command, ensuring it is followed and delivered so he can report on progress to the board. One of his most important duties is control of the financial state of the company and ensuring the delivery of information regarding this to the board. At all times directors must know that the credit the company is taking on will be paid on the due date or within a reasonable time thereof (see WRONGFUL TRADING).

Alternate

A director is permitted by law, provided the Articles also permit, to appoint an alternate to act in his place. An alternate director acts as a full representative for the appointee and has the right to receive all data sent to other directors. Such an appointment is usually made subject to the agreement of the rest of the board. Historically there have been relatively few alternate directors but this situation could change quite dramatically as a result of the recent extension of maternity leave and the pressure on PLCs to ensure 25 per cent of their boards are female by 2015. If during a director's maternity leave, she is not present in the workplace, does not attend board meetings etc., she is hardly complying with her '*duty of care*' as a director. It is not constructive (although possibly safer) for her to resign, and preferable for her to be able to appoint an alternate to act on her behalf during her leave. If the Articles do not allow for the appointment of an alternate director, they will have to be altered. However, the changes to maternity leave which allow a new mother to work for her employer for up to 10 'in touch' days during her maternity leave may overcome the problem.

Associate, local, regional, divisional

It is quite common for companies to allow senior employees (not on the board and not registered at CH) to use a job title which incorporates the word 'director'. This indicates that the company is granting to the person a high level of authority – commensurate to that of a director. Although executives using such titles are not legal or statutory directors, if they use the title in such a way as to suggest that they are, they could be deemed to have '*held* (themselves) *out to third parties that they are a director*' and be judged accordingly. In any event, almost certainly persons using such titles would be regarded as 'officers' of the company – and potentially liable as such – even though they had no say in decisions impacting such responsibilities. See WRONGFUL TRADING.

Courtesy titles

There are many, again not legally appointed, who use titles such as 'Director of ....' to indicate their level of authority. These titles can be given not only to a person who is not a board member but also to someone who may not even be an employee, yet third parties may be able to take such titles at face value.

Case study	Called a 'director', hence a director
	In *SMC Electronic Ltd v Akhter Computers Ltd* an employee used the title 'Director of Power Supplies Unit Sales' and signed a contract as such on behalf of the company. The Court held that the company could not repudiate the contract as it was reasonable for the other party to assume in dealing with a person with that title that they were dealing with someone with power to bind his company.

'De facto'

At the opposite end of the spectrum to non-directors calling themselves directors are those who are directing the activities of a company but have no wish to advertise that reality to the outside world; indeed they often wish to conceal their input altogether (possibly sheltering behind their *'front men'* appointees). However the fact of the matter (Latin *'de facto'*) is that they are directing operations – and are subject to the s.250 CA06 definition of a director as *'any person occupying the position of director by whatever name called'*.

Case studies	*De facto* directors
	In *HMRC v McEntaggart*, the Inland Revenue recovered £73,000 from the wife of a disqualified director. Since he was disqualified, he could not act legally as a director but was giving instructions to his wife who thus *'acted on his instructions'* meaning that ➡

Case studies	*De facto* directors – *continued*

under s. 15 of the Company Directors Disqualification Act 1986 she too could be held liable.

HMRC also successfully claimed £154,000 from her husband since – although disqualified – he was a *de facto* director. (A director acting whilst disqualified has unlimited personal liability for his actions in relation to the company.)

In *Secretary of State for Trade & Industry v Holler*, the company had become insolvent and the husband/father had been disqualified. However, his wife and son acted as if they were directors, taking decisions and requiring actions as directors. They were found to be *de facto* directors and were disqualified. A second son also acted but was not found to have been part of its corporate governance and therefore not a *de facto* director – and not disqualified.

The judge offered some guidance to determining whether a person was a *de facto* director:

- Was the person part of the corporate governing structure (if so he was probably a *de facto* director)?
- A distinction must be made between someone who participates in collective decision making at board level (who would be) and someone in management (who would not be).
- The decision is to be determined objectively on the basis of all relevant facts .A person may be a *de facto* director even though there is no day-to-day control of the company's affairs and/or he is involved in only part of its activities.
- Factors such as a family relationship may be relevant.

Conversely, in *Holland v The Commissioners for HMRC* it was held that a sole director of a holding company which was itself the sole corporate director of a number of subsidiary companies was not a *de facto* director of the subsidiary companies. It was said to become a *de facto* director the individual himself (not the corporate director) needs to have done something in relation to the affairs of the relevant company. This case pre-dated the CA06 requirement that there must be at least one real person on the board of every company.

Nominee

Major shareholders who wish to exercise some control over the board and/ or shareholders of joint venture companies often appoint their own nominee to a board. Directors nominated in this way owe obligations to two separate bodies (the company itself and their principal) and may need to take care to avoid a conflict of interests – as a result of their fiduciary duty the interests of the company of which they are a director must always be put first. A nominee director may have enhanced voting rights (e.g. a vote exercised by a nominee may rank greater than the combined votes of all other members) – if so, since the appointing body has 'board control', the results of the subsidiary may have to be consolidated with it.

Shadow

Section 251 CA06 defines a shadow director as '*a person in accordance with whose directions or instructions the directors of the company are accustomed to act*' – that is someone not recognised as a director but who is effectively controlling the board. The need to define and control such individuals reflects a continuing concern at a tendency of some major shareholders, creditors or others (e.g. customers) effecting control of the company and directing it (without any liability) whilst sheltering behind the appointed board (who could be liable). Without requiring such shadow directors to be recognised, the impact of the Insolvency Act 1986 (i.e. making directors personally liable to contribute to any shortfall due to the creditors in the event of their WRONGFUL or FRAUDULENT TRADING), is negated.

The definition of a 'shadow director' can cover a number of relationships – but there are exceptions. Thus, if a major creditor, instructed (or 'suggested') that the board should carry out a certain act on a one-off basis and the board did so, that person would probably not be a 'shadow director' – as '*accustomed to act*' implies a regular relationship. But if such control was ongoing (i.e. such 'suggestions' were made, and the board complied, regularly) a shadow directorship probably exists. Similarly if a major customer regularly required the board to act in a certain way and it did so, the customer could also become a shadow director. A company doctor – a person brought in to try to assist the company's survival – would almost certainly be a shadow director (if not properly appointed to the board) simply because of the control they would need to exercise. This was the Court of Appeal's decision in the case of *Tasbian Limited* where a company doctor negotiated with creditors, countersigned all the cheques and set up a new corporate organisation.

However, a bank manager requesting certain action as a result of influence gained because the company has borrowing facilities with his bank would not normally be a shadow, since this would be regarded as advice given in a professional capacity which is excluded by s.251(2), even if the board regularly acted upon such advice. In the same way, auditors or solicitors, sometimes have considerable influence and power, but are unlikely to be shadow directors.

In the *Deverall* case the Court of Appeal stated that the words *'directions or instructions'* needed to be interpreted objectively and could include both words and conduct. There was no need to show that there was an expectation that the comment would be complied with. Neither was it necessary to show that the board was subservient to the shadow. Courts will therefore seek to determine whether a person was a shadow director or not, by establishing the extent of their control or influence. The Court has also said that it would 'look behind the paperwork' at the reality of the situation.

Case study	Liable and penalised
	In *Re Mea Corporation, Secretary of State for Trade & Industry v Aviss*, A was director and sole shareholder of a parent company with two subsidiaries. B, who had been disqualified, was not a director of any of the companies but, with A, required all monies received by the three companies to be placed in a central fund.
	On the instructions of B, large amounts were paid from this fund to companies outside the group in which A had a substantial interest despite the protests of the directors of the subsidiaries (which could protect their positions – since acting in accordance with the instructions of a shadow director is itself an offence).
	The Court held A to be a shadow director of the subsidiaries and B to be a shadow director of all three companies. Both had failed to respect the *'separate legal identity'* of the three companies. A was disqualified for seven years and B for 11 years.

If a company becomes insolvent, the insolvency practitioner(s) appointed will seize as many assets as possible to try to satisfy the creditors. If it is felt that the directors have been guilty of WRONGFUL trading there is a possibility that their personal assets could also be seized. The existence of a shadow director would obviously be of interest to the insolvency practitioner since, if such a person can be proved to have been giving the board instructions or requests, they can be held financially liable in the same way as the directors whose details are lodged at CH.

Full personal details of a shadow should be entered in the register of directors and filed at CH (which would of course regularise the position) and any contract between the company and the shadow must be made available for inspection and the location notified to CH. If it is not possible to legitimise the directorship, for example, because the director refuses to sign the 'consent to act' line on the appointment form, or the board refuses to act, those officers aware of the situation should consider their own positions since they too have obligations – and personal liability – particularly if they act in accordance with the wishes of the shadow. It might be safest to bring the matter to the attention of the auditors. Since an audit certificate is required to cover the report of the directors which must state the names of all directors during the period) the auditors should refuse to sign, thus putting the company in breach of its filing obligations. Alternatively, the situation could be reported to a regulatory authority.

The person in breach is liable for both an initial and a daily fine (which continues until the breach is remedied). If the company secretary (or anyone else) has tried unsuccessfully to legitimise the matter internally first and then reports it externally, should a sanction be applied against him, he should be protected by the Public Interest Disclosure Act 1998 (PIDA or the 'whistleblowing' act). He could claim unfair dismissal – in respect of which there is no limit on compensation.

If the board of a subsidiary company is accustomed to act in accordance with the advice or instructions of employees (e.g. directors or senior management) of the parent company there is a possibility that the latter could be shadow directors of the subsidiary. It may be preferable to make the parent company itself a director of the subsidiaries. Any personal liability, in the event of failure of the subsidiary, that could otherwise have attached to such senior staff by reason of them acting, however unwillingly, as shadow directors, will then be borne by the parent company. Of course, this negates part of the reason for setting up a subsidiary in the first place. Under current law there is nothing to stop a holding company allowing a subsidiary to go into insolvent liquidation whilst having no obligations to that company's creditors – unless it has guaranteed the subsidiary's debts. However, a parent company itself will not normally be regarded as a shadow director even if it directs the activities of the directors of its subsidiary(ies).

Sole

LTDs were permitted by CA89 to have just one shareholder and have always been allowed to have just one director. Thus it is perfectly legal for an LTD to have the same sole person as shareholder (or guarantor) and director. However, if the sole director is killed or unable to act in some other way, so too is the shareholder and there is no-one able to appoint someone to replace the director. The company will be unable to continue to trade until the ownership of the share(s) is determined – a process which could take at least several weeks or months during which time the company could fail.

This is to some extent overcome by provisions in the new pro forma Articles which allow for the personal representatives of the deceased shareholder or guarantor to appoint a new director (presumably without awaiting grant of Probate or Letters of Administration). Company secretaries needing to deal with such 'personal representatives' would need to check their right to act if seeking to do so prior to the grant of Probate etc., and might require those representatives to sign an undertaking to 'hold the company harmless' for any liability incurred as a result of acting in accordance with their instructions. The situation becomes even more difficult if:

a) there is no company secretary;

b) the company is a guarantee company with a single guarantor who is also the sole director. At least when a sole shareholder dies the shares still exist and the question is one of ownership. When a guarantor dies the guarantee dies with him and the company has no members.

Note: CH recently stated that 650,000 companies (25% of the whole Register) had the same sole shareholder and sole director.

Silent or sleeping

Directors have a duty of care from which they cannot be absolved. If a person accepts the appointment of director they accept full legal liability for the actions of the company. If they fail to attend board meetings or to find out on an ongoing basis what is going on in their company they still have liability. Basically it is impossible for a director to delegate their responsibility (and liability) for operating the company. Ignorance of what is going on (as of the law) is no excuse.

Case study	Sleepwalking into liability
	In *Lexi Holdings Plc (in administration) v Luqman* there were two active directors (brothers L and W) and two 'sleeping' directors (their sisters Z and M). With W's knowledge L stole around £60,000 from the company. Judgement was originally obtained against both L and W for the amount stolen, but not against Z and M (even though they had breached their fiduciary and common law duties to the company). However, the Court of Appeal (since Z and M knew of L's previous convictions, of the creation of a fictitious directors' loan account, and of loans made in contravention of the Companies Act) held Z and M were in ➡

Case study	Sleepwalking into liability – *continued*

breach of their duty of care. As directors they had an obligation to seek advice about such matters and to inform the auditors – they could not '*do nothing*'. Z had to pay just under £42,000 and M just under £37,000.

This judgement referred to the case of *Re Westmid Packing Services Ltd (No 2)* which set out the principle that any director who allows themselves to be '*dominated or bamboozled by* [another director]' breaches their own duty as a director. Each director must be prepared to be independent.

Dividends

INTRODUCTION

A shareholder's investment can be rewarded by capital growth and/or by dividends paid out of profits. There is nothing to prevent the directors authorising and paying several interim dividends on their own authority in respect of the same financial year, since the recommendation of a dividend rests entirely with them. Control only passes to the shareholders when a final dividend for that financial year is proposed, since final dividends need shareholders approval. Even here their power is circumscribed in that they can only approve, reduce or reject the figure proposed by the board – they cannot increase the proposed dividend.

Taxation

Corporation tax is a complex subject and the advice of the auditors/tax advisers should be sought when considering the payment of a dividend so that the effects of the payment and the allied corporation tax payment are appreciated. Dividends are received by shareholders as a net amount, 'accompanied' by a tax credit (currently 10 per cent of the grossed up dividend). Thus in paying a dividend on 800 shares in Bloggs Products Ltd at a rate of 5.6p a share, a net payment of £44.80 is due to a shareholder. The shareholder would receive a dividend voucher showing this amount as the net payment but with an accompanying tax credit of £4.97 (the difference between the net dividend and its grossed up equivalent i.e. £49.77). The accumulation of the tax credits on dividends paid must be accounted for by the company under its corporation tax calculation and is usually paid quarterly using form CT61. Meanwhile the shareholder can use the tax credit to offset his personal tax liability.

Ability to pay

Companies can only pay dividends from earnings – not out of capital. Should current profits be insufficient to pay the amount recommended, previously undistributed profits (that is the balance of revenue reserves arising from the accumulation of previous profits) can be used for this purpose. Listed PLCs cannot pay a dividend unless the net assets (as defined) of the company

exceed the aggregate amount of their paid up share capital and undistribut-
able reserves by at least the amount of the proposed dividend (in other words
after the payment of the dividend there would still be a surplus).

Striking date

An effective date for payment of the dividend must be set together with a
date as at which members will be entitled to it – the dividend striking date.
Shares in listed PLCs can be bought and sold at any time but only members
on the register as at the striking date are entitled to the dividend. Whether,
when share ownership changes around the time of the striking date, the previous holder or new purchaser of shares is entitled to the dividend is a matter
for them, not the company, to determine. Such shares are quoted 'ex. div.'
or 'without the dividend' in the market once the striking date has passed.
Since the previous owner may still be sent the dividend, they may need to
account for it to the new member. If the share is quoted 'cum. div' it means
that if it is sold the purchaser will get the benefit of the dividend. Obviously
whether a share is 'ex. div.' or 'cum. div.' affects its price.

Tax voucher

In paying a dividend, the company has to prepare both a dividend voucher (a
cheque or account credit) and a tax voucher such as the drafts set out below.

Example	Dividend payment

Dividend No 4   **Bloggs Products Ltd**   **3rd July 2XXX**

The attached cheque is in payment of the FINAL DIVIDEND for
the financial year ended 31st March 2XXX at the rate of 5.6p per
share on the 800 Ordinary shares of £1 registered in your name
on 15th June 2XXX and payable on 3rd July 2XXX.

J Bloggs, Company Secretary

Name and address of shareholder

Reference	Holding	Tax credit	Net dividend
oyup12/g	800	£4.97	£44.80

(Dividend cheque)

Bloggs Products Ltd   3rd July 2XXX

(Valid 12 months)   →

Example	**Dividend payment** – *continued*

Ordinary shares dividend warrant

PAY   A. Shareholder   £44.80   Account payee only

For and on behalf of Bloggs Products Ltd

(Autographical signature)

Dividend payment No. 4.   Signed : J Bloggs

This voucher should be preserved safely. It will be accepted by HM Revenue & Customs as evidence of a tax credit.

Notes

1 The form of the dividend cheque should comply with the latest requirements of the Association for Payment Clearing Services.

2 The cheque is stated to be valid for 12 months as many shareholders fail to present dividend cheques for a considerable time. Although cheques are usually said to be stale after six months, discretion remains with a bank whether to accept or refuse a cheque which is older than six months unless it is stated (as here) to have a longer life.

3 Most companies prefer dividends to be paid by bank transfer direct to the accounts of their shareholders (i.e. via BACS) since it is less expensive than sending the dividend and tax voucher to the shareholder's address. Since however, the process by which the tax voucher is passed to the shareholder by their banks is often less than satisfactory when BACS is used, many private shareholders prefer to receive the dividend cheque and tax voucher direct.

Share accumulations

To encourage the extension, particularly, of private investor shareholdings, some listed PLCs offer their shareholders the option of taking new shares in place of the dividend or allowing the shareholder to invest the dividend in additional shares (a process which the company carries out for the shareholder). Under this 'dividend reinvestment' concept the value of the existing shares in the market is used as the basis on which new shares are valued. This value is then applied to the dividend generating a number of new shares that can be 'purchased' by surrendering the dividend. Members can simply nominate to receive up to that number of shares in place of part or the whole of the dividend with any excess dividend either being paid to them or carried forward to the next dividend payment and added to the amount then available for the same purpose.

Communication

Sending dividends to members provides an opportunity for company/shareholder communication. Details of discounts available on company products or services can be included, as can vouchers redeemable in the outlets of the company, notification of changes of address and even requests to be placed on the company's internal mailing list. These links can aid shareholder loyalty, which could be valuable should there be a hostile takeover bid.

The London Stock Exchange sends listed PLCs a Dividend Procedure Timetable each year. If it follows the LSE's dividend timetable, a company does not have to notify the LSE in advance provided the company secretary advises the Exchange the amount of the dividend, the striking and payment dates (which should not be more than 30 days apart) and a note of whether there is any 'share:dividend' exchange.

Refusal to pay dividends

Should a company be profitable and yet dividends are not being paid (without good reason – e.g. to accumulate funds for expansion or capital investment), other than an action re the DIRECTORS REMOVAL, the only recourse of a shareholder would be to the Court since this might be classed as abuse of a minority particularly if the directors are paying themselves reasonable (or excessive) amounts.

Financial year end

INTRODUCTION

Within nine months of its date of INCORPORATION a company must notify CH of the date to which its first accounts will be made up, i.e. its financial year end (or accounting reference date – ARD). If the company does not make such a notification, CH allocates an ARD which is the end of the month in which the anniversary of the company's incorporation falls. The accounts of a newly incorporated company must be filed not more than nine (or six if it is a PLC) months after the anniversary of its incorporation, or not more than three months after its first ARD whichever is the later.

Significance

LTDs are required to file accounts with CH by the end of the ninth (PLCs: sixth) months of their ARD. 'End of the month' means the last day of the calendar month six or nine months later, although since listed PLCs must publish their accounts on their websites within four months of their year end they may as well file them with CH simultaneously. Companies filing late are subject to fine. Since the preparation and auditing of the accounts can be an onerous task, due regard should be given to selecting an ARD which is convenient for this work, and is also appropriate for the business. A date just after the end of the busiest (and/or most profitable) period may be applicable (e.g. in retailing with a preponderance of pre-Christmas/New Year sales, choosing 31 January might be appropriate), although a great many companies use 31 March, thus making their financial years coterminous with the tax and fiscal years.

Change

During an accounting reference period and the filing period (that is before the end of the ninth (PLC: sixth) month in respect of those accounts, a company can change its accounting reference date (provided this would not mean an accounting period in excess of 18 months). The accounting period can usually only be lengthened once in five years, although the period can be shortened without limitation (an accounting period that has been lengthened could subsequently be shortened).

Notification

Once the ARD has been notified, any subsequent change in the date requires form AA01 (s.392 CA06) to be filed. For CA06 companies, their first accounting reference period must last not less than six but not more than 18 months from the date of incorporation and the accounts must be filed no later than 21 months after incorporation (i.e. no later than nine months after the anniversary of the company's incorporation).

Forms

INTRODUCTION

The new CH forms break with the tradition of using CA section numbers and instead use letters derived from the words describing the subject matter of the form. In the following list, forms that can be filed electronically are indicated by **E** – the position as at July 2011. CH has announced that it wishes to move to a completely electronic process by 2013. Electronic filing is available at CH from 7 a.m. until midnight, seven days a week.

Incorporation and updating

- Application to register a company IN01
- Change of registered office AD01 *(E)*
- Notification of Single Alternative Inspection Location (SAIL) AD02
- Annual return AR01 *(E)*

Name

- Exemption of use of 'limited' from name NE01
- Change of name by resolution NM01 *(E)*
- Change of name by conditional resolution NM02 *(E)*
- Notification confirming satisfaction of conditional resolution NM03
- Change of name by authority in Articles NM04
- Change of name by directors resolution NM05 (where required by Secretary of State or on company being restored to the register)
- Seeking comments from bodies on change of name NM06

Shares

- Return of allotment of shares SH01 *(E)*
- Notice of consolidation, sub-division, etc. of shares SH02
- Return of purchase of own shares SH03
- Notice of sale or transfer to treasury of shares by a PLC SH04
- Notice of cancellation of treasury shares SH05
- Notice of cancellation of shares SH06

- Notice of cancellation of shares held by or for a PLC SH07
- Notice of name or other designation of class of shares SH08
- Return of allotment of new class of share by unlimited company SH09
- Notice of particulars of variation of share rights SH10
- Notice of new class of members SH11
- Notice of particulars of variation of class rights SH12
- Notice of name or other designation of class of members SH13
- Notice of redenomination SH14
- Notice of reduction of capital following redenomination SH15
- Notice by Court applicants for cancellation of resolution re redemption or purchase of shares out of capital SH16
- Notice by company for cancellation of resolution re redemption or purchase of shares out of capital SH17
- Statement of capital SH19
- Application for trading certificate for PLC SH50

Directors

- Appointment AP01 *(E)*
- Appointment of corporate director AP02 *(E)*
- Change of details CH01 *(E)*
- Change of corporate directors details CH02 *(E)*
- Termination of appointment TM01 *(E)*

Secretary

- Appointment AP03 *(E)*
- Appointment of corporate secretary AP04 *(E)*
- Change of details CH03 *(E)*
- Change of corporate secretary's details CH04 *(E)*
- Termination of appointment TM02 *(E)*

Manager appointed re Companies (Audit, Investigations & Community Enterprise) Act 2004

- Appointment of manager AP05
- Change of service address of manager CH05
- Termination of appointment TM03

Filing

- Consent form for paper filing of PROOF filing member PR03

Accounting

- Accounting reference date – change AA01 *(E)*
- Dormant company accounts AA02

Mortgage/charge

- Particulars of charge MG01

Striking off

- Application to strike off DS01

Oversea company (OC)

- OC establishing a place of business in UK BR1

Charges

Charges are levied by CH for filing some items and were last reviewed in April 2011.

General Meetings

INTRODUCTION

Members control companies via Annual General Meetings (AGMs) and General Meetings (GMs). Pre-CA06 companies may find the latter referred to in their Articles as Extraordinary General Meetings (EGMs). An AGM must be held each year by all PLCs – such meetings (particularly if the company is listed) usually having a much higher profile than the AGM of the average LTD since not only do they tend to have many shareholders but also their results and discussion may generate media interest. At the AGM the corporate entity is 'on display', and needs planning and attention to detail to ensure that the company is presented in as advantageous a manner as possible. Under CA06, LTDs need not hold AGMs unless their Articles stipulate it or their members or directors require it. Where business is required to be transacted at times other than when it could be dealt with at an AGM, an (E)GM can be convened.

(a) AGM

Convening and content

Usually a PLC must give 21 clear days' notice of its AGM to all its shareholders. However, if the shareholders of a listed PLC have agreed and the company offers to all its shareholders the *'facility for shareholders to vote by electronic means'* then it need give only 14 days' notice.

An LTD must give 14 clear days' notice (s.307 CA06) or such longer period (e.g. 21 days) that its Articles require. 'Clear', for English and Welsh companies, means the day of the meeting and the day the notice is deemed served are in addition to the required period. For companies registered in Scotland, the day of the meeting can be counted as one of the notice days.

Shareholders of LTDs can waive the whole or part of the notice period for a general meeting provided the holders of at least 90 per cent (unless the ARTICLES require a higher percentage – up to 95 per cent) of the voting rights agree.

For PLCs, notice of the AGM can be waived only if there is unanimous consent of all members. Notice of (extraordinary) General Meetings can be waived providing 95 per cent of all the votes are in favour.

However under the Stock Exchange listing agreement, listed PLCs are required to give their members 20 business or working days' notice (i.e. they must exclude weekends and public holidays). Ideally, to avoid claims that insufficient notice has been given, it may be prudent to give in excess of the minimum notice periods. Also items sent by first class post are not deemed to be served until 48 hours later, and thus this period should be added to the calculation of the 'days notice' required. Notice is not normally validly served on a day on which there are no postal deliveries (that is weekends and Bank Holidays).

Traded companies must also include in the Notice: the address of the website with meeting information, the 'strike date' from which the right to vote will emanate, statements re. proxy appointment forms and procedures for members attending and voting.

Business

At the AGM the following business must be transacted, although this is not exclusive, and, if other matters are timely, there is no reason why they should not be included in the notice and considered at the meeting.

- Receipt and consideration of the accounts and balance sheet and audit report.

The word 'approve' should not be used. There is a widespread misconception that a company's shareholders approve the report and accounts. In fact it is the board that must approve the report and accounts and then present them to the AGM. If the members purport to vote not to 'approve' the report and accounts, it has no effect on those documents which remain the version that must be filed with CH within the required time limits.

- Approval of any DIVIDEND on the shares. Normally the payment of interim dividends is the prerogative of the board and needs no shareholder approval. However, shareholders do have the right to approve, reduce or reject a final dividend recommended by the board. There is nothing to stop the board resolving to pay an interim (or second interim) dividend on their own authority, and not propose a final dividend.
- Election or re-election of directors. If the ARTICLES require a proportion of the directors (often a third) to retire by rotation at each AGM, the third of the directors who are the longest serving must retire and, assuming they are eligible and wish to do so can put themselves forward for re-election by the shareholders. Directors appointed since the last AGM must also retire at the next following AGM and (if they wish and are eligible) can seek re-election. Retiring by rotation is on the decrease for companies other than charities, some guarantee companies, and listed PLCs (where under the Listing Agreement a proportion of directors are required to retire and seek re-election each year).
- Election or re-election of AUDITORS.

- Authorisation of the directors to agree the remuneration of the Auditors – business which is normally delegated to the directors. Companies whose turnover is less than £6.5 million are not legally required to have their accounts audited (unless they are also subject to the requirements of the charity or financial services regulators).

Preparation

The AGM is usually the only occasion in the year when the company could be said to be 'on show'. Where members not on the board are likely to attend, attention needs to be given to every aspect of the meeting's presentation. Using a checklist such as the following may be appropriate. Preparations should be monitored by the board/company secretary on a regular basis.

CHECKLIST   Preparation for annual general meeting

Item	Responsibility
Decide date and time	Board
Visit venue, check facilities	Co.sec. / board
Book venue (6/12 months ahead) – check:	
✓ room and overflow facility	
✓ air conditioning/ventilation	
✓ acoustics/amplification	
✓ accommodation including catering/toilet facilities	
✓ notice boards/room directions	
✓ tables for signing in	
If product/photo display required	Marketing dept
✓ display tables or electronic equipment	
Stipulate to venue management:	Co. sec.
✓ timetable for arrivals	
✓ serving tea/coffee	
✓ lunch (if required)	
✓ likely departure	
Delegate items to staff:	As allocated
✓ greeting arrivals (especially 'speakers')	
✓ ensuring arrivals sign in (taking attendance cards)	
✓ ushering to seats	
✓ care of registers & proxies	
✓ acting as teller(s) (in event of VOTING AND TAKING A POLL)	
✓ care of statutory books, service contracts, minute book	
✓ liaison with catering	
✓ spare copies of annual report, publicity handouts	

Arrange 'speakers'	Co. sec.

✓ 'tame' members (and back up in event of absence), who will actually propose and/or second the various resolutions to avoid it looking like too much of a one-person show (i.e. the chairman's)

Anticipate and prepare for any hostility	Chairman

✓ liaise with advisers (see VOTING)
✓ preparation of answers to awkward questions

If chairman is new to running formal meetings:

✓ preparation of chairman's crib (i.e. a script to cover each   Co. sec.
part of the meeting – see BRIEFING THE CHAIRMAN)

Promulgate timetable and checklist	Co. sec.

✓ briefing on preparations, likely problems etc. (i.e. a meeting scenario) for board and advisers

Liaison with:	Finance director

✓ auditors (have a right to attend and may read the Audit Report)
✓ solicitors, stockbrokers (for listed PLC)   Co. sec.
✓ public relations (and, through them, media representatives)   Corporate PR.
✓ Company registrar (including printing of DIVIDEND   Co. sec.
cheques and tax vouchers, and arrangements for granting authority to post)

Make transport arrangements	Transport mgr.

✓ for directors, staff, guests, major shareholders etc.

Arrange for:

✓ display of products/tour of premises (either actual or   Director
electronic)
✓ press release   Corporate PR.
✓ if required, draft and agree with chairman in advance, possibly amending should this be required following the meeting.

Documentation

Notice

The AGENDA and NOTICE of the meeting are usually included in the ANNUAL REPORT although there is no requirement for this and they could be sent separately, which some listed PLCs now do, particularly if an informal letter inviting (i.e. urging) shareholders to attend the meeting and/or explaining the business accompanies them.

Letter of invitation

With the formal notice, a number of listed PLCs, particularly those with large numbers of private (i.e. non-institutional shareholders) send a semi-personal 'letter of invitation' to shareholders to attend the meeting, which can explain the logic and reasoning behind business to be transacted – e.g. changing the ARTICLES etc.

Intention and attendance cards

Companies with large numbers of shareholders, many of whom may wish to attend the meeting, send their shareholders 'intention of attending' and 'admission' cards. Shareholders are urged to return the 'intention' cards in advance, to provide a rough 'number of attendees', knowing which is useful for security, accommodation, catering etc. Using 'admission' cards on arrival can aid swift admittance, and also assist identification when there is a need for increased security. Obviously no shareholder without a card should be barred from entry – processing their admittance may simply take more time.

Questions

Shareholders can ask questions at the AGM. Shareholders of 'traded' companies (that is PLCs whose shares are listed on the main Stock Exchange market) are however not able to ask questions which are:

- undesirable in the company's interest or the meeting's good order:
- only answerable by interfering with the preparation for the meeting;
- answerable only by disclosure of confidential information;
- already answered in the 'frequently answered questions' (FAQ) section of the company's website.

Questions do not necessarily have to be answered at the meeting. The chairman could state they will be answered later and/or posted on the FAQ.

Proxy

Proxy cards will have been sent with the agenda or notice of meeting and should be lodged with the company secretary or the share registrar of the company, and these should be checked and an analysis of the support for and opposition to each resolution passed to the chairman before the meeting. The proxy cards themselves should be available at the meeting and those processing attendance need to be able to cross-reference the proxy cards with the attendees' lists, in case someone who has already lodged a proxy, also attends. Whilst there is nothing to prevent this, obviously their votes must not be counted twice. A 'change of address' notification could form part of the proxy card.

A member of a company can appoint more than one proxy. Thus a shareholder could appoint a proxy for several tranches of the same holding (e.g. 100 different proxies each acting for one share of a holding of 100 shares). Whilst this could be useful for voting on a show of hands, since all 100 would then be counted, this is fairly pointless since the proxy (if they disagree with the result of a show of hands vote) is usually empowered to demand or join in the demanding of a poll in which case all the votes could be counted.

Some listed PLCs have changed their ARTICLES OF ASSOCIATION so that voting can no longer be effected by show of hands (which only grants one vote per person) at all, but only by poll (one vote per share) thus ensuring all resolutions reflect the true voting strength.

Informal communication

Since such meetings may be fairly formal, a custom has been growing with listed PLCs for members of the board to make themselves available at the AGM venue, say, 30 minutes before meetings (and/or for some time afterwards) so that shareholders can talk to them. At least one leading listed PLC invites shareholders to send it details of any 'shareholders topics' for consideration at the AGM. The advantage of 'drawing' any hostility from the more public domain of the meeting in this way should not be underestimated, although directors of listed PLCs need to be careful regarding any comments they make at such meetings, to avoid breaching INSIDER DEALING legislation. For most LTDs the AGM is likely to be a less formal event and such informal contact can be achieved relatively easily and with fewer 'leakage' concerns.

Developments

Some companies have been investigating 'holding' their AGM in more than one location (e.g. using a number of regional meeting points) to save excessive travel of shareholders based remotely from the meeting location. Such meeting points are linked by closed circuit television to the central location where the board (and perhaps a high proportion of shareholders) might be present.

Case study	Meeting remotely
	In *Byng v London Life* the Court of Appeal held that that a shareholders' meeting could be held in more than one place provided there were *fully functional mutual audio-visual links* in all locations. Thus it would not be possible to hold a general meeting validly using only an audio or written (e.g. via email) link.

Using two or three locations is possibly appropriate but any more could pose considerable problems. Before taking advantage of such a ruling, legal advice would need to be taken, and it might be preferable for the ARTICLES to be changed to avoid any challenge, and to address the situation regarding the possible invalidation of the meeting should one or more of the links between the venues break down.

(b) General Meetings

Definition and description

Under CA06 any meeting other than the AGM is a General Meeting although for pre-CA06 companies such meetings are usually referred to in their Articles as Extraordinary General Meetings. Obviously for companies which do not hold an AGM, those owning (and who are not on the board of) such companies would not normally meet those running it even to discuss routine business. Should there be no obligation to hold an AGM and/or the timing of that meeting is inappropriate for the consideration of business requiring shareholder decision, an (E)GM can be convened. Minutes must be taken and kept for at least 10 years.

Convening

An (E)GM can be convened by:

- the board;
- the members in accordance with the ARTICLES;
- for an LTD, those holding 10 per cent of the members' voting strength (unless no general meeting has been held for at least 12 months, in which case the required percentage is only 5 per cent);
- for a listed PLC, those holding 5 per cent of the voting strength;
- the AUDITORS, should they resign and/or feel there are matters which should be brought to the attention of the members; and
- the Court.

Members' request

If the board receive a members' request to convene an (E)GM then it must do so within 21 days of receiving the members' request and the meeting itself must be convened for a date within a further 28 days (that is the meeting must be held within a total of 49 days from the request date). Minutes of the meeting must be taken and made available to the members (should they wish to inspect them) for two hours every business day.

Should notice of the meeting have already been sent out and the members require an amendment to a proposed resolution this should normally be treated as a new resolution and any specific requirements of the Articles must be complied with. Unless the company agrees to waive them, any costs must be borne by the shareholders making the request. The question of notice must also be addressed since, unless the required percentage of shareholders agree to waive the normal notice requirements, insufficient notice (see below) may have been given.

If the board becomes aware of member concerns which could lead to a request for a meeting and/or a resolution or amendment, it may be advisable to try to discuss requirements in advance, since requisitioning a meeting can be expensive. A shareholder holding more than 10 per cent of the shares in Millwall Football Club's parent company requisitioned a meeting regarding development plans for the club. His proposals were rejected, but convening and running the meeting cost the club over £50,000.

Notice

An (E)GM normally only requires 14 days' notice. Traditionally some resolutions relating to specific business have required longer notice in their own right, e.g. special resolutions required 21 days' notice. Notice periods for all resolutions and meetings (other than PLC's AGMs which still require 21 days' notice) have been rationalised at 14 days under CA06. However, this relaxation is subject to an individual company's Articles and, if the Articles specifically require a special resolution to be subject to 21 days' notice, that amount of notice must be given unless and until the Articles themselves are changed. An (E)GM of an LTD can be held with shorter or no notice provided 90 per cent (or any higher percentage stipulated in the Articles) of the voting rights agree. A shareholder unable to attend a general meeting has a right to lodge a PROXY stipulating how he wishes his votes to be cast.

Gifts, ethics and interests

INTRODUCTION

CA06 imposes controls regarding conflicts of interests, disclosure of benefits provided for a director or obtained by virtue of the directorship of a company, whilst the Bribery Act 2010 adds a new dimension regarding giving and receiving gifts and inducements which could affect business decisions. It is advisable for a code dealing with such matters to be adopted, promulgated and policed. Of course the impact of such a code should not necessarily be restricted to directors. The fact that a code had been adopted should provide some basis for a defence – the legal maxim *'in litigation the person with the best paperwork stands a better chance of winning'* is apposite.

The Bribery Act 2010

This Act came into operation on 1 July 2011 and defines bribery as:

- giving or offering a financial or other advantage to another person;
- requesting, accepting or receiving a bribe;
- bribing a foreign official;
- failure by a commercial organisation to prevent bribery by a person who provides services to it (which could include employees, agents or consultants).

The last offence places an obligation on organisations to take reasonable steps to ensure all those interfacing with third parties (which could include directors, employees, agents or consultants) do not bribe or receive bribes.

In order to successfully use the defence that *'reasonable steps were taken to prevent it'* the organisation must be able to show that:

- it regularly assesses the nature of bribery risks to which it is exposed;
- prevention of bribery is a top level consideration and the commitment to operating without bribery is clearly communicated to everyone;
- there are adequate policies and practices that cover all parties to a business relationship;
- it has implemented its anti-bribery policies and procedures and these are set out in practical terms (i.e. examples are provided);
- it monitors its requirements to ensure compliance.

Some companies now require claims for expenses and the form to be completed by new directors (in DIRECTORS – APPOINTMENT) when completed annually, to state what entertaining has been provided and/or enjoyed, although normal business entertaining is not prohibited by the Act. As one commentator stated *'the Government has made it clear that it has no intention of seeking to prohibit corporate activities aimed at building corporate relations and promoting business'*. However, it will still be an offence to provide 'hospitality' if it can be proved that it was being provided to persuade someone not to act 'in good faith, impartially, or in accordance with a position of trust.'

There is concern that an organisation can be held to be criminally liable for the actions of people acting on its behalf – e.g. agents. Thus there will need to be considerable checking when entering into new markets, acquiring new businesses and entering into joint ventures and/or new partnerships.

Codes of Ethics

The chairman of the first corporate governance committee – Sir Adrian Cadbury – once stated *'from a company's point of view, codes of conduct are a form of safeguard for their reputation'*. Loss of, or damage to, company reputation was placed top of a list of risks that could affect a company detrimentally in a recent survey. Those who control organisations are expected to act in a responsible manner and to ensure that all those they employ act similarly. Companies produce wealth and, as a result, become powerful; the danger with such a situation being, as economist J K Galbraith once said, that *'the greater the wealth, the thicker will be the dirt'* – perhaps somewhat pertinent given the recent failures of formerly highly regarded financial undertakings headed by people paying themselves very handsomely. Any code can only be as effective as:

- the clarity with which it is promulgated;
- the willingness of those affected to comply with its requirements; and
- the effectiveness of the policing of its requirements.

Boardroom compliance

To combat any suggestion of providing bribes as well as bringing the expectation of ethical attitudes and actions to all involved, it may be prudent to promulgate a code of ethics.

Example	Code of ethics

1 Standards

This [organisation] operates under high quality standards – of products, of services and of customer care, and requires these standards to be adhered to at all times in all its dealings.

2 Morality

The organisation will not:

- trade with any regime or organisation that is regarded as oppressive and/or which does not recognise human rights,
- trade with any weapons producer,
- speculate against the currency of its own country,

and will endeavour to prevent its activities being used for any illegal purposes including bribery, money laundering and/or drug trafficking.

3 Personal obligations

All employees are expected to:

- be loyal to the organisation in all their endeavours on its behalf,
- be honest and diligent, and maintain high standards of dignity in undertaking their duties and responsibilities,

and should not:

- act in any manner that will or could damage the organisation's reputation,
- accept, offer or give any bribe or inducement from anyone or to anybody (or any person or organisation acting on their behalf) involved in any way with the organisation,
- permit any activity which might result in a conflict of interests with this organisation, or use any organisational information or material for personal gain.

4 Inducements

Other than properly authorised trade and retail promotions, no inducement may be offered to or given to any customer or outlet whereby they will be induced or encouraged to place an order for or take any product or service offered by the [organisation], or to any supplier or creditor to obtain improved terms of trade. Such activity is proscribed by the Bribery Act 2010 and could result in criminal prosecution. ➡

Example	Code of ethics – *continued*

5 Entertainment

i. Whilst it is acceptable to entertain a customer or supplier to lunch or dinner to discuss normal contractual matters, this must be at places and to the limits laid down in the [organisation's] gifts/entertainment guide. On no account must the limits and guidelines included in that guide be broken without prior written approval of [name].

ii. In the event of any person considering that he needs to entertain or provide a gift for a customer and that the limits are inappropriate (for example the matter concerns an attempt to compensate for previous poor service, quality etc.,) the written authority of a member of the board should be obtained and indication of any limitation agreed and this authority referred to in the subsequent expenses claim.

6 Hospitality

Employees are allowed to accept hospitality from major customers and suppliers in terms of lunches and/or dinners or other similar value entertainment, to a maximum of [number of occasions] per third party organisation per year. In the event that the value obtained is in excess of that laid down in the company entertainment guide, this fact must be made known to a board member as soon as possible. If the entertainment provided is considered to be in excess of that warranted by the circumstances, the director responsible may need to contact the third party to explain the policy.

7 Anti-competitive practices

This organisation operates in a competitive industry and welcomes healthy competition. On no account may any employee or person acting on behalf of the organisation enter into or agree to enter into an arrangement whereby the effect is to price-fix, arrange collusive tendering, split or allocate markets or customers with a competitor, abuse a dominant market position or act in any way which constitutes a breach of the anti-competition legislation and/or is to the detriment of a consumer. Any suggestion of such activity from a third party should be reported immediately to [name].

Example	Code of ethics – *continued*

8 Legal compliance

The [organisation] operates within the [specify] industry and is required to and wishes to comply with all laws, regulations and codes of practice etc. It seeks to trade legally, fairly, openly and honestly with all third parties and to give value for money in all its dealings. It requires and expects its employees to carry out their work and responsibilities and to conduct their relationships and dealings with third parties in accordance with these precepts. All dealings must be conducted openly and fairly in such a way that should every aspect of the transaction become widely known (for example in the media) this would not cause any embarrassment, injury or damage to the reputation of the [organisation] whatever.

9 Respect

All employees are required to act responsibly, decently and with due regard for the dignity and rights of others in both business and personal dealings. In many instances personnel (particularly senior personnel) will be seen as acting on behalf of, or by virtue of their position in the [organisation], in place of the [organisation], the reputation of which must be protected at all times.

10 Whistleblowing

All employees at whatever level in the [organisation] are encouraged to report any activities which seem to them to be in breach of this code to [director]. Such reports will be treated as confidential and provided they are made in good faith and not made with the aim of personal gain, the person making the report should not fear reprisals or detriment.

To try to ensure adherence to required ethical conduct some companies require their employees to sign the code, some even requiring this to be an annual undertaking. It may be advisable to point out that failing to comply with 7 and 8 above could not only result in the application of disciplinary sanctions but also to criminal penalties – including imprisonment.

Whistleblowing

An increasing number of companies (including all listed PLCs since they are obliged to do so under the listing agreement) have adopted whistleblowing codes so that employees becoming aware of wrongdoing are encouraged to make a 'qualifying disclosure' (QD). A QD is any information which tends in the reasonable opinion of the worker (which is an objective test in each case) to show a 'relevant failure' which include:

- a criminal offence has been, is being or is likely to be committed;
- a miscarriage of justice has occurred, is occurring or is likely to occur;
- someone has failed, is failing or is likely to fail to comply with a legal obligation to which they are subject;
- health and/or safety of any individual has been, is being or is likely to be endangered;
- the environment has been, is being or is likely to be damaged;
- information relating to any of the above has been, is being or is likely to be deliberately concealed.

Compensation for successfully claiming unfair dismissal because of whistleblowing is unlimited.

Case study	Theft and fraud
	Antonio Fernandes was the financial controller of Netcom. His managing director gave him petty cash slips on two occasions without any supporting receipts. The amounts claimed were in excess of £200,000. When he protested that such claims were almost certainly a fraud on HMRC since they could not be properly claimed as being wholly and exclusively in the proper execution of his duties, he was told by the managing director, and subsequently by the American owners of the company to 'keep your nose clean and pay it'. He refused and was told to resign. When he did not he was dismissed. In one of the first claims under PIDA, he was awarded £293,000 compensation.

Gift policy

Many employees and directors experience a situation where a customer, adviser or supplier wishes to reward them personally for good service etc., and in principle and moderation there should be nothing wrong with this. However, it is all too easy, if the gift is substantial, for it to become not so much a 'thank you' for past service but a bribe to obtain advantage in the future. Adoption of a gift policy may be helpful both as a guide as to what can be accepted and a way of tactfully refusing larger items.

Example	Gift policy

i   Other than at Christmas [and/or other religious/national celebrations where there is a custom that presents are exchanged], employees are not allowed to accept or retain gifts made by any customer or supplier or other third parties, generated as a result of the business relationship. If such gifts are delivered and it seems potentially damaging to the relationship to return them, then, subject to the approval of [director] the gifts may be retained and will be handed to [the Social Club] for use as raffle prizes or disposed of in a similar way. The director will contact the donor and explain what has occurred and why (i.e. it is in accordance with internal rules).

Practical guidance: A bottle of wine or spirits once a year can be accepted – a bottle every week should not – and must be disclosed.

ii   At Christmas [other religious/national celebrations], employees are allowed to accept the normal gifts to a maximum of [amount] per donor. If gifts above this level are received then, subject to the approval of the [director], they may be retained.

Practical guidance: a gift of value £20 may be acceptable once a year – a gift of £200 might not other than in very exceptional circumstances which should be reported.

iii   If multiple gifts are received to mark good service which has been provided by a number of employees, these may be retained and distributed to the employees concerned provided the value per employee does not exceed the guidance laid down in the entertainment policy.

Practical guidance: A case of wine at Christmas is acceptable but should be distributed between the team. A case of wine every week/month would not be acceptable and should be reported.

iv   The attention of all employees is drawn to the danger of a customer or third party using the previous or anticipated delivery of gifts or inducements as a bribe or to exert pressure (either overt or latent) to obtain concessions (e.g. orders, better terms, preferential treatment) or any other consideration; or such persons using the threat of or actual publicity concerning the previous acceptance of a gift or lavish entertainment as pressure to obtain such concessions etc.

➡

Example	Gift policy – *continued*
	In all circumstances the response '*I cannot comment further – I must contact [director] to discuss this matter*' should be made.
	Practical guidance: Being entertained at a sporting or social activity once a year is acceptable. Accepting such invitations more often/regularly would not be acceptable. An all expenses paid trip to see the Beijing Olympics would probably have been unacceptable although a day trip to the London Olympics would probably be acceptable.
	v Any suggestion of using facilities owned, occupied or made available to a third party (for example a holiday villa or other property, concessionary travel, etc.) either on a free basis or for any consideration which seems or is less than the market price, should be communicated to the [director] at whose discretion the matter can proceed or be concluded.
	Practical guidance: Such a scenario is unacceptable, but a short, expenses paid visit, made because it is genuinely necessary to check facilities that might be used by the organisation should be acceptable.
	vi Any employee feeling unsure about any of the foregoing or that they are being placed in an 'awkward' position by a third party, should report the matter to [named person]. This guidance is best summarised as '*if in doubt, shout*'.

Although this is a policy drafted to provide internal guidance, there is no reason why it could not also be distributed to suppliers, customers etc., so that the incidence of them making a gesture that would breach the rules can be avoided thus preventing embarrassment. It is also a method of advertising the subject organisation's wish to act and be seen to act ethically at all times.

Interests

Directors' conflicts of interests are strictly controlled by CA06. The detailed obligations are set out in DIRECTORS – PAYMENTS, LOANS AND INTERESTS. However, many companies may wish to restrict executives other than the board from having such interests and thus potential conflicts. Accordingly publication of guidance regarding the company's attitude to such matters may be advisable – for example in the employee handbook or similar procedure manual. In addition use of the form set out in DIRECTORS – APPOINTMENT on taking up the position and possibly annually thereafter should be considered.

Example	Control of conflicting interests clause

1 No-one working for or employed by, or providing services for the [organisation] is to make, or encourage another to make any personal gain out of its activities in any way whatsoever without this being agreed to by [named person/board].

2 Any person becoming aware of a personal gain or interest (or potential gain or interest) as a result of which they would benefit is required to notify [name]. Only if it is agreed by [person/board] will such a matter be allowed to subsist.

3 Anyone being in a situation such as is outlined in 2 who does not report the matter will be regarded as having committed an act of gross misconduct for which the usual penalty is dismissal.

4 Anyone reporting a matter which could involve a benefit being made by or given to another and/or which could conflict with that person's obligations, provided there are reasonable grounds for such suspicion, will be protected.

5 All employees are expected to report any suspicion or knowledge of wrongdoing to [named person].

Inevitably since directors are effectively in control of their company's assets the possibility of them (or their connected persons) acquiring such assets no longer required within the company (or selling personal assets to the company) is likely to arise. Whilst assuming that an 'arm's length' valuation is obtained, and that since there is nothing in the Articles to prevent such a transfer, such a transaction could proceed, it would be prudent:

- for a disinterested quorum of the board to resolve that the transfer go ahead;
- for details to be entered in the register of directors' interests (see STATUTORY BOOKS);
- for the matter to be disclosed to the auditors.

Prior approval of the members is required if the value of the asset exceeds £100,000 or is 10 per cent or more of the company's net assets (and exceeds £5000).

INTRODUCTION

Other than buying the shares of an existing company, a company can be acquired from a company formation agent, solicitors, etc. on an 'off the shelf' basis for a cost of up to £200, or set up following the checklist below. CH offers 'same day' incorporation, as well as electronic incorporation, services. However, the latter is probably only economically usable by company formation agents since software systems need to be compatible with and approved by CH for this service to work effectively.

CHECKLIST   Incorporation

✓ Decide on NAME, with alternative choices.

✓ Apply to CH for clearance of name. If it is required to change an existing company's name, and the date of change is critical it may be safer to form a shell company with the required name and then for both existing and new companies to pass special RESOLUTIONS exchanging names on the same date. If an original name is pre-ferred, it may be advisable to try and incorporate the company with that name without checking (using CH 'same day' incorporation service). If the application goes, through, then the name is protected immediately. If it is rejected then little, other than the filing fee, has been lost. Even checking a name out may allow someone else to slip in first – although this possibility is, to some extent, prevented by the company names tribunal. Alternatively, a preferred name can be checked for availability/usage using the CH Webcheck service.

✓ Describe activities or objects (if required). Traditionally these details were set out in the MEMORANDUM and it was usual for them to cover virtually every conceivable activity the company could ever enter into. For CA06 companies, objects clauses are unnecessary (other than for charities) but, if required, must be included in the Articles. The objects clauses of pre-CA06 companies are now deemed to be part of their Articles.

✓ Decide location of the company's registered office which (pending ratification of European Union proposals allowing freedom of relocation within the EU) must be within the country of incorporation.

✓ Purchase STATUTORY BOOKS in hard copy or set up electronic versions. These are Registers of:
  ● members (shareholders or guarantors)

- directors and company secretary
- directors' shareholdings (PLCs only)
- substantial interests in shares (i.e. those held by other shareholders)
- debenture and/or loan holders (if any), and
- CHARGES
- directors' interests (in the shares of their company). This is no longer required for LTDs. Since, however, companies must be advised of third parties etc., in which their directors may have an interest – and thus a potential or actual conflict – it would be best if the company kept a record of such information. This register (with the word 'share' deleted from its title) could suffice for that requirement.

✓ Minute books for meetings of both members and directors will be needed as may a seal and register (and/or register of items signed as deeds).

✓ Determine share capital if required (or for a guarantee company the amount of each guarantee). There is no lower limit on the amount of an LTD's share capital, but for a company to be a PLC, a minimum of £50,000 issued share capital of which 25 per cent or more is paid up in cash must be subscribed. A company formed under CA06 need not have an 'authorised' share capital – the share capital of such a company can be decided by the directors (subject to any shareholder limitations).

✓ Determine any rights of shares, other than the ordinaries.

✓ Arrange initial subscribers. Until CA89, every company had to have two shareholders, but that Act made it legal to operate a company with only one shareholder – a single member company.

✓ Draft MEMORANDUM and ARTICLES OF ASSOCIATION of which the final versions need to be signed by the promoter(s) (and dated and witnessed). The Memorandum of a CA06 company needs little drafting as it contains only the type of company (PLC, LTD – limited either by shares or guarantee) and its country and date of registration (with the copy sent to CH also stating the promoter(s) name(s)). Originate the company's Articles possibly using the drafts accompanying the Act and/or customising clauses. A charitable company must adopt an objects clause and include it within its Articles.

✓ Appoint initial directors of whom full personal details (name, address, date of birth, occupation) will be required both for the register of directors and formation publicity (although a service address rather than a director's private address can be used for public disclosure).

✓ Complete and submit form IN01 (s.9 and s.14 CA06) to CH with fee and a Statement of Compliance (s.1068 CA06). CH has powers to:
  - stipulate in which form it must be lodged (this could mean that such documents must be lodged electronically (see s.1069) which is the intention by 2013)
  - require standard contents
  - require it to be authenticated by a particular person.

✓ A PLC must obtain a 'certificate to commence trading' from CH, before trading.

If a PLC trades before it has this certificate the directors can be held liable for its debts etc.

✓   Open bank accounts, appoint auditors, solicitors, obtain a VAT number, notify HMRC, although the Revenue is automatically notified of the formation of every company and writes to companies requiring information etc.

Certificate of Incorporation

Evidencing the formation and existence of the company, CH issues a Certificate of Incorporation which states:

1   The company's name (in upper case although this does not prevent it using upper and lower case as long as the name itself is identical).
2   The registered number. This entirely distinct (and never re-used) number remains unchanged with the company throughout its life (no matter how often its name is changed). There are proposals (no date yet set) to add computer check digits to all company numbers to aid filing at CH.
3   The date of incorporation.
4   That the company is limited by shares or guarantee or is unlimited.
5   Whether it is an LTD or a PLC.
6   The country of registration (England and Wales, Scotland or Northern Ireland).

The Certificate is conclusive evidence that the legislative requirements have been met and the company is registered under the Act.

Name

The name of the company, as shown on the Certificate of Incorporation, must be used (but no longer on the outside of buildings):

■   at every place of business. In default, every director and the company secretary are liable to an initial fine plus an additional fine for every day this is not effected;
■   on all business letters, purchase orders, notices, website and official publications;
■   on the common SEAL (and any securities seal) of the company;
■   on all invoices, bills of exchange, purchase orders, orders for money etc.

Failure to comply renders those at fault liable to initial plus daily fines.

Date of incorporation

This date (D) is used as the start point for filing time limits.

- D: Incorporation – company is formed, liability of the members is limited, etc.
- D plus 9 months: Notify Registrar of Accounting Reference Date (i.e. FINANCIAL YEAR END)
- D plus 12 months: Latest date for making up first ANNUAL RETURN
- D plus a year plus 9 months (if LTD) or 6 months (if PLC) – file accounts.

Preservation

A replica of the Certificate of Incorporation is often inserted as the first page of the printed Memorandum and Articles. On any change of company's name, CH issues a Certificate on Change of Name which then stands in place of the original Certificate of Incorporation. The Certificate of Incorporation (or Certificate on Change of Name) should be kept safely and permanently.

CH company incorporation service

Although anyone can set up a limited liability company most people use formation agents or solicitors to act for them, tailor-make their Articles etc. Such a service is now also available from CH. Its Web Incorporation Service can form a company for just £18.

However, anyone wishing to use this alternative should be aware that the company *must* use the standard set of Articles accompanying CA06 which may not be appropriate in all cases. However, there is nothing to stop a company being set up with those Articles and then passing a Special Resolution (filing it with CH within 15 days) altering them if the brief 53 regulations (rather than 118 in Table A of CA85) do not suit (contact www.businesslink. gov.uk).

Insider dealing

INTRODUCTION

The principle of trading on the Stock Exchange is that it provides a 'level playing field' for both buyer and seller by making the most up to date information available to everyone. This means that deals can be effected between parties having common knowledge. The reality may be somewhat divorced from that and progressively the situations in which deals are done where one party has the benefit of information not available to another has been restricted by the insider dealing legislation.

Origination

The Criminal Justice Act 1993 created three prohibited insider dealing situations:

- If an individual who has inside information deals in securities using such information. It is an offence if a director of a listed PLC knows that information to which he is party would affect the price of the shares were it to be made public, and traded in the shares.
- If an individual who has inside information encourages another person to trade in the shares he may be guilty of insider dealing and if the person who is encouraged to deal knows that the data is 'inside information' because the informant is in a position to have access to such information then that person may also be guilty.
- If a person discloses price sensitive information to another person other than in the proper performance of his duties. Thus, if a director told their spouse or partner who then traded in the shares on the basis of the information then that person would be guilty. If the director's spouse or partner told a friend and that friend knows the director's position in the company and thus that the source of the information is likely to be authoritative, then if they trade in the shares, they may also be guilty. Thus a person in no way connected to the company (other than by knowing the source of the data) can be guilty of insider dealing. Similarly if a director has a professional adviser – e.g. an accountant – looking after the director's interests and they learn the information and trade then they too will be guilty.

For those found guilty the penalties are severe – up to seven years imprisonment and/or a substantial fine.

Case studies	Should have known better
	McQuoid, a solicitor working for a PLC, tipped off his father-in-law that his employer was about to be taken over. His father-in-law bought over 150,000 shares and made a profit of nearly £50,000. They both received jail sentences of eight months.
	Calvert, after working for nearly 40 years for leading stockbrokers, Cazenoves, (and about to retire) made £104,000 tipping off a friend. He was found guilty of five counts of insider dealing and jailed for 21 months.
	Christian and Angie Littlewood (jailed for three years and a 12-month suspended sentence respectively) and Helmy Sa'aid (jailed for two years, deported to Singapore and fined £640,000) admitted carrying out a £2 million insider dealing scam (relating to tips about takeover bids of eight companies) over several years.

There are some defences including 'that the act of trading would have taken place whether the inside information had been known or not'. This should cover the situation where the person concerned needs to sell shares in order to raise money for a specific (and time-related) purpose. In addition, if a director disclosed the information in the ordinary course of business not believing it would be used for the purposes covered by the Act then that could be a defence.

The whole aspect of the control and prevention of insider dealing was given increased impetus as a result of the passing of the Financial Services and Markets Act which covers not only directors of listed PLCs but also their employees, advisers and private individuals. The thrust of the legislation is to try and enhance the principles of the Criminal Justice Act 1993 referred to above.

Thus a listed PLC must:

- comply with the updated listing rules of the Stock Exchange;
- abide by the requirements regarding the dissemination of 'price sensitive information' (PSI);
- avoid breaching the principles of the 'market abuse' regime; and
- avoid breaching the wider financial promotion regime which now covers all corporate communications.

Market abuse

'Insider dealing' is replicated – but extended. Thus market abuse occurs:

- If a person has information not available generally and that person deals or encourages another to deal. There is no requirement for profit to be made from the action or even for the information to have been price sensitive.
- If a person's behaviour will give a false or misleading impression of the price or value of shares. Thus a listed PLC could commit market abuse by failing to advise the market of material matters or giving misleading or false announcements.
- If a person's behaviour is likely to interfere with or distort the proper operation of market forces.

General compliance with the Listing Rules and Takeover Code then will probably be a sound defence as will be the case if the actions are not below the 'reasonably accepted standard' of behaviour.

Intent

The offence of 'market abuse' does not require intent and thus a person can be liable even if they unknowingly break the rules. Of more concern may be the EU's proposed directive on market abuse (i.e. insider dealing and market manipulation) which does not require that the person intended to commit market abuse at all. The EU suggests that if a person makes an untrue statement believing it to be true that is market abuse – and the offender is liable. So draconian are these rules that companies should ensure everyone affected knows the detailed requirements. The following checklist for action may be of assistance.

CHECKLIST   Internal action

✓   The existing requirements regarding 'insider dealing' should be revisited and revised.

✓   All those involved in market operations need to understand the requirements – particularly the concept of lack of intent.

✓   Check advisers have installed more vigorous verification procedures regarding company announcements to ensure no breach occurs.

✓   Ensure all involved understand the requirements of the 'PSI' regime (see Financial Services Authority 'Code of Market Conduct' which gives examples of market abuse).

✓   Check all issued information (including any posted on the company's website) for compliance and accuracy.

✓   Re-issue internal guidance regarding directors' and employees' rights and actions vis-à-vis trading in the company's shares ensuring that full reference to the new rules is included in that guidance.

Share trading

Inevitably, listed PLCs' directors hold shares in their companies. This poses them a problem in terms of the timing of any purchases and/or sales since almost inevitably at every stage in their company's financial calendar they will have access to information which, if released, might affect the share price. In recognition of this the Stock Exchange listing agreement suggests that directors should observe a two-month 'dead period' before the publication of interim or preliminary announcements during which time directors should not buy or sell any of their company's shares other than for the most urgent reasons. In addition, most companies now require their directors to notify the chairman every time they trade in shares or options.

Postscript

The FSA is so concerned that insider dealing is widespread, that having already insisted in 2010 that emails and calls using landlines must be taped, in 2011 they added a requirement that mobile phone calls and emails etc, must be taped if they relate to deal orders and customer transactions.

Interests in shares

INTRODUCTION

That someone holds (or adds to or disposes of a holding of) shares (particularly if it is a material number or percentage) in a listed PLC can have an effect on the market value of such shares, as well as being of interest to those dealing with the company or preparing to buy or sell such shares. In the interests of creating a '*level playing field*' of knowledge for all investors, those whose share interests exceed certain levels are required to advise the company which must, having recorded the information, then advise the Stock Exchange. Obviously changes in shareholdings of directors of the company can have an even greater impact on the shares' market value.

Major interests

Members whose shareholding reaches or exceeds 3 per cent of the issued shares of a listed or quoted PLC must, under the Listing Agreement requirements, notify the company of the total of their interest. In addition, whenever their holding above this level increases or decreases so that a whole percentage point is altered (that is it goes from (say) 3 per cent to 4 per cent, or down from (say) 7 per cent to 6 per cent), that change must also be notified, as must any development which takes their interest below 3 per cent. All such notifications must take place within two days.

In addition, the company is legally required within three days of receipt of such information to record in its register of substantial interests in shares, the date, the name of the shareholder and the data itself – and, under the Listing Agreement, to inform the Stock Exchange.

Non-material holdings

Non-material holdings of 10 per cent or more must also be notified. A non-material interest exists where the named holder acts (for example as a trustee) and has no personal interest in the shares. If both material and non-material holdings are in existence then it is necessary to disclose the aggregate if this reaches or exceeds 10 per cent, even though the constituent parts separately need not be declared. For example, if the material interest was less than 3 per cent and the non-material interest was just over 7 per cent, but their total is less than 10 per cent, there is no obligation to disclose either interest under the individual notification requirements. However, if in aggregate they exceed 10 per cent both interests must be disclosed. This situation must be monitored since if (as in the above example) there was an increase in the non-material holding this could push the total of the two interests over the 10 per cent disclosure threshold. The effect of a sudden disclosure of an interest of over 10 per cent when none was formerly recorded could have a material effect on the share price – even though in fact there has been very little change! There is now an additional requirement to notify non-material interests at a 5 per cent level but not at the intervening percentage points between this level and 10 per cent.

Discovering the true ownership

Companies who believe that the owner of the shares (by the notified name) is not the actual owner are permitted to serve a notice on the disclosed owner (who it suspects may be a nominee) requiring disclosure of the person who has beneficial ownership. The notice, permitted under s.793 CA06 is required to be complied with within two days of being served. It is not unusual to find one nominee holds it for another nominee and so on, and to find that the true owner is not disclosed until after several notices have been served in respect of the same holding.

Example	**Draft s.793 notice**
	Name of Company
	Address　　　　Date　　　　Reference　　　　Person dealing
	Name of shareholder
	Address
	Companies Act 2006, s.793.
	(Description of type, classification, etc. of shares e.g. 'XXX Ordinary Shares')
	We have registered a holding of (number and description) of the above shares in your name. As authorised by section 793 of the Companies Act 2006, we require you, within two days by letter, fax or telex, to provide us with the answers to the following questions:
	1. In how many shares of the above description do you currently have an interest?　　　　　　　　　　　　　　➜

Example	Draft s.793 notice – *continued*
	2. What is your interest in such shares?
	3. If you have disposed of the shares, on which date(s) was your interest disposed of, and, if you are aware, who now has that interest?
	4. Please state the full details of any agreement or arrangement of which you are aware regarding the exercise of any voting rights in respect of such shares.
	Yours, etc.

Failure to provide adequate answers to such questions or even to obtain a reply to the request can lead to the company having the right to disenfranchise the shares, although the Stock Exchange requires a 'cooling off' period for further negotiations before this can be implemented since it prefers not to have franchised and disenfranchised shares in the market simultaneously.

Directors' holdings

Listed PLCs having been informed of a director's interest in the shares of the company (or of any change) must place such details in the register of directors' share interests within three days. For such companies, the holdings (and any changes thereto) of directors in their company's shares must also be advised to the Stock Exchange within five days of the transaction. There is also a requirement that for a period (usually two months) before the announcement by the company of what could be 'price-sensitive' information (e.g. the announcement of results) that directors should not trade in their company's shares (see INSIDER DEALING).

Under FSA rules and in compliance with the Disclosure and Transparency Rules, should a director of a listed PLC use his shares as security for a loan or similar then that must be advised both to the company within four days (and he should gain clearance for his action from the board prior to implementation) and the company must disclose the fact to the Stock Exchange.

However, following the case in late 2008 of David Ross (former deputy chairman of Carphones Warehouse) who used shares in that company as security for a large loan, the FSA admitted that although its rules regarding disclosure were as set out above, there was no sanction should a director fail to comply! The fallout from this high profile breach prompted the FSA to announce a two-week amnesty in January 2009 for companies that had failed to disclose such actions of their directors. During that amnesty over 50 companies '*came clean*' and made such a disclosure.

The FSA has now clarified the rules and as a result, directors must now disclose to the company if and when they pledged shares for a loan. Such disclosure must be made within four days of the event, and the company must then inform the Stock Exchange. Failure to do so renders both company and director liable to an unlimited fine.

Memorandum of association

INTRODUCTION

CA06 abolishes the need for companies (other than charities) to have or retain objects clauses which for companies formed under earlier Acts are set out (and form the major part of) their Memorandum. For a CA06 company, however, although there is still an obligation for a company to have a Memorandum, it is reduced to just a few lines – and virtually duplicates the content of the Certificate of Incorporation.

Content

The Memorandum of a CA06 company must state:

1 The names of the promoters, although once INCORPORATION is completed this is of purely academic interest. Formerly at least two members were needed to sign the Memorandum, although the Memorandum of a single member company needed only to be signed by one person. Under CA06 a single person can form any type of company.

2 For a company limited by shares: the number of shares taken by each promoter, although this is of interest only on formation since thereafter additional shares can be issued. In the Memorandum of a company limited by guarantee, the maximum amount of the guarantee(s) must be stated. A CA06 company does not need to have an 'authorised share capital' unless the shareholders require it, in which case it must be set out in the Articles.

3 The name of the company which must include the word 'limited'. This indicates that the liability of the members is limited to the amount of their investment.

4 The name of the country (England and Wales, Scotland or Northern Ireland) in which the REGISTERED OFFICE is to be situated. Pending the implementation of EU proposals to relax this restriction, a company registered in England and Wales, Scotland or in Northern Ireland can have its registered office only in its country of registration. Although the actual address of the registered office need not be stated in the memorandum, under s.9 CA06, on INCOPORATION a note of this address must be filed with CH using form IN01. Any alteration in the address of the registered office of the company must be filed with

CH on form AD01. On the change of a registered office, a 14-day period is allowed, during which both old and new offices are valid for the service of notices. A CA06 company's Memorandum is unalterable.

Pre-CA06 companies

In addition to the above, pre-CA06 companies' Memorandums were (and still are unless altered) required to contain:

- a statement of the total number of shares (and their various categories if applicable) that the company was authorised to issue. Whilst this is valuable information to creditors, since (at least in theory) it shows some of the funds available as security for their debts, the amount and type of share capital has always been subject to alteration. If the company is to be formed as (or re-registered as) a PLC, the share issued capital must be at least £50,000 of which 25 per cent (i.e. at least £12,500) must be paid up.
- the objects of the company. These, often extremely numerous, clauses are a public statement of the business the company was formed to undertake, and effectively act as a limitation on its directors' authority to conduct business and as a contract between the company and the outside world. Under CA89, companies were instead permitted to have a short form 'objects clause', e.g. *the company will be a general commercial company*. Effectively this would mean that it would be very unlikely that the company could ever act beyond its powers. Such a clause was rarely used mainly since banks were averse to lending money to a company if its aims or objects were unrestricted. Such concerns over using an abbreviated objects clause reflect the original purpose of stating the objects – to protect those dealing with the company by confirming the nature of its business. It may be feasible to use the abbreviated clause for a subsidiary, or joint venture company where lenders' concerns could be overcome by the parent(s) giving guarantees. Section 39 CA06 states that (other than for charitable companies) the validity of an act done by a company cannot be questioned on ground of 'lack of capacity'. Companies that wish to (or must, if a charity) retain objects clauses must include them in the Articles. The objects clauses of pre-CA06 companies that do not change or re-write their Articles are simply now deemed to be part of their Articles.

Minutes

INTRODUCTION

The company secretary is usually responsible for the administration of both members' meetings (AGM and (E)GMs) and board meetings and composing the record of the proceedings of both. The clear recording and promulgation of decisions made by the members and the board are a legal requirement under s.248 CA06. However, in addition to providing a record of board decisions, minutes can also provide contemporaneous and written evidence that the directors were complying with their duty of care; grant authority for directors or others to carry out acts on behalf of the company, and act as a means of progress-chasing decided business. Since CA06 sets out explicit duties of directors, minutes addressing the manner of compliance with these requirements may also help prove that the board was aware of and complied with such obligations. Minutes should, therefore be compiled with care, read by the board with similar care and be corrected/approved appropriately. Minutes do not have to be handwritten and may be best kept in secure loose-leaf folders so that minutes of subsequent meetings can easily be added to create an ongoing record.

Content

Generally minutes should record:

1 *The Constitution* under which the meeting is taking place. This may be fairly obvious for a board meeting since the directors are meeting with the authority of their appointment (and in accordance with their duty under company law) to take decisions to operate the company on behalf of and for the benefit of the owners, whilst taking into account the interests of the other company 'stakeholders' (employees, creditors, consumers and the environment). Where there is a meeting of, for example, a sub-committee of the board, the terms of reference of that committee might usefully be set out in the minutes of its first meeting as well as in the minutes of the appointing body (see BOARD MEETINGS).

2 *The administration*: when and where the meeting took place and who was there. Minutes should record the board members 'present', as well as advisers 'in attendance' and any comings and goings of members during the meeting (and the points of the meeting at which such entrances and exits occurred).

3 *The information*: data (e.g. reports) on which decisions were taken (including a note of whether these were tabled or distributed previously). The information that was provided demonstrates the basis on which decisions were taken, and, by exception, what information was not available to the board (which might be of considerable importance should the company get into difficulties – see WRONGFUL TRADING).

4 *The official back-up*: details of which registers were sealed, initialled, etc. and which reports were considered.

5 *The decisions*: whilst the content will differ according to individual company requirements, it is usually considered preferable for minutes to record decisions (and any dissent therefrom) rather than discussion and arguments for and against the matter and reasons for arriving at it. It is generally agreed that the briefer the minutes the better – although, ideally, they should contain sufficient information to enable a third party to understand the reasons for decisions taken, which may mean at times that some limited (and occasionally detailed) commentary should be included to explain the basis for such decisions. This is a particular requirement for companies operating under FSA rules.

6 *The authority*: minutes (of both board and general meetings) should be signed as a true record of the preceding meeting at the next following board meeting. Under s.249 CA06, signing the minutes grants them status as evidence (in Scotland, sufficient evidence) of the proceedings, and they can be produced as such in Court. Some Articles stipulate that if the minutes are approved and signed then they will be conclusive evidence of the proceedings, meaning that it will be virtually impossible to challenge them later.

7 *The record*: Once the minutes have been drafted they should be approved in principle by the chairman with drafts sent out to all members. Ideally this should happen within three to four working days of the meeting. If (a) board member(s) object(s) to the wording proposed, and the objection has general support, the minutes should be changed. Although this can be done by alteration, it may be preferable for a fresh version, incorporating agreed change(s), to be prepared.

If members wish to make more substantial amendments this may require further drafts until there is a consensus that the record is an accurate reflection of what was agreed. Seeing decisions in a written format can sometimes generate a rethink!

Sending the minutes out as soon as possible after the meeting means they may be able to act not just as a record of the board decisions, but also as prompts to those required to effect the decisions, not least since some members' recollection of what they agreed and/or were required to do may be hazy. Those in receipt of such copies may also need to be reminded of the need for adequate security. Minutes should be a true fair and accurate record which is of particular importance should the company need to produce a certified copy of a minute to a third party, for example to evidence a member's authority to sign a contract, ratify a bank mandate etc.

The following examples should be regarded as guidance only, since the style adopted may not suit every company. Under both versions, references to explanatory notes have been included – indicated by the numbers in brackets shown on the right hand side of the page, the notes being set out following each draft.

Example	Draft minutes – I

ANY COMPANY LIMITED   182(1)

MINUTES of a BOARD MEETING held on 30th March [year]

At [address] at 10.00 a.m.

Present: XYZ (in the chair)

ABC

DEF

GHI

In attendance : JKL (company secretary)

(Mr. TSS, auditor was in attendance for items covered by Minute 3 i and ii)   (2)

An apology for absence due to illness was received from UVW and this was accepted. Those present signed the attendance book.   (3)

The board reminded themselves of the seven duties of directors set out in the Companies Act 2006 and confirmed that in taking all decisions they would continue to take account of these duties and bear in mind the disparate interests of the company's stakeholders.   (4)

1   MINUTES

The minutes of the board meeting held on 29th February [year] previously distributed were taken as read, approved and signed.   (5)

2   DIRECTORS INTERESTS

The register recording interests of board members as advised to the company was laid on the table.   (6)

3   RISK CONTROL

The Secretary tabled an updated statement of risk control which would form part of the forthcoming Annual Report, as a result of an investigation and report recently   →

Example	Draft minutes – 1 – *continued*

completed by the Risk Control sub-committee of the Board. This was ratified. It was noted that an updated Delegated Authority chart had been issued to all employees and agents, drawing attention to the instruction that on no account should bribes be offered or taken. (7)

4   SHAREHOLDER MATTERS

It was resolved that a share transfer covering 500 Ordinary shares in the company from Mrs MNO to Mr PQR be and it hereby is approved and that a share certificate in the name of Mr PQR be issued and the required entries be made in the Register of Members. The secretary was asked to write to Mr PQR welcoming him as a shareholder.

Action: JKL (8)

A report from the company secretary recommending that responsibility for the share registration work of the company be placed with Share Registrars Ltd. was accepted and the terms of the contract approved. The company secretary was requested to make the necessary arrangements in liaison with the chairman.   Action: JKL

(Mr DEF, having previously notified the company that he had a consultancy agreement with Share Registrars Ltd did not take any part in this discussion or decision.)   (9)

5   FINANCE

i) Management accounts.

The accounts for the month of February and the cumulative 11 months were tabled and discussed in detail. The favourable comparison with budget was welcomed, as was the managing director's opinion that the trading and financial situation would continue to show improvement, both in real terms and against budget. It was noted that the situation regarding discounts and promotional payments was still being clarified and additional controls would be introduced from the commencement of the new financial year.

A number of estimated provisions were listed for possible incorporation in the year end accounts.   Action: ABC

ii) Depreciation.

It was agreed to change the company's accounting policies so that depreciation would be charged on vehicles, office

Example	Draft minutes – I – *continued*

equipment and computers at 33.3 per cent p.a. straightline. It was noted that this change would have to be recorded in the published Accounting Policies.

iii) Capital expenditure.

a) It was agreed that a further five production units at a cost of around £4000 each could be purchased in stages over the remainder of 2XXX to allow the sale of [detail]. Mr UVW (whom failing, the company secretary) would authorise each item bearing in mind the effect on cash flow.

Action: UVW/JKL (10)

b) The chairman referred to Capital Expenditure Project form number 13/2XXX for the investment in [detail] which projected a first year return of 14 per cent rising to 17 per cent in year 2 on a fully absorbed basis. The project was approved for implementation no earlier than 31st December [year].

Action: ABC

iv) Cash flow. The latest projection for the period ending 31st December [year] was tabled, discussed and approved.

v) Investigations for the replacement of the company vehicles allocated to six area managers would be carried out. The guidance of the auditors as to the company's and individual's tax situation would be sought.   Action: GHI

vi) Bank Mandate. The secretary reported that the company's bankers had requested that a new mandate on the main drawing account be completed. It was resolved that the company operate the No 1 Main Drawing account in its name with the Finance Bank Plc on the terms and subject to the restrictions set out in a new mandate, a copy of which initialled by the chairman for the purposes of identification is attached to these minutes, and that the secretary be and he hereby is empowered to take such actions as might be necessary to give effect to this resolution.   Action: JKL (11)

vii) Borrowings. The secretary reported that in the absence of Mr UVW he had negotiated an additional £100,000 overdraft facility with the Finance Bank on the same terms as the existing facility. This additional borrowing was available for the eight weeks until end August [year]. Although he had expected to receive documentation requiring board approval to evidence this borrowing this had not arrived before the meeting.

→

Example	Draft minutes – 1 – *continued*

It was resolved that the chairman, ABC and UVW (whom failing the company secretary) be and they hereby are empowered to sign such documents and take such actions to provide the company's bankers with the documentation they required in order to facilitate the advance of this additional borrowing requirement.

The secretary was instructed to let each board member have copies of the relevant items and documentation when these were to hand.

The secretary confirmed that even with this additional borrowing the limits in the Articles had not been breached.

Action: XYZ, ABC, UVW, JKL (12)

6 CURRENT TRADING

The managing director reported that [synopsis of report.........]. An analysis showing the deterioration over a five-year period of sales of the main product was tabled and it was agreed that the deadline for delivery of supplies of Project X needed to be brought forward to compensate for the expected shortfall in sales in the latter part of the calendar year.

Action: ABC

DEF requested that his dissent from this course of action be noted in the minutes with the note that in his opinion not enough was being done to incentivise the sales force and he had serious doubts concerning the effectiveness of the recently appointed sales manager.   (13)

7 PERSONNEL

A report from the divisional director (Personnel) had been sent to all members and the contents were accepted. It was agreed that negotiations should commence with employee representatives to try to agree the wage increase with effect from 1st July [year] along the lines outlined in the report.

It was noted that all employees and agents had been reminded of their obligations in compliance with the Bribery Act.

8 PROPERTY

The following items were noted: (14)

[Facility address]: Little progress had been made on any of the pending rent reviews which would update the list accompanying the agenda for the meeting other than the following: ➡

Example	Draft minutes – 1 – *continued*

[Facility]: Approval was granted to a letter of response to the landlords requesting that an extension to the user be agreed.

[Facility]: Evidence thought to be misleading had been submitted by the landlord's agents.

[Facility]: The landlord's agents had reduced their figure for the reviewed rent to £13,500. Negotiations continued.

The sale of [facility] was proceeding with exchange of contracts expected for mid-July and completion by 1st August. It was noted that receipt of the sale monies had not been built into the cash flow forecast and that if this sale completed as anticipated the additional overdraft facility would not be needed.

The possibility of selling the business and licensing or underletting the lease at [facility] was being pursued urgently.

Insurance: The secretary would draft a letter to be sent to all landlords of leased premises requesting that the interest of the company be noted on the insurance policies to ensure any liability in the event of loss was minimised.   Action: JKL

(Mr DEF apologised and with the permission of the chairman left the meeting.)   (15)

9 SAFETY MATTERS

i) The monthly report was accepted, no actions being required.

ii) The secretary reported

   (a) that he had investigated the requirements of the current health and safety legislation regarding fire precautions in the workplace and tabled a brief synopsis of the action he felt it was necessary for the company to take in order to comply with the requirements. The board requested him to obtain detailed cost estimates for the various requirements with, in each case, an indication of the proposed timetable for implementation of the recommendations.

   (b) that he had commissioned reports to determine whether there were any asbestos containing materials in the company's properties.   Action: JKL (16)

10 SEALING

The secretary produced the Register of Sealing (and documents signed as deeds) to the board and approval was granted to the affixing of the company seal to items

Example	Draft minutes – 1 – *continued*

numbered 345 to 357 and 359 to 361, and approval
granted to the signing as a deed of item 358. The chairman
was authorised to sign the register in evidence of this
approval.   (17)

11 BOARD MEETING TIMETABLE

The dates of future meetings of the board were confirmed
as 28th April, 30th May, 30th June, 28th July, 31st August,
29th September, 25th October, 23rd November, and
21st December.

The secretary was requested to inform Messrs DEF and
UVW of these dates as soon as possible.   (18)

Chairman ....   28th April [year]   (19)

Action points: (20)

Welcoming shareholder	JKL	[Completion date]
New Share Registrars	JKL	[Completion date]
Provisions in accounts	ABC	[Completion date]
Capex products purchase	UVW(JKL)	[Ongoing]

and so on.

Notes

1   Ideally minute pages should be consecutively numbered to try to prevent fraudulent alterations. The subject of each minute (where applicable) should be indexed and a degree of cross-referencing provided. Some companies use the financial year to delineate minutes e.g. 2011/X etc. – changing to 2012/X for the first board meeting in the new financial year.

2   Stating the exact period of attendance of advisers, and even of members if not present for the whole meeting, is advisable.

3   It is arguable that only if an apology for absence is accepted that the absence is acceptable. In some boards if no apology is made, that fact is stated in the minutes (i.e. *'No apology was received from ...'* which underlines the implied obligation for directors to be present). Under reg. 81 of Table A of CA85, if a director does not attend board meetings for six months or more without permission of the board, he can be removed from the board.

It may also be advisable for directors to sign an attendance book

– although it would not normally be necessary to minute this if done as a routine. Some charities require this.

4   CA06 places explicit duties on directors and to be able to demonstrate that they were aware of these duties wording such as this could be inserted in the minutes once a year as a reminder (and in the minutes of any board which a director is attending for the first time so that newcomers have the point brought to their attention).

5   Ideally the chairman should initial each page of the minutes except for the last which should be signed. See 19 below.

6   Listed PLCs, and companies with shareholders not on the board, should consider incorporating in their ANNUAL REPORT a statement of risk and control mechanisms devised as well as the fact that these are regularly assessed by the board. Being able to use the defence (e.g. for an allegation of bribery) that *reasonable steps have been taken* would seem to indicate that it needs a constant re-assessment of the possibility and a repeated reminder that it must not occur. Board attention in this way may be of assistance in meeting this aim.

7   Under CA06 there is an implied requirement to record items in which directors have an interest – e.g. indemnities, loans, potential and/or actual conflicts of interest etc. It may be prudent to maintain a register of directors' interests into which details of such items are entered and to have this available at each board meeting so that all members are aware of each of their interests. This may also assist the secretary should an item of business require a 'disinterested quorum'. This register can be updated regularly if the concept of requiring directors to complete a statement of their interests each year is adopted. (See form in DIRECTORS – APPOINTMENT.)

8   Directors of many LTDs have the right to refuse to allow transfer of shares to a person of whom they do not approve. It is probably unlikely that an LTD would need to retain external registrars to deal with its share registration work as is suggested here – although this is often used by listed PLCs.

   In addition, placing the initials of the person due to deal with the item enables the minutes (already a document of record and reference) to act also as a means of encouraging prompt action.

9   Depending on the Articles' requirements, it is important that any director with an interest in the subject matter should declare that interest and that the point be noted. DEF's interest with Share Registrars should have been entered in the register of directors' interests – see 7 above.

10 Framing a decision in this way leaves some leeway for delay should the circumstances at the time warrant such delay and also covers the situation should Mr UVW not return.

11 Where a lengthy document is required to be approved, rather than repeating the whole item in the minutes, it could be copied and

attached to the minutes. It should then be numbered either consecutively after the last page number for that meeting's minutes, or take the number of the past page and 'a', 'b', 'c' etc., added with a designatory letter for each page of the item. Banks may wish to have a set form of resolution adopted for the approval of their mandate and similar forms.

12 Reference should be made to the Articles to ensure the board are acting in accordance with them. They often set out the requirements and restrictions on board activities, particularly constraints on the maximum the board can borrow on behalf of the company. If such pre-set figures need to be exceeded, the Articles should be changed otherwise the directors will be acting *ultra vires* and could be held personally liable to repay the excess borrowed.

13 In the event that any director wishes to exercise his common law right to have his dissent recorded, this must occur.

14 To save the time of the meeting, it may be possible to distribute a report (as here) with the agenda and simply report on any update since the date of the agenda.

15 Ideally all directors should be present for the whole meeting – and there is a presumption that this is the case. If it is not possible, the time that a director left (or arrived, if late) should be noted in the minutes.

16 The Health and Safety Executive has recommended that safety should be a regular item for discussion by the board. This is sound advice not least since it may be valuable evidence that the company took and takes safety considerations seriously. It might be best if there were a regular safety report – at the very least the board could review the results of the regular 'Responsible Persons' inspections regarding fire safety required to be carried out at every place of work.

17 Although not a statutory requirement, the use of a register of seals (and/or of documents signed as deeds) and subsequent board approval of all entries provides board authority for the items. It also enables details to be noted of items signed as deeds where the use of the seal has been dispensed with. The chairman should sign under the last number authorised at the meeting and should add the date. Ideally the number of each seal entry in the register should appear on the item sealed as a further cross-reference of authority.

18 Meetings arranged in the absence of a colleague can clash with other commitments already entered into, hence early advice of meeting dates is essential. The dates of board meetings may best be arranged on a rolling 18-month basis, with the immediate six months dates fixed, the following six months subject to some leeway and the third six months indicative only. Progressively each six-month section becomes firmer with additional outline indications tacked on.

19 Inserting a place for the chairman to sign and adding the date (of the next planned meeting) emphasises the importance of signing as well as improving the presentation of the minutes themselves.

20 Some companies that utilise the actions points concept (see 8 above), additionally list these at the end of the minutes and insert a required 'completion date' for each.

These minutes are based upon those successfully provided for the boards of actual companies so the style and format can be said to be an effective way of drafting minutes. This is not to say that there cannot be other equally effective versions. It is up to a company's board to decide the way it wishes to record its deliberations and to adopt a suitable style. However, the importance of proper meeting control and minute taking is perhaps underlined by the comments made by the DBIS inspectors' report on the Phoenix/MG Rover collapse. One could be forgiven for describing it as an excellent example of *'how not to do it'*. There the breaches were stated to include:

- convening board meetings without notifying all directors entitled to be there;
- not taking minutes of board meetings at which important matters were *'decided'*;
- false minutes (e.g. directors being shown to be present when they had no knowledge of the meeting and, in some cases, were out of the country);
- directors voting on matters in which they had a interest;
- directors benefiting from decisions in which they had an interest;
- minutes not being approved at a subsequent meeting, and so on.

One commentator stated that *'it would seem to offer an open and shut case for the directors of MG Rover Group to be disqualified for life'*.

Example	Draft minutes – 2

ANY OTHER COMPANY LTD   431(1)

MINUTES of the [x]th ANNUAL GENERAL MEETING

held on Thursday, 24 October 2XXX at [address] at 10.00 a.m.

Present: ABC (in the Chair)

HIJ

KLM

NOP

12 shareholders

In attendance :   AAA (Secretary) and BBB (Auditor)

 1 NOTICE

      The secretary read the notice of the meeting   (2)

Example	Draft minutes – 2 – *continued*

2 DIRECTORS REPORT for the year ended 30 June 2XXX

The chairman referred members to the Report and Accounts for the year ended 30th June 2XXX and the balance sheet as at that date. He requested BBB (of accountants – name) to read the audit report which he did. (3)

The chairman proposed, NOP seconded and it was resolved unanimously that the report and accounts of the company for the year ended 30th June 2XXX and the balance sheet as at that date be and they are hereby received. (4)

3 DECLARATION OF DIVIDEND

The chairman referred to the payment of an interim dividend in January 2XXX and to the fact that the board were recommending payment of a final dividend of 2p per ordinary share. He proposed, KLM seconded and it was resolved unanimously that the company should pay a final dividend on 27th October 2XXX in respect of the year ended 30th June 2XXX of 2p per ordinary share to the holders of ordinary shares registered on the books as at 1st October 2XXX. (5)

4 RETIREMENT BY ROTATION OF DIRECTORS

The chairman stated that in accordance with the Articles of Association and as set out in the notice of the meeting, Mrs EFG and Mr KLM were retiring by rotation and each being eligible, had submitted themselves for re-election. The chairman proposed, Mr HIJ seconded and it was resolved unanimously that the re-election of both retiring directors could be put to the meeting as one motion. (6)

The chairman proposed, Mr K Jones, a shareholder seconded, and it was resolved unanimously that Mrs EFG and Mr KLM be and they hereby are re-elected directors of the company.

5 AUDITORS

It was proposed by Mrs EFG, seconded by the chairman and resolved nemo contendare that Messrs [Name] be and they are hereby re-appointed auditors of the company until the conclusion of the next following AGM on terms to be agreed by the directors. (7)

The meeting terminated at 10.25 a.m.

Chairman .... 29th November 2XXX (8)

Notes

General: Under CA06, an LTD no longer needs hold an AGM unless its members (or the company's Articles or the directors) so require. If an AGM is held then minutes must be taken and preserved for 10 years (although it may be wise to preserve them in perpetuity):

1   The pages should be numbered consecutively. Often minutes of general and board meetings are kept in the same folder and numbered consecutively as a single complete record. This can pose a problem should a member wish to inspect them, since although members have a right to see the minutes of general meetings, they have no right to see the minutes of board meetings. Thus the minutes would have to be separated and the page numbering might look somewhat odd. Minutes of meetings of shareholders must be kept at the registered office. There is no restriction regarding the location of minutes of board meetings, although in view of their content they should be kept securely.

2   There is no requirement to read the notice of the meeting but it can be helpful (if only to cover the arrival of latecomers).

3   Similarly there is no requirement for the auditors to read the audit report (which they will already have had to sign) but again it does little harm and, at the very least, identifies the auditor to the members.

4   The members have only a right to receive accounts already approved by the directors – they have no right of approval or rejection. Under common law, when the chairman proposes a resolution a seconder is unnecessary. However, since few members may know this it may be better to arrange seconders and for them to be shareholders who are not directors, giving, at least, the appearance of democracy.

5   The members can approve, reduce or reject a final dividend: they cannot increase it. Using a 'striking date' prior to the meeting should enable all the calculations to be carried out, and even cheques drawn, on the assumption that the dividend will be approved. Once this happens, the cheques can be signed and despatched (or the amounts transferred via the banking credit system) so that members receive them on the due date. Listed PLCs must give notice to the Stock Exchange of a board meeting at which there will be consideration of dividend declaration and of its approval.

6   The re-election of directors *en masse* can only take place if the meeting has previously approved (as here) that the re-election can take place in this way.

7   '*Nemo contendare*' is Latin meaning no one objected to the proposal. Thus, although everyone voted in favour of all the previous proposals, in this instance, whilst no-one voted against, one or more members abstained.

8   Best practice suggests that the minutes of AGMs and (E)GMs should be approved and signed by the chairman at the next following board meeting (i.e. not waiting until the next following general meeting).

Names and name changes

INTRODUCTION

A company's name, registered number and office and country of incorporation are set out in its Certificate of Incorporation which evidences its existence, rather like a 'corporate birth certificate'. Such details are constantly required to be used by the company, as a legal person, to ensure those dealing with it know who it is and where to contact it. This satisfies the basic principle that everyone has a right to know the identity of the person with whom they are trading. There are strict rules regarding the name a company can use – see CH guidance note GP/1. For active companies the corporate name must be displayed at every location at which a company's business is carried on. Whilst some companies use their corporate name as a well-marketed and well-known trading name, others have high-profile product names, but virtually unknown corporate names.

Publication

The corporate name, registered number and office, and the country of incorporation are required to be shown:

- at the registered office (or SAIL used for records inspection);
- at all places where business is transacted (although no longer on their exterior);
- on all business letters and purchase orders;
- on all official publications and notices;
- on any website operated by the company (where the VAT number, if applicable, must also be stated);
- on all bills of exchange, promissory notes, cheques, money orders, etc.;
- on all invoices, receipts and letters of credit.

These rules also apply to all communications with third parties. Thus communications sent by fax or email to a third party must also comply with disclosure requirements. It is not necessary for a business card or compliment slip to bear these details, although if such a slip was used to handwrite an offer or confirm a contractual commitment this could create a 'business letter' which might have to comply.

Business names

Formerly, where any business traded under a name which was not its corporate name, under the Business Names Act 1985 (BNA85) it was required to state this fact and, if it was a company, it was also required to state the corporate name, registered number and office and country of registration on all business letters, orders, invoices, purchase orders and demands for payment of debts. Although BNA85 has been repealed, its requirements are repeated in ss.1192–1199 CA06. This is curious since this legislation is binding on all organisations trading under a name which is not that of a real or legal person and means that organisations that are not companies are also bound, although it is extremely doubtful if a sole trader, partnership, etc., using a trading or business name would think of checking company law for their obligations!

Example	**Statement of corporate name and registration**
	BLOGGS PEGS is a business name of BLOGGS LTD
	[Registered in England, No.111222333, registered office address]

A company must also display at all premises where business is carried on, its corporate name and an address where official documents can be sent or served, and, should anyone request that information, it must be supplied in writing within five days (failing to do so renders the company liable to a fine). Thus a retail company must display in every shop a notice stating the corporate name and address for service of documents, again complying with the basic rule, that even if the transactions are of tiny worth, everyone has a right to know the legal identity and address of the 'person' with whom they are trading, and to know to what address any formal communication (e.g. regarding a dispute) must be sent. Such units are also required to display in their windows, the name of the owner of the shop. It must be said that both requirements are more noted for breach than observance. Further, in *DTI v Cedenio* it was held that a sole trader did not breach BNA85 where, in a business letter, although he stated that he was the author of the letter he did not state that he was the proprietor of the business; neither was he obliged, having given an address for the business, to state that this was an address on which legal notices could be served. This ruling seemed to undermine the whole principle behind the business names' legislation.

Choosing and changing its name

I A company can choose and change its name to another provided the proposed name does not offend certain rules.

2 The name must not:
- duplicate an existing name (on the company register);
- be misleadingly similar to an existing company's name;
- be offensive or criminal (both in accordance with criteria as laid down by the Secretary of State);
- infer a local or central government connection;
- and must contain
- certain words as required by the Secretary of State (e.g. Limited, Ltd or LTD, Public Limited Company, Plc or PLC, etc., as applicable);
- other restricted words only provided the permission of bodies controlling such use has been obtained and not withdrawn.

It is also wise to check whether any company is already using the name as a registered trade mark, since attempting to use a protected name may generate an infringement or 'passing off' action. This can be effected using the Companies House Webcheck service.

There is a trend to use combinations of letters and symbols to form 'original' company names. Since some of these symbols have caused problems at CH there are restrictions regarding their use.

3 The company needs to pass a special RESOLUTION at a general meeting. Under CA06 only 14 days' notice is required but if the Articles specify it requires 21 days' notice the latter must be given, unless notice was waived in whole or in part. Alternatively the resolution could be passed by written resolution provided 75 per cent of the total voting strength is in favour.

4 Within 15 days of the passing of the resolution, a printed copy of it, certified as such by the secretary or a director, together with the current fee, must be filed at CH.

Example	**Meeting notice and draft resolution**
	Any Company Ltd
	Notice is hereby given that a(n)
	(Extraordinary) General Meeting of the company
	will be held on Monday, 18th December 2XXX
	for the purpose of considering, and if thought fit passing the following resolution as a SPECIAL RESOLUTION
	'THAT the name of the company be changed from Any Company Ltd to Another Company Ltd'
	By order of the board
	Name, Secretary 16th November 2XXX

Example	Wording for CH notification
	SPECIAL RESOLUTION ON CHANGE OF NAME
	Companies Act [1985 – 1989] OR [2006]
	Company 0009876543 ANY COMPANY LTD
	At a(n) (Extraordinary) General Meeting of members of the above-named Company, duly convened and held on 18th December 2XXX the following SPECIAL RESOLUTION was duly passed:
	THAT the name of the company be changed to
	Another Company Ltd
	Signed.................... Secretary 30th December 2XXX

> Accompanying the resolution must be form NM01 (Notice of change of name by resolution under s.78 CA06).
>
> **5**   CH issues a Certificate of Incorporation on Change of Name.

If the date of the name change is critical, or the company wishes to ensure that no one else can use the new name before the change can be effected, it may be safer to form a shell company with the new name and then for old and new companies (by both passing special resolutions) to exchange names simultaneously.

Control

For many years companies have been required to change their names if:

- the name is too like that of another company;
- information provided to support the use of the name was misleading;
- any description of activities in the name is misleading;
- the name of an oversea company is such that it could not have been approved for use in the United Kingdom.

There is detailed guidance on 'sensitive' words in the CH Guidance Note. However, control over company names is now exercised by the Company Names adjudicator's office and additionally, if a company wishes to use, and thus objects regarding, a name already registered, it may be able to challenge the existing name. The person owning the existing name will only be able to resist the challenge if it can show:

(a) the name was registered before the objector obtained any value or goodwill in it;

(b) the company using that name has already operated under the name and/or has incurred costs preparing and/or using the name;

(c) the company was registered in the ordinary course of company formation and is available to the objector on commercial terms of company formation;

(d) the company was formed in good faith;

(e) the objector's interests are not adversely affected to any significant extent.

However, if the objector can prove that the purpose in registering the name was purely to obtain value from a subsequent legitimate user, the tribunal can order the original company to change its name and if it does not comply, the tribunal will effect the change, allocating a name of its own choosing! This legislation is retrospective so even companies formed speculatively before October 2008 could be affected.

Unfortunately this 'too same a name' protection does not extend to companies registered in the separate jurisdictions of the Isle of Man, Jersey and Guernsey, which, if they trade on the mainland through a third party (i.e. they do not have a place of business in Great Britain which would classify them as an oversea company – see TYPES OF COMPANY) cannot be prevented from using the same name as a company registered in Great Britain.

Case study	Not too similar?
	To date the Tribunal has heard over 100 cases and most applicants have won (i.e. the decisions went against those who had previously set up speculative companies). However, in the case concerning Zurich Insurance Company (ZIC) against 'Zurich Investments Ltd' (ZIL) the applicant (ZIC) lost.
	ZIL had been set up in the Isle of Man and it was later decided to change the name of a UK company to ZIL. The Tribunal felt that this was purely an administrative action not intended to conflict with (the already existing) ZIC and one made 'in good faith'. Subject to appeal by ZIC, ZIL can continue to use that name although many might feel that ZIL would surely have some connection to ZIC which it does not!

'Too similar' name objection and monitoring

Although CH is not permitted to allow the registration of a company name which is the same as or 'too like' an existing company name, there have been instances where this has taken place. Companies have 12 months within which to object to the registration of a new name which they feel is too like their own. Once the 12-month period has expired there is no right to require a change. Companies concerned to protect their name may wish to monitor the list of proposed company names regularly so that any objections can be lodged before the time limit expires. There are a number of formation agents etc., who, for an annual fee per name being protected, offer a 'company name watch service'. Alternatively, using the CH website, anyone can check the current register and therefore see whether there is a new company with a 'too similar' name.

Although registering a company name at CH should protect that name in terms of preventing another company using it as their corporate name, this does not necessarily prevent others using it commercially. Trade Marks are distinct from company names and action to protect such assets may be necessary.

Case study	Need to protect name
	In *IBM v Web-Sphere Ltd*, IBM registered 'Websphere' for software products as a Community Trade Mark (CTM) in 1998. In 1999, a competitor company, Publiweb Ltd, changed its company name to Web-Sphere Ltd and registered three domain names using their new corporate name. A CTM owner is entitled to prevent other parties using an identical mark in relation to identical products (and may be able to prevent use in relation to similar goods). IBM sued Web-Sphere Ltd for passing off their product as if it were IBM's. Web-Sphere tried to use the argument that this could not be so since it was merely using its 'company' name but this failed and the company was held to have infringed IBM's CTM. The High Court also held that it was entitled to require Web-Sphere to change its name and to cease using the domain names. (This pre-dated the setting up of the Company Names Adjudicator's office.)

The Businesslink company name and trade mark checker (**www.busi nesslink.gov.uk/nameandtrademark**) incorporates data from both CH and the Intellectual Property Office and enables users to check registers of company names and trade marks simultaneously, thus trying to avoid unnecessary applications or subsequent challenges. A recent survey by the UK Patent Office discovered that over 80 per cent of small and medium sized organisations had not registered the name of their business as a trade mark; 44 per cent did not think they had enough protection and 1 per cent didn't know whether they had protected their name.

Postscript

If the company has permission to omit 'Limited' (or 'cyfyngedig' for Welsh companies) from its name (which can be effected by submitting form NE01 to CH) and the Secretary of State has determined that permission to omit should be rescinded, or where a company has been restored to the register having previously been removed from it, the directors can resolve to change its name and then lodge form NM05 with CH.

■ If the Articles of the company permit a name change other than by special resolution form NM04 can be used to notify CH.

■ If a company wishes to change its name to one which requires permission from a third party, form NM02 can be used to notify CH (thus presumably preventing others using the name); with form NM03 used if and when the required permission is granted.

Nominee shareholdings

INTRODUCTION

Although rendered unnecessary by the Companies (Single Member Private Limited Companies) Regulations 1992 which allows UK companies to have one member, there are many, mainly subsidiary, companies, where their parent company owns (say) 99 shares and another party (a director) holds the remaining share as a nominee for the parent. This was (and still is) a perfectly legitimate device (although now unnecessary) to comply with the previous requirement that every company should have at least two members.

Directors as nominees

There is no reason to continue with the device of someone holding a share simply to create the '2nd shareholder' as companies are now allowed to have just one member – thus becoming a 'single member company' (SMC). If the company originally had two shareholders and the single share is transferred to the parent, the required entries are made in the register of members, and CH is informed, the company becomes an SMC. In such an instance, in the entry providing details of the sole member in the register of members the phrase 'On [date] this company became a single member company' must be entered. If an SMC subsequently acquires additional member(s) the note 'On [date] this company ceased to be a single member company' – and the effective date of change – must be added to the former sole member's account and CH must be informed.

A difficulty may arise where a director (or some other appointee) is the nominee holding the single share and a disagreement arises and they leave, or are told to leave, the company. In order to register the transfer, either to another nominee or to the parent company, the nominee's signature is required on a stock transfer form, which may be difficult to obtain and a refusal to sign might be used as a lever to obtain an enhanced settlement.

Administration

If it is decided to create a nominee holding or to appoint a new nominee, a declaration of trust together with an undated stock transfer form (STF) relating to the share(s) and signed by the nominee should be obtained. Provided the nominee has previously signed an STF then should the majority owner ever wish to change their nominee (or simply to transfer the share into its own name), the name of a new holder can be inserted, the form can be dated, and lodged with the share certificate to effect the transfer. Obviously such a signed STF should be preserved safely. No stamp duty is due.

Example	Draft declaration of trust for nominee shareholder
	This Declaration of Trust is made by me (NAME) of (ADDRESS) on this (DATE) concerning the ONE share of (NOMINAL VALUE) held by me in (COMPANY).
	I confirm that I hold the above share on behalf of, and as Trustee for (NAME and ADDRESS OF BENEFICIAL OWNER) who is the legal owner of the share. I confirm that any dividends received by me in respect of my holding this share on behalf of the said (OWNER) will be immediately remitted by me to (OWNER), or immediately disposed of in accordance with any instructions issued by (OWNER).
	I also confirm that on receipt of instructions from (OWNER) I will immediately transfer the share as directed, in anticipation of which instructions I have today signed a stock transfer form which has the identity of the transferee left blank.
	Signed .... Witness.....................................

INTRODUCTION

The word 'proxy' has three separate but inter-related meanings. It is the:

a) right given to a member of a company to authorise another person to vote in their place in respect of their shareholding (or part of it);

b) form evidencing that appointment; and

c) person who is appointed as a member's proxy to exercise that member's voting rights to the extent of and in accordance with the authority granted to them.

Authority

Most ARTICLES confer an authority on the members of the company to appoint another person to act as their proxy (on their behalf) and may stipulate the requirements re. drafting and submitting the proxy forms. It is usual for a company to despatch a proxy form with the notice of the meeting and to state that it must be lodged (usually at the registered office or office of the share registrar of the company) by a set time before the meeting. Under reg. 62 of Table A of CA85, the time for lodging cannot exceed 48 hours before the meeting (or 24 hours where the poll is taken after the meeting). In the CA06 pro forma LTD Articles, any time limit can be set by the company in its Articles, so companies adopting the pro forma set would need to add specific requirements in this regard. Although it is administratively preferable for members to use the standard printed form, the use of an alternative is usually allowed provided the instructions are clear.

Form

Proxies can be either general or specific. A general proxy simply appoints another person to act and vote on behalf of the member in accordance with their (the proxy's) own views – which may of course have been dictated to them by the member previously). Specific proxies, or two-way proxies, allow the member to indicate, for each resolution to be considered by the meeting, how the votes must be cast.

Example	General proxy

GENERAL PROXY   Bloggs Manufacturing Ltd

I, [name] of [address] being a member of Bloggs Manufacturing Ltd hereby appoint [name of proxy], or failing him/her, [name], as my proxy to vote in my name and on my behalf at the [type of meeting e.g. ANNUAL, EXTRAORDINARY] GENERAL MEETING of the company to be held on [date] and at any adjournment thereof [as he thinks fit].

Signed.................................   Date....................................

Example	Specific proxy

SPECIFIC PROXY   Bloggs Manufacturing Plc

I, [name] of [address] being a member of Bloggs Manufacturing Plc hereby appoint [name of proxy], or failing him/her, [name], as my proxy to vote in my name and on my behalf at the ANNUAL GENERAL MEETING of the company to be held on [date] and at any adjournment thereof as is stated below :

Resolution 1 Adoption of accounts for the year ended

30th June 2XXX and Balance sheet as at
that date   FOR / AGAINST*

Resolution 2 Payment of dividend   FOR / AGAINST*

Resolution 3 Re-election of directors

        J Bloggs   FOR / AGAINST*

        A N Other   FOR / AGAINST*

Resolution 4 Re-election of Auditors   FOR / AGAINST*

Resolution 5 Authority for directors to agree
the auditors' remuneration   FOR / AGAINST*

Signed.......................................   Date...................................

* Delete as appropriate. Unless the way a vote is to be cast is indicated, the proxy will vote as they think fit.

Proxy administration

1   It is usual to insert 'the Chairman of the meeting' as the first choice proxy with space to allow the member to delete this and insert an alternative.
2   A proxy need not be a member of the company.
3   Listed PLCs must use the specific or two-way proxy not the general proxy (so that the voting intention of the member in respect of each resolution is clear) and can be counted in advance of the meeting.
4   Where there are large numbers of members it may be helpful to suggest that members give the person acting as their proxy, a copy of the form of proxy to aid identification when attending the meeting.
5   Proxies should be date and time stamped on receipt. It is possible for a member to file a subsequent proxy (before the final time limit) in which case the later proxy revokes the earlier.
6   An analysis of the proxy forms should be made as soon as the required time of deposit has passed so that voting strength both for and against (where specific proxies are used) is known in advance.
7   The ARTICLES should be checked for clarification of whether or not a proxy is to be counted towards meeting QUORUM requirements.
8   Under the Electronic Communications Act, companies are allowed to let their members submit proxy forms by electronic means.
9   Under CA06 members are allowed to appoint more than one proxy – each representing part of their holding.

Revocation

Proxies are revoked by:

- the submission of a later proxy in place of one filed previously;
- the death of the member provided this is known before the expiry of the time limit for filing proxies;
- the attendance by the member in person at the meeting, although it would be safer to check the position (i.e. who is going to vote) if both member and proxy are present.

Operation

The use of the authority vested in a proxy (person) by the proxy (form) depends on the ARTICLES:

- in an LTD it is usual for the proxy to have the right to speak as well as vote, but not to be able to vote on a show of hands (although the proxy can request or join in the request for a poll);

■ in a PLC usually the proxy can vote on a show of hands but does not have the right to speak except to request or join in the request for a poll.

Calling for a poll

The full power of shareholding can usually only be felt when a poll is called since then all votes eligible (rather than one 'hand' per shareholder regardless of whether they have 10 shares or 10,000) can be counted. A poll can usually be demanded or called by:

■ the chairman;
■ any two members (which includes representatives of corporate shareholders); or
■ any member(s) holding 10 per cent or more of the share capital.

The pro forma Articles for an LTD accompanying CA06 also allow 'the directors' to demand a poll.

Thus an individual proxy unless speaking for member(s) holding 10 per cent or more of the share capital, can only join in the request for a poll.

Some listed PLCs have changed their Articles and abolished voting by show of hands. All votes are conducted by poll and thus business is resolved by (potentially) the full voting strength.

Representatives

Institutional members should not complete a form of proxy, but appoint a representative. This requires a resolution of the board of the member institution which appoints a named individual to act on its behalf. Such a representative acts in all respects as an individual member with all rights of a member.

Electronic proxies

The EU Shareholder Rights directive requires listed PLCs to give their members at least 21 days' notice of a general meeting, but this can be reduced to 14 days provided:

■ the shareholders have firstly approved (by special resolution), every year, the shortening of such notice; and
■ shareholders are able to cast their votes by electronic means available to all of them.

The wording for such a resolution could run:

'That any meeting other than the Annual General Meeting of the company be properly convened providing 14 days' notice is given to members entitled to attend and vote.'

Quorum

INTRODUCTION

As a precaution against major decisions being taken by a minority of the members of a board or general meeting during the absence of the majority for whatever reason, the concept of there needing to be a quorum (minimum number) of members present, is widespread.

Board meetings

The ARTICLES may stipulate a quorum; the CA06 draft Articles for an LTD state that the quorum can be fixed from time to time by the directors themselves but it must never be less than two (and if it is not fixed, it will be two) – which are virtually the same provisions as those in Table A of CA85. Reference should also be made to any Article governing directors' interests, since some state that if a director has an interest in an item for discussion then they may not be counted as part of the quorum for that item – that is there must be what is called a *'disinterested quorum'* for that item. If so, at least the required minimum number of directors who are not interested in the matter must be present. If the number of directors is small and the quorum requirements are high, a director being disqualified from being counted in the quorum could mean there is delay in gaining proper authority for decisions. Failing to abide by the requirements of the Articles renders those responsible personally liable for any losses occasioned thereby since they are acting *'ultra vires'* (beyond the powers given them by) the Articles.

General meetings

Other than in a single member company where the sole member is the quorum (in which case all decisions taken by such sole member should be recorded either by means of a written resolution or by minutes of that person's 'meeting') normally the quorum is two persons personally present. Thus, in such circumstances, the attendance of a proxy may be insufficient to generate a quorum if only one other member is present in person.

Case study	Ignorance is no excuse
	In *Smith v Henniker-Major* a director wanted the company to follow a course of action which he knew his colleagues would not support. Failing to notify his colleagues that he was convening a board meeting, acting on his own, he purported to pass a board resolution approving the matter. However, he overlooked that the Articles stipulated that the quorum for a valid board meeting was two directors. Not only was failing to give notice of the board meeting to his colleagues a breach of company law, he was also acting *ultra vires* his company's Articles. The Court of Appeal stated that the 'resolution' he purported to pass was a worthless piece of paper. In addition, since the director had acted in breach of the Articles, he was personally liable for any loss occasioned as a result of his action.

Conducting business

Usually, if within 30 minutes of the time set by the notice of the meeting, a quorum is not present, the meeting cannot proceed and must be adjourned. However Table A of CA85 stipulates that if a quorum was present at the commencement of the meeting but then later the meeting ceased to be 'quorate' (i.e. to have a quorum, the minimum required not being present) because a person forming part of the quorum left (or was disqualified, for example because of a conflict of interests), then, providing there are at least two members present, a meeting can continue.

Single member quorum

In a company where more than one member is entitled to attend, the Court has power to authorise the holding of a meeting even though it is known in advance that only one person will be present (either in person or by proxy). Thus in a case where the minority shareholder refused to attend meetings at which the business to be conducted was his dismissal by the majority shareholder, the Court allowed the majority shareholder to act alone to conduct the business.

If there is only one holder of a class of shares (e.g. preference shares) the decision of that person on behalf of the whole class (see CLASSES OF SHARES AND CLASS MEETINGS) will be binding even though no 'meeting' as such has taken place.

Record inspection and retention

INTRODUCTION

As a legal person, a company is obliged to make the details in its STATUTORY BOOKS available to numerous persons, organisations and regulatory bodies. This includes those with 'internal' rights (shareholders, creditors, and auditors) as well as those with 'external' rights (regulatory bodies) whose numbers have doubled during the past two decades according to surveys conducted by the Federation of Small Businesses. In addition there are many other records which need to be preserved for various lengths of time.

Policy for document and records preservation

To ensure that the documents required to be made available are protected and able to be displayed, companies could adopt a policy such as the one shown below.

Example	Company policy for document protection
	Document and records preservation [Company] PLC/LTD
	1 Responsibility for preserving the various books, registers and records of the company, in order to comply with legislation and business practice is devolved to [the company secretary].
	2 Such responsibility includes
	● ensuring safe storage with reasonable accessibility whilst the items are current,
	● provision of adequate back up systems capable of providing current record data, should the original be lost for any reason,
	● preserving records in accordance with a procedure and timetable to be devised, and in those archives.
	3 The various terms of retention as set out in *The ICSA Guide to Document Retention* (subject to any extension, but not contraction, of the suggested time limits for reasons particular to the company) are to be adhered to at all times. ➜

Example	Company policy for document protection – *continued*
	4 Suitably secure premises/facilities will be utilised for this purpose. Such premises etc. need to be protected from rodents, fire and flood, intruders etc.
	5 Checks will be made that all records held electronically can still be accessed before any change of system/software is implemented.
	6 [The company secretary] will monitor changes in requirements and effect appropriate alterations.
	7 [The company secretary] will be required to report annually to the board on compliance with the requirements of this procedure.

Promulgation

It is not simply a case of the board and company secretary knowing the company's obligations, but also ensuring that those responsible for admitting visitors to the company know how to deal efficiently with such enquiries. A well-rehearsed procedure is advisable. Some years ago a national newspaper bought shares in FTSE 100 companies and then tried to inspect their records. Although many companies dealt with the request professionally, some did not – quite illegally.

Until the introduction of CA06 anyone wishing to inspect the register of members was able to do so for '*two hours every business day*'. CA06 has changed that right so that if the board do not feel the request is for a '*proper and fit purpose*', they can reject the request and apply to the Court for power to resist the inspection.

The remaining records are available as before – for example, members have a right of access to all registers, and creditors have a right of access to the register of charges. In fact personal inspections are rare and most people wishing to check such data will prefer to access the company data filed at CH electronically, even though it may be somewhat out of date (i.e. the share-holders' names will be that disclosed by the most recent annual return which could be over a year old).

Suggested procedure

I   Identify all those having a right of access and the records to which such rights apply.

2 The credentials of the person requesting access to the records (i.e. their relationship to the company) should be checked in order to ensure that they have the right to access (or make a request to access) the record requested. Shareholders' names should be checked against the members' register, creditors against the purchase ledger, debenture/ loan holders against their register, and so on.

3 They should be conducted to the interview room. Those with a right of inspection (members and creditors) will be interviewed by the company secretary, whom failing the assistant company secretary, whom failing the chief accountant.

Should the visitor require copies of the documentation, charges as laid down may be levied. An invoice should be raised and a cheque/ cash/credit/debit card authority obtained before the visitor leaves [or before inspection]. A company representative should remain in the interview room during the inspection/copying to ensure the protection of the record. A note of the inspection should be made in the visitors book and the fact reported at the next following board meeting.

Those without an immediate right of inspection will be advised that their request will be passed to the board for decision and they will be advised of the decision within 48 hours.

Notes

The charges for inspection and copying (there is no obligation to provide copying facilities) are as follows. The company can also charge for any costs incurred in delivering a copy.

a) Register of members: inspection – £3.50 each hour or part thereof; copies – £3.50 for first 50 entries, £31.50 for next 950 entries or part thereof, £20 for next 4,000 entries or part thereof and £25 for every subsequent 5,000 entries or part thereof.

b) Directors' service contracts and/or indemnity provisions, resolutions and meetings, report under s.805: inspection as above; copies – 20p per 1,000 words or part thereof.

c) Register of debenture holders: inspection as above, copies – 10p per 500 words in the trust deed.

'Internal' bodies access

These records are shown below with details of those with rights of access. Unless otherwise stated the records should be held at its registered office or SAIL. If such records are held in a non-legible form, the records should be held at the registered office and CH informed. If a SAIL is used all the records must be held there.

A

Register of members must be held at the Registered Office (RO) or SAIL

Access: on application to the directors.

The board must within five days allow the inspection or apply to the Court (telling the person wishing to inspect that it has done so) for permission to resist the inspection because they feel it is 'not a fit purpose'.
   'Fit purposes' could include:

- to check correct personal details;
- to contact other shareholders for pressure purposes;
- for regulators checking money laundering;
- in consideration of a takeover;
- for research;
- for stockbrokers before a transaction;
- to enforce a judgement (e.g. a stop notice).

Whilst the reasons for resisting an inspection could include purposes that:

- are unlawful;
- would breach the Data Protection Act;
- enable a third party to check credit or identities of shareholders;
- facilitate the marketing of investments or commercial products;
- might result in the threatening, harassment or intimidation of shareholders;
- seek to market securities, and so on.

When wishing to resist an inspection, taking legal advice may be appropriate.

Note: There is further guidance as to 'proper purpose' tests on the ICSA website (**www.icsa.org.uk**)

B

Register of directors and secretary (RO or SAIL)

Register of directors' shareholdings (RO or SAIL) – PLCs only

Register of significant shareholdings/substantial interests (RO or SAIL) – listed PLCs only

Overseas branch register (with register of members)

Reports on disclosures under s.793 CA06 notices (listed PLCs only) (RO or SAIL)

Contract/Statutory declaration for purchase by company of own shares

Access: by members – every working day. By others – on application to the directors.

C

Minutes of General Meetings

Directors' service contracts (RO or SAIL with register of members) (must also be available for inspection at AGM)

Access : by members only (who must also be sent a copy if requested).

D

Register of charges (RO or SAIL)

Access : by members and creditors.

E

Register of debenture/loan holders (RO or SAIL in place where register of members is held)

Access : by members, and debenture stock/loan holders.

F

Statutory declaration of payment out of capital for redemption or purchase by company of own shares (RO or SAIL)

Access: by members and creditors.

Additional requirements

The notes in the first part of this section cover only those corporate records where there is a requirement to preserve them and to make them available for inspection. The preservation of a considerable number of other records is required – to comply with legislation, for commercial reasons and since they form part of the history of the company. The time limits applicable to preservation for legislative demands vary widely which adds complexity to the obligation.

Detailed consideration is essential for the safe protection and accessibility of such records. In view of any space limitations the possibility of record preservation via microfilming or recording on disk might be examined although great care should be taken and reference should be made to the British Standard BS6498 on the 'Preparation of Microfilm for use in evidence' and their 'Code of practice on the legal admissibility of information stored on electronic document management systems'. Under the Civil Evidence Act 1995 computer-generated records are admissible as evidence.

Retention periods

Generally records such as those stated above must be held for at least the life of the company. However, since a company is a legal rather than a real person, it can not only 'die' (be dissolved, liquidated, wound up, struck off etc.) but, by order of the Court, it can also be resuscitated (see RESURRECTION OF COMPANIES) for the purpose of facing a liability claim. It may be safest (other than for companies which have never traded) to retain such records for at least (say) six years (the time limit for resuscitation) beyond the life of the company. Since resuscitation or resurrection is effected to enable a company to respond to a liability claim it would be prudent to keep liability insurers records for the same length of time. Records other than those stated above may be held for shorter periods and guidance should be sought in each case.

Access of 'external bodies'

A considerable number of other regulatory bodies have rights of access to the company premises, records, etc., and it is essential to be prepared for such visits and to brief those responsible in the company to deal with them.

Procedure

1   Representatives of organisations on the following list have a right of access to company premises, may have a right to inspect records and interview employees and may also have a right to remove records, data and registers, etc. Denial of access to some bodies can itself be a criminal offence.
2   The receptionist/gate keeper on duty should establish the agency the visitor(s) represent and inspect their credentials to ensure their *bona fides*. They should be conducted to the waiting room and the relevant company representative should be contacted. The contact will then be responsible for dealing with the enquiry.

(a) Government and statutory regulatory agencies

Department of Business, Innovation and Skills (DBIS), Financial Services Authority (FSA), Serious Fraud Office (SFO), Office of Fair Trading (OFT)/ Competition Commission (CC), European Union inspectors (EU).

Scope:

- *DBIS*: Under company legislation, DBIS has power to investigate company affairs, ownership, dealings in shares, including insider dealing. Exact nature of investigation must be ascertained.
- *FSA*: Under the Financial Services Act 1986, the FSA has powers to investigate the affairs of all companies operating under its aegis. In addition, the FSA has authority under the Financial Services and Markets Act 2000 to regulate all financial business in the UK and investigate instances of market abuse and manipulation including insider dealing. It has a wide range of disciplinary and enforcement powers. (See USING THIS BOOK re the proposed changes to the FSA.)
- *SFO* has powers, wider in many cases than those available to the police or FSA, under the Criminal Justice Act 1987, to investigate matters of fraud likely to total in excess of £2 million and to be of public concern.
- *OFT* has an obligation to investigate whether supplies of goods or services breach the principles of the Fair Trading Act 1973 – and is now the policing arm of the Competition Commission.
- *CC*: The Competition Commission (acting under the Competition Act 1998 and the Enterprise Act 2002) can investigate (and gain access to inspect records etc.) any company which is suspected of infringing the prohibitions set out in those Acts.
- *EU* inspectors have rights (without notice) to enter the premises of organisations of member states under the Communities Act 1972. In doing so, the inspectors are supposed to act in accordance with the laws of the member state (and in concert with the domestic regulatory agency) concerned, although this does not always happen.

Persons dealing:
Company secretary (whom failing assistant company secretary, whom failing chief accountant).

Actions:

- Telephone chairman and board, corporate lawyers, and public relations staff (in case media require information).
- Meet representatives and endeavour to ascertain requirements.
- Check requirements with corporate lawyers.
- Endeavour to assist investigators whilst minimising the potential damage to the company name and reputation.
- Write report of visit, requirements, action carried out, records inspected/removed.

WARNING

 Taking legal advice may be essential since those questioned may not have a right to silence (i.e. refusing to answer questions felt to be self-incriminatory can generate sanctions including imprisonment). It is also essential to try to obtain copies of everything seized during such a search, although some agencies will not allow this and undertake to provide copies of the documents seized within a week.

(b) Statutory reporting agencies

HM Revenue & Customs (HMRC), Health and Safety Executive/Local Authority (HSE/LA), Trading Standards Officers (TSO), Pensions Regulator (PR), Rating authorities (RA).

- *HMRC*: Powers of access tend to be exercised by the Audit Department of the Inland Revenue, or the Compliance units of the Dept of Work and Pensions (DWP), which are charged with the duty of checking the validity of the way an employer has paid and deducted tax from employees and workers. The DWP has a right under the National Minimum Wage legislation to check that employers are paying at least the wage rates specified to those entitled (and to sponsor criminal prosecution if not) – which may be extended to investigations regarding payments made to apprentices.
- *Customs and Excise* has wide powers of access in respect of its VAT collection duties which emanate from its previous and existing role as Excise officers. The penalties for, even totally accidental, errors, in VAT collection and payment are severe despite recent amelioration.
- *HSE and/or LAs* have rights under the Working Time Regulations 1998 to inspect records of hours worked by those opting out of the maximum 48 hours worked per week rule.
- *TSOs* have rights under the Consumer Protection Act 1987 to ensure compliance with such legislation.
- *PR* has rights under various Pensions Acts to check compliance, in particular that pension contribution deductions made from employees wages have been paid to the appropriate trustees and that, where necessary, access to the provider of a stakeholder pensions is provided and the deductions made are being paid over.
- *RA* have a right of access for the purpose of checking the valuation for the purposes of the Uniform Business rate (or any appeal in respect thereof).

Persons dealing:
Chief accountant/personnel director (whom failing finance director, whom failing company secretary).

Actions:

- Meet representatives and establish nature of enquiry.
- Provide information required.
- Advise chairman and board and corporate lawyers (via company secretary).
- Ensure if errors are found that systems are changed to avoid a repetition, whilst those responsible should be disciplined if procedures have not been followed correctly. Inland Revenue have a right to pursue an employee if through their actions – rather than those of the employer – tax has been underpaid in respect of payroll liabilities.
- Write report of visit, action required and effected.

(c) Emergency and utilities services

Fire, police, Health and Safety Executive, Factory Inspectorate, Environmental Health Officers, gas, water and electricity utilities

- *Fire*: right of access to premises mainly for the purposes of checking compliance with the Regulatory Reform (Fire Safety) Order 2005 (i.e. that there is a Responsible Person appointed for every location and that they regularly conduct inspections of the premises).
- *Police*: unless in the belief, or in connection with such belief, that a crime has been or is about to be committed, or is being committed, or in 'hot pursuit' of a suspected person, or accompanying Government and Statutory Regulatory Agencies the police have no immediate right of access to premises other than with the permission of the owner/ occupier.
- *Health & Safety Executive (HSE), Environmental Health Officers (EHOs)* and Factory Inspectors have a range of powers which vary from industry to industry. Operators of large (and potentially hazardous) facilities are obliged (under the Control of Industrial Major Accident Regulations 1988) to file and keep up to date details of plans and emergency evacuations etc. which will require an interface with the appropriate department which may well wish to check the site. EHOs also have rights of access under the Food Safety Act 1992 to check that food preparation and serving areas are suitable. HSE inspectors have a right of inspection of Certificates of Employers' Liability Insurance (hard or electronic copy).
- *Utilities* have rights of access to read meters and, if leaks / breaks are suspected, to rectify on an emergency basis which could even entail forced entry.

Persons dealing:
Personnel director (whom failing company secretary, whom failing personnel manager).

Actions

- Meet representative and establish problem.
- Rectify if required and possible.
- Update procedures, if required.
- Write report of visit and action effected.

(d) Others

- *UK Border Agency*: to check the right to work (and the copy documentation related thereto) in the UK of all employees (and ex-employees for up to two years after they have left), and, if using immigrants from outside the EU, that the employer has the appropriate licence.

Persons dealing:
Personnel/HR manager (whom failing company secretary).

Action:
Be prepared to produce copies of relevant evidence (in a form which cannot be altered) and, if applicable, the licence.

- *Department of Transport*: to inspect transport (fleet) operator's licence and administration.

Persons dealing:
Department of Transport: transport manager (whom failing company secretary).

Action:
Be prepared to produce operators licence and back-up records etc.

- *Local Authorities*: have an increasing range of obligations – see above. In addition they are responsible for ensuring compliance with environment protection legislation.

Persons dealing:
Personnel/HR manager, whom failing company secretary.

- *Landlords and agents*: to inspect condition and use of premises, assess value for insurance, prepare dilapidations ('wants of repair') reports, under the provisions of leases and licences.

Persons dealing:
Company secretary (whom failing assistant company secretary, whom failing chief accountant).

Action:

- Meet representatives – since most leases state that (say) 48 hours notice of such inspections must be given there should be no need to allow

immediate access unless it is an emergency. Good landlord/tenant relations may require a positive and helpful approach.

■ If a dilapidations notice and schedule of 'wants of repair' (that is a
requirement to put or keep the premises into good order and repair) is
to be served, refer to the lease for the procedure to be followed.

Any other bodies with rights of access for particular industries (e.g. Charities
Commission for charitable companies, etc.) should be identified and added
to the list, which may also need customising to fit individual companies'
requirements.

Registered number and office

INTRODUCTION

On INCORPORATION each company is allocated a 'registered number' by CH. This number is never changed (and never reissued even if the company is wound up or dissolved). Companies must also nominate a registered office – which must be within their country of registration – and advise CH then – and later should the company wish to change the address (which can only be within the country of registration).

Consistent identification

Although a company can change its name (by special resolution), its business (by changing its objects clause, if it has one), its type of registration (e.g. an LTD can RE-REGISTER as a PLC and vice versa etc.), and its ownership, etc., the one constant evidence of its existence is its unique and unalterable registered number which is never re-used by CH. Under s.1066 CA06, CH has powers to add check digits to a company's registered number to facilitate electronic filing and access. There are currently no plans for this, and if it were implemented, a three-year period (during which both old and new numbers would be acceptable) would be allowed whilst letterheads and other stationery stocks could be exhausted and equivalents with the new number printed.

For the purposes of the official lodgement of papers (matters concerning the corporate entity, legal actions, notices, etc.) and to comply with the principle that all those dealing with the company have a right to know with whom they are dealing, every company must have a registered office. The registered office can only be situated within the country in which the company is incorporated (although there are EU proposals that would allow a company to move its registered office within the EU – in which case it would then be bound by the corporate laws of the country to which its principal office was relocated). On registration, the registered office must be advised to CH (form IN01), and all subsequent changes of address must be notified on form AD01 (s.87 CA06). The country of registration (but not necessarily the address within that country) must be stated in the Memorandum. Around 50 per cent of companies registered in England and Wales have their registered office in London or the south-east of England.

Promulgation

The company name is required to be displayed at every place at which the company undertakes business (but no longer on the exteriors), however, the fact than an address is the registered office of the company must be displayed on the exterior of that location (although not if it is a domestic residence). Details of the registered office must also be shown on all invoices, order forms, letterheads, websites and monetary documentation. This includes fax and external email communications where software should be changed to incorporate these legal requirements as standard. There is no requirement to put these details on business cards or compliment slips. Under CA06 the Secretary of State has powers to stipulate where the company name must be displayed.

Changing the location of the registered office

Any alteration in location of the registered office must be filed with CH using form AD01. Registering the change is not simply a question of legal compliance, there is a practical aspect. All communications from CH are sent to the registered office. If it is changed and there is no postal redirection, official communications may go astray. This could result in the company failing to file its accounts within the required time limit, in turn leading to prosecution and fines for the directors – and even to the company being struck off the register (thereby incurring costs for reinstatement).

On notifying CH of a change of registered office, a 14-day period during which both old and new offices are valid for the service of notices is allowed. If a company is required to move in an emergency (for example because of a fire, flood or other disaster, etc.), the penalties for failing to notify the change of registered office to CH are waived provided notification of the new office is made within 14 days of the enforced move being known.

'Company hi-jacking'

There have been a number of instances of unauthorised persons filing a change of registered office form at CH, altering the registered office address to a location under their own control. From that location they proceed to trade and take on credit as if they were the original company. Anyone suspicious, on checking the company's file at CH would find the change of address filed, as they might think, correctly. The fraudsters then abscond owing substantial sums to unpaid creditors who would understandably think they were owed the money by the original company. Despite representations the Government has decided (at least for the time being) against rules that would allow CH to correct data, so regular checking of the company's details on file might be prudent. Alternatively, the company can add its own name (with a stated address) to CH's Monitor service so that all changes to the records are notified to a stated address (i.e. other than the registered office), or use the CH PROOF service, under which the company commits to file all items electronically which (needing both an authorisation code and a password) should provide greater protection than the paper system. Having signed up to this system any subsequent hard copy notification will be rejected by CH.

Administration

The registered office is required so that third parties know where official or legal notices can be served. However the means by which such documents are processed after delivery also need to be given due attention as there have been instances where documents requiring instant action have been filed rather than actioned.

Case study	Expensive inactivity
	In a case concerning an unpaid claim made on a leading UK insurance company, documents giving notice to the company of a legal hearing for a winding-up order against it, legitimately served by the creditor in north-east England, were filed rather than actioned. Because there was no response, the winding-up petition was listed for a court hearing, to the considerable embarrassment of the company, whose bankers then indicated that unless there was immediate clarification they might need to dishonour the company's cheques. The judge refused to accept the company's explanation and promise to pay, to allow delisting of the application, unless the company produced the creditor in Court to confirm personally that he had been paid. At its expense, the company had to transport the creditor to London and accommodate him in a hotel prior to the hearing!

A responsible person should oversee the receipt of post and ensure such notices are brought to the prompt attention of someone in authority.

Disclosure

As the registered number helps identification of the legal person and the registered office confirms the location of that legal person, both must appear on all business letters and communications, invoices, websites, statements and order forms etc. In view of the requirement also to state the country of incorporation, it is normal to use a form of words such as the following, and to instruct printers to incorporate them on all such business stationery.

Example	**Wording for incorporation on company letterheads etc.**
	Bloggs Manufacturing Co.Ltd. Registered in England No 123456789
	Registered office: Bloggs House, 1, Bloggs Rd, Bloggsville, Bloggshire, BL1 SH1.

Notes

1 The names of directors are not required to be shown on letterheads, unless one is named, in which case all must be named. However where the printing of a name merely indicates a personalisation of corporate notepaper (e.g. 'from the office of [name of director]') DBIS has stated that this is not normally regarded as being a breach of this requirement.
2 Fines can be levied against both company and officers for failure to comply with all requirements.

Registrar of companies

INTRODUCTION

The UK Registrar of Companies (CH) is an Executive Agency of DBIS and maintains records on around 2,650,000 'current' companies, (including up to 600,000 that are dormant), and over 2,000,000 dissolved companies. It is a repository of data on those companies and provides public access to their records. The '*quid pro quo*' for the limiting of the liability of the shareholders is '*disclosure of information*', which explains the increasingly strict attitude to time limits on putting data into the public arena – particularly companies' financial results and the annual return.

Locations

The main company registry for English and Welsh companies is in Cardiff:

> Companies House
> Crown Way
> Maindy
> Cardiff CF4 3UZ
> **www.companieshouse.gov.uk**
> telephone (to all departments): 0303 1234 500

There is a single satellite office in London at:

> 21 Bloomsbury Street
> London WC1B 3XD

The records of companies registered in Scotland are located at 37 Castle Terrace, Edinburgh, EH1 2RB, and the records of companies registered in Northern Ireland are located at IDB House, 64 Chichester St, Belfast, BT1 4JX.

At each location, search, inspection and copying facilities (subject to charge) are available for all callers, usually between the hours of 9.30 and 4.00, Monday to Friday (excluding Bank Holidays). CH offices clear their letterboxes at midnight each day. Items placed in these boxes, even if posted there after normal office hours, provided it is before midnight, are regarded as being filed on that day.

The service

Information on CH requirements and data available is freely available and includes:

1 Guidance notes on a variety of subjects.
2 *Monitor* – a free service which enables subscribers to nominate certain companies in which they are interested so that each time an item is filed in respect of such companies, they are automatically sent a copy.
3 *Direct* – a subscription service which enables subscribers who wish to obtain information on any company on a regular basis to do so at any time by direct access. Charges are deducted from a float paid in advance to the Registrar.
4 *WebCHeck* is a web-based service which enables those paying by credit card to access information on companies electronically and virtually instantaneously.
5 *'Scan on demand'*. Since 1995 all company data has been reconstituted in virtual format and is available on demand. Earlier records are progressively being reconstituted in virtual format. Where this has not taken place records are available on microfiche. Until all files are available electronically, CH operates a service whereby copies of data not available in virtual format can be requested electronically, accessed and scanned and then made available (on an individual basis) electronically.
6 *'Register'* – is a free journal for CH customers which is available in electronic format to those wishing to add their names (via the CH website) to the electronic (only) mailing list.
7 *PROOF* stands for PROtected Online Filing facility. Companies which sign up to this service commit themselves to file all documents electronically. Thus any paper documents (if, for example, filed by fraudsters to try and 'hijack' the company – see REGISTERED OFFICE) would be rejected.
8 CH produces a CD-rom every month containing details of all the active companies on the register as well as those in liquidation, receivership, as well as details of all companies dissolved, struck off, etc., in the previous 12 months. The information includes the name, number and address of the company and its type, its year end or accounting reference date (ARD), and dates of the latest annual return and accounts.

Filing requirements

All CH required data is subject to two requirements. It must be filed on or before time, and in an appropriate format.

Hard copy documents must be submitted:

- bearing the company's registered number;
- on plain white matt A4 paper between 80 and 100 gsm weight (or else of a background density not greater than 0.3);
- using black ink, with clear legible writing of uniform density or in printed format (but not on a dot matrix printer);
- letters must not be smaller than 1.8 mm with a line width of not less than 0.25 mm;
- have a margin all round not less than 10mm wide.

Documents submitted other than in the above formats (including the customary four-colour glossy reports of listed PLCs) will be rejected.

Hard copy forms, returns etc., can be sent by post or delivered by hand to each office. Those wishing to file electronically must apply to CH to obtain an authorisation code and a user password to be used for each filing. See FORMS.

Receipt

CH does not issue a receipt if filing by post or delivering hard copy documents (i.e. not using the electronic process where there is an automatic email receipt). Since it is advisable to be able to evidence receipt (to resist a claim of late or non-filing), either the name of the subject company should be added to the Monitoring service referred to above, or a covering letter in duplicate should be sent with each item filed. The original letter should request that CH receipts the copy letter (or a copy of the form) and returns it. CH is prepared to do this (by affixing a bar code sticker to the copy letter) provided a stamped return envelope is provided. Alternatively blank forms POST 31 are available for similar processing, or CH can simply affix the bar code to a duplicate copy of the form itself.

Example	Letter to CH requesting receipt for item filed
	LETTERHEAD
	Registrar of Companies
	Crown Way, Maindy
	Cardiff CF4 3UZ
	Dear Sir
	A Bloggs & Co. Ltd Reg. Number 12345678987
	I enclose form [number, in the following case AP01] relating ➜

Example	Letter to CH requesting receipt for item filed – *continued*
	to [specify subject, e,g in this case, 'the appointment of an additional director to this company's board of directors'].
	Kindly acknowledge receipt by signing and returning the attached copy letter. A stamped addressed return envelope is attached.
	Yours faithfully
	J. Bloggs
	Secretary
	Enc. Copy letter
	Form [number]
	Reply paid return envelope
	[On copy in addition to the above wording]
	I acknowledge receipt of the document referred to above.
	Signed ....
	Registrar of Companies

CH wishes to move to a complete electronic basis by 2013 when filing hard copy will no longer be possible.

Much of the data required to be filed is subject to time limits, with fines for breaching such limits and/or non-compliance. There are at least four separate filing time limits:

- most forms must be filed within 14 days;
- certain ordinary resolutions (i.e. increasing the share capital, authorising the directors to allot shares, authorising a voluntary winding up, and revoking an elective resolution) as well as all special and extraordinary RESOLUTIONS must be filed within 15 days;
- details of charges must be filed within 21 days (if not the charge cannot be filed and the company will have to apply to the Court to explain the reason for the delay);
- details of shares issued (but not those transferred) and the annual return must be filed within 28 days.

It may be simpler to assume that all items are subject to the 14-day limit. Fines for late filing most of the forms are rarely applied. However, the accounts and the annual return must not be filed late, since this can generate a fine. Those responsible can also be subject to personal fines, whilst under s.3 of the Company Directors Disqualification Act 1986, anyone responsible for (amongst other offences) *'persistent late filing'* at CH can be disqualified from acting as a company officer of all UK companies.

Accounts

Although smaller and dormant companies can claim exemption from having their accounts audited, they must still file their accounts with CH. LTDs must file within nine months of their Accounting Reference Date (ARD – see FINANCIAL YEAR END) and PLCs within six months of their ARD. A late filing penalty (of varying amounts depending how late the accounts are being filed) is applied, simply by the issue of an invoice.

There is a strict approach to the time limits. However, if it is the first time a company has late-filed and the delay is not more than three days; or the accounts were filed in time but had to be returned for amendment and the corrected accounts are returned within 14 days, the penalty may be waived. In addition to the late filing penalty on the company, individuals responsible may be made subject to personal fines in the criminal court (i.e. resulting in them having a criminal record) and CH may take action to strike the company off the record. If the company is subsequently restored to the register, penalties may be required in respect of the late (or non) filing of data during the period the company was 'off the register'.

If there are exceptional difficulties in filing the accounts by the due date, providing CH is contacted *before* the deadline for filing, it may be possible to obtain an extension. If this is carried out by telephone it would be advisable to record all the details including the date and time of the call in a letter or email to CH. All calls to CH are recorded and kept for a year.

Appeal

If a company has a complaint against a CH procedure – or member of staff etc., it can appeal to the CH adjudicator at the CH office. A report on the previous year's appeals and complaints is provided by the Adjudicator in the Companies House magazine, *Register*.

Dormant companies accounts

A company which has not traded (i.e. has had '*no significant accounting transactions*') within the year being reported on, can claim exemption from audit (by passing a special resolution exempting itself from appointing auditors) and need only file with CH an abbreviated balance sheet and notes (i.e. there is no requirement to file a profit and loss account or a directors' report, although the latter must be sent to the members). If the dormant company does not wish to prepare a set of accounts, form DCA can be completed instead, although CH recommends that this form should only be used where the company has never traded and should not be used for companies that have traded previously.

Routine filing matters

A company is required to prepare an ANNUAL RETURN made up to the anniversary of its incorporation and to file it within 28 days of that 'return date'. Thereafter the company must make subsequent returns to dates no later than the anniversaries of previous 'return dates', and file such returns within 28 days of those dates. The return date can be brought forward before the anniversary of the previous return – but not deferred.

For companies filing electronically, the procedure is that CH sends a reminder that the annual return (form AR01) is due. Via the website, the company can simply amend any out of date data on the electronic record and pay a £14 fee.

However, companies wishing to file hard copy (until 2013) have to download a blank return form, complete all the details themselves and pay a filing fee of £40. Around a third of all hard copy annual returns have to be rejected and returned because they are unsigned and/or are not accompanied by a cheque or contain incorrect information. In around 3000 cases each year CH claims to receive cheques without the return and, in some cases, completely empty envelopes! Cheques should bear the company registration number on their reverse as very often the cheque is drawn on an account other than one in the company's name.

If a company wishes to bring forward the date of the next return (and did not notify this on the previous return) it can download a blank form for completion. Failure to file the annual return can involve those responsible being fined, being given a criminal record and can even involve the company being struck off the register.

Non-form filing

As well as the forms which must be filed, companies are also required to file:

- **details of their Constitution** (the Memorandum and Articles) and any changes thereto. Such changes will normally require special resolutions which will also need to be filed. It is not possible to alter the Memorandum of a CA06 company.
- **certain ordinary RESOLUTIONS**. The following resolutions must be filed within 15 days: those that authorise:
  - an increase in the authorised share capital,
  - the directors to allot shares, and
  - a voluntary winding up of the company,
  or
  - revoke an elective resolution (although to a large extent such resolutions are effectively rendered unnecessary by CA06);
- special resolutions and extraordinary resolutions (although again the latter are effectively rendered obsolete).

Format of resolution for filing

The following is a draft of the format that should be acceptable.

Example	Wording of resolution for filing at Companies House
	Company Name Registered number [12345678987]
	Ordinary/Special/[Extraordinary] Resolution(s)*
	of [Company Name]
	At a general meeting of the members of the above-named company duly convened and held on [date] at [time] at the registered office of the company [address], the following resolution(s) was/were* duly Passed:
	THAT .... [detail]
	Signed............................... Director/Secretary *
	Date..................................
	* delete as applicable

INTRODUCTION

There are around 2.6 million UK LTDs but only around 25,000 PLCs – of which fewer than 2,500 are PLCs listed on either the main stock market or quoted on the Alternative Investment Market. Most companies never change their 'status'. However, a small number of LTDs become PLCs and an even smaller number 'go public' by applying for a Stock Exchange (SE) listing or quotation, which is achieved by making at least 30 per cent of their shares available publicly. In floating its shares on the SE, a company makes itself subject to the requirements of the SE listing agreement, as well as to tighter controls regarding disclosure of information etc. A tiny number of listed or unlisted PLCs 'go private' (i.e. revert to being an LTD). Many LTDs re-register as unlisted or unquoted PLCs simply to gain increased prestige in the eyes of those with whom they are dealing since they believe those with whom they trade will perceive the letters PLC at the end of the company's name as being indicative of greater size, strength and reliability.

Private to public

To re-register an LTD as an unlisted PLC (ss.90-96 CA06) the company must:

1 Have an issued share capital of at least £50,000 of which 25 per cent or more must be paid up in cash. If there is insufficient capital then the members must first pass an ordinary resolution (which must be lodged with CH within 15 days) increasing the authorised and issued capital.
2 Pass a special RESOLUTION, which could be a WRITTEN resolution, stating that it wishes to re-register as a PLC.
3 Alter its MEMORANDUM and ARTICLES, changing its NAME so that it ends 'public limited company' (or 'plc', 'Plc', or 'PLC' or 'CCC' standing for Cwmni Cyfyngedig Cyhoeddus if it is a Welsh plc), insert a statement that it is to be a PLC, and remove any restrictions (e.g. the directors right to refuse a share transfer) which are incompatible with PLC status. A company which does not have its Memorandum in the format required under CA06 will be required to transfer its objects clause into the revised Articles.
4 Appoint a company secretary if it does not have one.
5 File a copy of the change of name resolution with CH within 15 days of it being passed, together with:

- a printed copy of the Articles and (if appropriate) amended Memorandum
- an auditor's statement regarding an accompanying balance sheet which must not be more than six months old, reflecting the tighter timetable for filing of PLCs accounts, and must bear an unqualified auditor's report and show that net assets exceed the paid up share capital and reserves;
- if part of the paid up capital is represented by a consideration other than cash, the company must obtain and submit an expert's opinion on its value;
- the appropriate fee.

6   CH then issues a certificate of re-registration as a PLC.

Public to private

To re-register a PLC as an LTD (see ss.97–101 CA06) the company must:

1   Pass a special resolution (which could be written) resolving that the company is to be an LTD, thus changing the name from ending PLC to LTD.
2   Alter the name in the Articles of Association, and (for pre-CA06 companies) in the Memorandum.
3   Send to CH (within 15 days) a copy of the change of name special resolution and the altered Articles and (if appropriate) the Memorandum.

There follows a 28-day delay to allow time for any minority shareholder who wishes to apply for cancellation of the resolution. However, if all members of the company endorse the special resolution the 28-day period can be waived. CH then issues a certificate of re-registration in the new LTD status and name.

Unlimited companies

An LTD can re-register as an unlimited company (ss.102–104 CA06), an unlimited company can be re-registered as an LTD (ss.105–108 CA06), and a PLC can become an unlimited company (ss.109–111 CA06).

INTRODUCTION

Owner control of companies is exercised in general meetings or by written RESOLUTIONS. There are several resolutions: ordinary, ordinary with special notice (i.e. additional requirements and details required if proposing the removal of a director or auditor), extraordinary (which have to some extent been rendered obsolete under CA06), special and written. Whilst normally resolutions are initiated by the directors, it is possible for an (extraordinary) GENERAL MEETING to be required to be convened by the members to consider a resolution that they wish to propose.

Ordinary

Any resolution which is not special or extraordinary is 'ordinary'. At a general meeting ordinary resolutions are used to obtain approval by means of a simple majority of the votes that are actually cast in person or by proxy. Any shares not voted are effectively disenfranchised – but that is the choice of the shareholder in deciding to abstain. The following ordinary resolutions must be filed with CH within 15 days of being passed:

- for a pre-CA06 company with a share capital, any resolution increasing it (since the effect of increasing the share capital means a change to the MEMORANDUM of the company);
- a resolution authorising the directors to allot shares (unnecessary for companies formed under CA06 unless required by the company's Articles);
- a resolution voluntarily winding up the company; and
- a resolution revoking an elective resolution.

'Simple majority' means a majority of the votes that are actually cast either in person or by proxy. Hence if only some of the votes are cast, then an ordinary resolution is passed if 50 per cent plus 1 of those cast, are in favour.

Special notice (of an ordinary resolution)

Certain ordinary resolutions require special notice being given to the members – that is at least 21 days' notice with full details of the proposal and any objections or representations of the other party(ies). It is required for:

- any resolution relating to an auditor other than re-election or to settle their remuneration; and
- the removal of a director (see DIRECTORS – REMOVAL).

Special

Special resolutions are required to:

- alter the objects clause;
- alter the Articles;
- change the name of the company;
- RE-REGISTER an LTD as a PLC, an unlimited company as an LTD or a PLC as an LTD;
- disapply any pre-emption rights of shareholders (i.e. a right of pre-emption means that existing shareholders have the right of first refusal to subscribe for any newly issued shares in proportion that their own shares bear to the total issued);
- authorise the purchase by the company of its own shares or the provision of assistance to allow the purchase of its own shares. Under the Companies (Acquisition of Own Shares) (Treasury Shares) Regulations 2003 a company can purchase (out of its distributable profits) a maximum of 10 per cent of its issued share capital. The shares purchased are held 'in treasury' in the company's own name. They are not cancelled since this would lead to a reduction of capital which is subject to the rules set out below. No voting or dividend rights attach to shares held in treasury. This may be a simple method of acquiring shares for later use (for example in an employee share scheme) rather than needing to issue more shares;
- reduce the company's share capital. For a PLC, a resolution to reduce share capital can normally only be effected with the approval of the Court to a scheme of arrangement, and provided the Articles allow for it (if they do not they must first be changed). The reduction is only effective when CH issues a certificate to this effect. However, under CA06 (s.943) an LTD can reduce its share capital by special resolution and either going to Court or by the directors swearing a solvency certificate (stating under all the directors' names and the date) that each of the directors has formed the opinion that there are no grounds on which the company would be unable to pay its debts for the year ahead, or, if the winding up of the company is expected to commence within a year, that the company will be able to pay its debts;
- any resolution relating to business stated in the Articles to require a special resolution.

Under CA06, the notice required for special resolutions is reduced from 21 to

14 days' notice (unless a company's Articles specify the longer period). The approval of 75 per cent of the votes cast in person or by proxy is required.

Copies of all special resolutions must be filed with CH within 15 days of the date of the resolution.

Extraordinary

An extraordinary resolution is needed to resolve:

- any matter stated by the company's Articles to require an extraordinary resolution;
- that a company cannot continue in business by reason of its liabilities and should be wound up;
- to grant certain powers to the liquidator in a members voluntary winding up;
- that assets of the company in a winding up can be distributed to the members *in specie*.

Extraordinary resolutions require 14 days' notice and the approval of at least 75 per cent of the votes cast by members present in person or by proxy. However, since all resolutions (subject to Articles requirements) now require 14 days' notice there is no longer any difference between the requirements for special and extraordinary resolutions, both of which must be filed within 15 days.

CA06 ignores extraordinary resolutions presumably assuming special resolutions will be used. However, a company should refer to its Articles since, if they stipulate certain business must be passed '*by an ExtraOrdinary resolution*', this must be followed.

Written

To reduce time and resources that LTDs were perceived to waste in convening meetings to gain their shareholders' agreement to business, CA89 authorised members to pass resolutions without meeting. Copies of the proposed resolution must be sent to all members (either electronically or in hard copy) with a note of how to indicate agreement (s.296) and a cut-off date, after which, if not ratified, the resolution fails. If no cut-off date is specified the proposed written resolution fails 28 days after the date (the circulation date) the resolution is dispatched. Where the members are distant from the company it may be advisable to send hard copies by recorded delivery so that some record of posting exists, and to suggest that the same precautions are taken when returning the signed copies. It might also be advisable to request that shareholders who are not known personally to the company, have their signatures witnessed.

Originally, written resolutions required unanimous agreement – if just one member did not agree, or simply did not reply, the resolution failed. However under s.288 CA06 written ordinary resolutions can now be passed if there is a simple majority (50 per cent plus one or more) of everyone entitled to vote, whilst written special resolutions are passed if there is 75 per cent support from everyone entitled to vote. Thus there needs be a higher level of agreement compared to the situation where the same resolutions are considered at a meeting where a simple majority for an ordinary resolution or 75 per cent for a special resolution is needed, but only of the votes actually *cast*.

Under the Companies (Resolutions of Private Companies) Order 1995, although the company auditors must be sent a copy of the resolution (failure to do so attracting a £500 fine) the auditors no longer have the power to state that if the resolution 'concerned them' the written process must be abandoned and a meeting convened.

Once the resolution is passed, a copy certified by a director or the company secretary must be recorded in the minute book. If the resolution is such that, had it not been passed using the written process it would need to have been passed as a special resolution, or would have been passed as an ordinary resolution which was required to be notified to CH, then CH must be notified within 15 days.

A written resolution cannot be used to remove a director (s.168) or auditor (s.510) from office. Such a proposal can only be effected at a meeting with the resolution subject to the special notice requirements.

In addition, there are special rules (mainly relating to the need to provide full explanation) regarding using written resolutions in the following circumstances:

- disapplication of pre-emption rights;
- financial assistance for the purchase of own shares;
- purchase of own shares;
- payment out of capital;
- approval of directors' service contracts.

Members holding 5 per cent or more of the voting strength of the company can request that a written resolution be put to the members. A lower percentage can be required if the Articles so permit.

Wording

Legal advice may be advisable when framing the wording for a resolution relating to other than routine items, as clear wording is essential and to ensure the operative date is also clear. Thus it may be better, rather than resolving:

'That the report of the directors and the annual accounts for the year ended 30th June 2XXX, together with the Balance sheet as at that date are accepted',

to word the resolution:

'That the report of the directors and the annual accounts for the year ended 30th June 2XXX, together with the Balance sheet as at that date be and they are hereby accepted'.

The word *'hereby'* indicates that the resolution was passed on and became effective on that date. However, with resolutions where the operative date is dependent on the actions of some third party (for example, the change of the company name is not effective until the date of the Certificate of Incorporation on change of name issued by CH) the wording might be:

'That the name of the company be changed from ANY COMPANY LTD to ANY OTHER COMPANY LIMITED and that the new name be operative from the date stipulated by the Registrar of Companies.'

Filing with CH

The following resolutions must also be filed:

- any resolution passed unanimously which would otherwise have been a special resolution;
- any resolution passed unanimously by a class of shareholder which would have required a specified majority; and
- any resolution directed by the Secretary of State requiring the directors to change the company name to include the word 'limited'.

The following format should be acceptable.

Example	Resolution
	SPECIAL RESOLUTION ON CHANGE OF NAME
	Companies Act [1985] or (2006]
	Company 00123456789 ANY COMPANY LTD
	At an [Extraordinary] General Meeting of members of the above-named company, duly convened and held at [address, usually the Registered Office] on [date] the following SPECIAL RESOLUTION was passed:
	THAT the name of the company be changed to ANY OTHER COMPANY LTD
	Signed..........................Secretary [Date..............]

Minority protection

Any resolution (or any other action e.g. the payment of an interim dividend) the effect of which is that a member with a minority shareholding is disadvantaged is illegal – for example if A holding 90 per cent of the shares purports to pay a dividend but only to those holding more than 10 per cent of the shares. The minority shareholder could bring an action for unfair prejudice. If the majority shareholder were also a director, there could also be a basis for a DERIVATIVE CLAIM as this could amount to a breach of trust and/or breach of statutory duty (which is to treat all members equally).

The Elective regime

To relieve LTDs from perceived administrative obligations (particularly companies where all the shares were held by board members), CA89 introduced the 'elective regime' which allowed shareholders (if acting unanimously, i.e. every entitled vote has to be in favour) to 'elect' to allow their company to take certain actions. Whilst such resolutions could be passed at a meeting, they could also be passed by a written resolution (which also originally required 100 per cent unanimity) in which case the members did not even have to meet. CA06 allows LTDs not to hold AGMs, so to a large extent elective resolutions have been rendered superfluous.

Under the Companies (Resolutions of Private Companies) Order 1995, provided all the members agree, the requirement to give 21 days' notice of an elective resolution could be waived.

The elective regime was restricted to:

- give, renew or extend the directors' five-year authority to ALLOT shares. The effect was that the directors could allot shares either within a limitation either in time or number of shares (within the limits in the Memorandum unless those requirements were first changed), without convening a meeting and seeking such permission from the shareholders at the time. CA06 companies are not required to have an authorised share capital and the directors can issue shares they feel are warranted (any required control over shares to be issued etc. would need to be inserted in the Articles);
- dispense with laying the accounts before the AGM. When such a resolution was adopted the accounts were still required to be sent to each member. CA06 abolishes the need for LTDs to hold AGMs unless the Articles state one must be held (or the directors or shareholders want such a meeting). The accounts must still be sent to the owners;
- dispense with holding an AGM. The business normally undertaken at the AGM is fairly routine. In any event under CA06, LTDs do not need

to hold AGMs unless their Articles state they must have one, or their shareholders or directors state that they want one;

■ reduce the percentage required for sanctioning short notice of an EGM from 95 per cent to 90 per cent. This has also been overtaken by CA06 which allows short notice providing 90 per cent of the voting rights agree (although a company's Articles can stipulate a higher threshold up to 95 per cent);

■ dispense with annual re-appointment of auditors (in which case the auditors are deemed to be re-elected automatically). If an LTD does not hold AGMs the auditors simply continue in office.

All elective resolutions were required to be filed at CH within 15 days of being passed. If passed at a meeting, the minutes evidencing the adoption of the elective resolution(s) must be prepared and filed in the ordinary way. If passed using a written resolution, the requirements relating to recording of such resolutions apply.

If an LTD re-registered as a PLC, elective resolutions ceased to be effective. An elective resolution was also able to be revoked by the members passing an ordinary resolution (which itself had to be filed with CH). Of course the effect was that a shareholder who acquired shares after an elective resolution had been passed was subject to it unless and until he could muster sufficient support to pass an ordinary resolution of revocation.

Postscript

CA06 is silent concerning elective resolutions and effectively abolishes the concept (unless of course the principle has been written into the Articles), although if all the members are in agreement, obviously they can resolve all legal business. If unanimity is not possible, either the written resolution process could be used or a meeting could be convened.

INTRODUCTION

If a claimant wishes to lodge a liability claim against a company no longer on the active register, it is possible, so that the action can be defended, for a defunct company to be resurrected with the Court's authority. The time limit is six years, although the Court can extend this. However, companies that were defunct before 16 November 1969 (i.e. 20 years before the date the original rule regarding resurrection came into force) cannot be resurrected.

Action

The actions that could generate application to the Court for resurrection are those concerned with claims for damages in respect of personal injuries or claims under the Fatal Injuries Act 1976 or Damages (Scotland) Act 1976 and would mainly be generated by application from or on behalf of former employees who, for example, have become subject to a condition which surfaced after the company was removed from the register but which can be proved to have originated prior to that date. For example, it can take many years for diseases caused by industrial activity (e.g. mesothelioma, caused by inhaling asbestos fibres) to manifest themselves. If it is alleged that the condition was caused by a company now defunct, the company can be resurrected to face the claim brought by the injured party. However, under the Third Parties (Rights against insurers) Act 2010 those who allege loss against a company that is insolvent or cannot meet a claim for damages can sue its insurers directly i.e. the company would not have to be resuscitated to face the action.

Administration

Shareholders or guarantors allowing their companies, or parent companies allowing their subsidiaries, to be struck off should ensure they keep details of insurers, as well as the various records of the defunct company in case such an action is brought in accordance with this relaxation. It may be prudent to keep (securely) company statutory books, etc., for 'life of the company' plus (say) 6 years (in view of the Court's powers to extend the period during which resuscitation can take place). A number of commercial organisations provide such safekeeping facilities.

Certificates of Employers' liability insurance

The principle of allowing company resurrection to face liability claims flows from the realisation (as above) that some claims for liability may not arise for some time after they originated. From 1999 the annual Certificates of Employers' liability insurance were required to be kept for 40 years and had to be displayed at every place of work. The requirement to keep these certificates has been abandoned, as has the obligation to display the annual certificates, provided the details are kept electronically on a system to which every employee has access. It might be prudent, despite the relaxation, to continue to keep a copy of each future certificate – possibly with the statutory books.

INTRODUCTION

The UK Corporate Governance Code states '*the board is responsible for determining the nature and extent of the significant risks it is willing to take in achieving its strategic objectives. The board should maintain sound risk management and internal control systems*'. Whilst '*comply or explain non-compliance*' is an obligation for listed PLCs the identification and control of risk should be just as much an objective for other companies – indeed it may be even more essential for smaller companies. Obviously it includes directors taking steps to preserve and protect the assets of the business as well as seeking to minimise potential losses by creating contingency and crisis plans. Planning for recovery from disasters seems logical – although a survey by accountants Deloitte and Touche found that 30 per cent of UK companies had no disaster plans at all.

The Turnbull recommendations

The Turnbull committee, which originally reported on risk and recovery, stated that:

- internal risk control should be embedded in the company processes. It should not be seen as a separate exercise and for this reason the board should regularly review contingency and disaster plans;
- risk control should be responsive to changing circumstances in particular related to new risk areas (which need to be regularly identified);
- companies should customise their own plans – and regularly update them.

These aims should be valid for all companies but particularly in companies where there are shareholders who are not directors, since they have every right to expect the directors (i.e. their appointees) to protect the assets they jointly own – and to hold them responsible if they fail to do so because of their alleged negligence. The requirements can be summarised as:

- allocating responsibility to a board member who should report to the board regularly;
- giving the requirement a priority;
- involving management all levels;
- identifying clear objectives and demonstrating how these are being satisfied;

- identifying all risk areas and prioritising the risks so identified;
- establishing risk management and reduction programmes and procedures;
- regularly updating the detail (considering as part of this process all new risks and threats).

Full details of the report (which concludes with a 'Twenty Questions' type checklist) are available from Institute of Chartered Accountants in England and Wales:

PO Box 433
Moorgate Place
London, EC2P 2BJ
website **www.icaew.co.uk**

Risk awareness updated

The original recommendations were revised so that listed PLC boards were required to:

- continually review their application of the guidance and treat the internal control statement as an opportunity to inform their shareholders about how they manage risk and internal control;
- apply the same standard of care when reviewing the effectiveness of internal control as when exercising the directors' general duties;
- confirm in the annual report that necessary action has been or is being taken to remedy any significant failings or weaknesses identified from their review of the effectiveness of the internal control system;
- include within the annual report such information as considered necessary to help shareholders understand the main features of the risk management processes and system of internal control.

It has been suggested that:

a) risk should be a regular agenda and board discussion item (see MINUTES);
b) a risk register should be compiled with all invited to contribute;
c) there should be regular discussion of existing, and identification of new, risks;
d) those involved should be trained in the discipline;
e) the process should be subject to consideration regarding improvements.

Stakeholder interests

Failing to devise disaster or contingency plans could be costly – and, in addition, shareholders could sue the directors for a breach of the requirement to act in their best interests. Under CA06, it is easier for a shareholder who believes that the company has suffered loss because of the activity(ies) (defined as *'an actual or proposed act or omission involving negligence, default, breach of duty or breach of trust'*) of a director, to initiate legal action (a DERIVATIVE CLAIM) against the director on the company's behalf.

CA06 also places obligations on directors, not only to act in the best interests of the shareholders and to take account of the interests of their employees and creditors, but also to consider the impact of the company's operations on the environment and the community at large, and the desirability of the company maintaining a reputation for high standards of business conduct.

Case study	Being prepared pays dividends

Gee Publishing formerly occupied a five-storey building next to Canary Wharf in part of London's docklands. One Thursday in February 1996, I delivered the final manuscript of a new employment law loose-leaf manual to Gee's offices. 24 hours later I saw, on television, that office devastated by one of the largest IRA bombs ever exploded on the mainland. Since the previously blue glass fronted but now wrecked building was designated a 'crime scene' by the Police, Gee were not allowed back into the building (even if only to collect files and papers) for six months. Yet early the following Monday morning I received a phone call from my editor checking that I had another copy of everything passed to her the previous Thursday.

Gee had realised that, being located immediately next to a very recognisable landmark (Canary Wharf), they were vulnerable, and had developed a detailed contingency plan. Over the weekend they had sourced, and relocated to, temporary (now their permanent) offices. Whilst inevitably there was disruption and losses of some records etc. a substantial part of the business was up and running without missing a single working day – indeed within one working hour of the explosion. Such reaction is only possible within such a short time if there is a detailed recovery plan – and suitable stand-by facilities whether that be an office, hard copy records, back-up computer records etc.

Of course the parent company shareholders could not hold Gee's directors responsible for the bomb – but they could hold them responsible for failing to plan on a 'what if' basis so that the business could recover more swiftly than otherwise.

Insurers are increasingly enquiring about their insureds' disaster recovery planning, the answers to which could affect premiums. Many organisations – particularly those operating in the financial services sector – in London and other major centres now keep 'ghost offices' available for activation in the event that their main office is subject to terrorist activity either by being directly affected or simply from them being denied access to the site.

Nigel Turnbull, speaking at the launch of the annual Risk Management Survey, stated *'Boards should review risk management processes on a monthly basis'*. However, according to a recent survey (conducted by the Institute of Chartered Accountants in England & Wales), only 47 per cent of boards review risks monthly, most boards look at the issue once every four or six months and 10 per cent consider it only once a year.

The FRC suggests many risk statements are not as required and comments *'Any board should be able to describe in their accounts, simply and clearly, the principal risks and uncertainties facing the company ... too many do not. Boards who retreat [behind standard wording] give the impression that they have not themselves understood the risks they face.'*

The following questions could be addressed:

- 'Do the disclosures state clearly which are the principal risks and uncertainties?'
- 'Have these been the subject of recent board/audit committee discussions?'
- 'Is the description of each principal risk and uncertainty sufficient for shareholders to understand its nature and uncertainty?'
- 'Are risks described in a manner consistent with the way they are discussed in-company, and in the rest of the report?'
- 'Are there risks not covered within the business review?'
- 'Is there a description of how the company manages each of the principal risks and uncertainties?'

The Walker recommendations

The Walker committee recommended that boards should appoint risk committees comprising at least three directors with a majority of non-executives, one of whom should take the chair. The committee should regularly advise the board on risk tolerance and exposures and be expected to advise on risks endemic on acquisitions and disposals. It should also provide a risk report for inclusion in the annual report which:

- describes the strategy within a risk management context and explains the membership of the risk committee;
- incorporates information on key risk exposures inherent in the strategy;

- explains how risk is assessed over time and whether external advice is sought, etc.;
- It is also suggested that the chairman of the risk committee should be prepared to answer questions at the AGM.

(See ICSA Guidance on terms of reference for a risk committee.)

'The buck stops in the boardroom'

Safety-related legislation has been introduced recently which could involve directors facing imprisonment if they are found guilty of not being sufficiently pro-active in restricting risks in the workplace. The adoption of risk identification principle leading to risk assessment, the consideration of such items regularly (and constructively) at board meetings and the promulgation and policing of risk reduction or control procedures etc. could be a valuable foundation for a defence against such claims. The old adage 'in litigation the person with the best paperwork stands a better chance of winning' is apposite.

Case study	Cost of a cavalier attitude
	The first prosecution under the Corporate Manslaughter Act resulted in a company being fined £385,000 for negligently causing the death of Alexander Wright. He was a junior geologist working in an unsupported pit which collapsed on him. The company's attitude to safety was described as 'cavalier'. The case against the director personally was abandoned in view of his ill-health.

INTRODUCTION

Using a seal to evidence a person's agreement to a contract originated over a thousand years ago when, to indicate their agreement, those who could not read or write pressed signet rings into hot wax on the document. A company can effect its agreement to a contract by having its seal impressed onto the document. Using the seal, evidenced by an entry in a register of seals ratified at a board meeting, is an effective control over – as well as being a useful record of – the commitments entered into by the company.

Adopting the seal

Subject to the Articles giving authority for its use, a seal bearing the name of the company should be produced at a board meeting, and a resolution passed adopting it as the common seal of the company. An impression of the seal should appear on the minute page alongside those words. If the company changes its name and wishes to continue using a seal the process should be repeated with the new seal.

Requirement for use

Originally seals were used to create deeds which were needed for:

- freehold property transactions and leases lasting three years or more;
- sales and purchases of British ships (or shares in such ships);
- 'gratuitous promises' i.e. transactions where there is no consideration for the value being given; and
- confirmation of the legitimacy of share certificates. The Articles of many pre-CA06 companies limited by shares state that a share certificate is only a valid document of title if it bears the common seal of the company. A company deciding to dispense with using a seal – see below – would need to change its Articles as otherwise it would not be able to validly issue share certificates.

Sealing procedure

To ensure adequate time is allowed to gain board authority to the item, the following procedure could be used.

1 Documents required to be sealed should ideally be submitted at least two weeks before any critical date.

2 Affixing the seal can be witnessed by two directors, a director and the secretary. With Articles authority, the seal can also be witnessed by one director and a person authorised by the board – usually known as an 'authorised countersignatory'. Many large companies that need to undertake a great deal of sealing delegate witnessing the seal to officers rather than a second director or the company secretary. If documents are to be signed 'as deeds' rather than sealed then they can only be witnessed by two directors or by one director and the company secretary or in Scotland (only) by one director and an authorised countersignatory.

3 At least one signatory must know personally of the content of the item to be sealed.

4 Other than for the approval of the following items, a brief synopsis of the content of the document must be prepared and initialled by the director ultimately responsible for the commitment of resources, etc., evidenced by the document. This synopsis should be kept in the register of seals until the sealing has been approved by the board, and will be preserved subsequently for [three] years.

   a) Share certificates. Many companies use a securities seal which is affixed by the person looking after the company's share registration work under terms of authority granted by the board.

   b) Renewals of leases, or new leases which have board approval.

   c) Agreements where the capital value in total (either separately or should the document be one of a series, cumulatively) is less than (say) £5000.

5 The register of seals (and/or of documents signed as deeds) will be completed with every item sealed being given a sequential number. The same number will be placed on the document itself and also on any synopsis. Using such a Register is not a legal requirement but has many practical advantages not least, being a record of all the items sealed or signed as deeds, and it can avoid giving details of all items sealed at a board meeting – the register can provide the details to interested parties.

6 The register of seals will be produced at each board meeting so that all members (if they wish) can inspect details of all items sealed between board meetings. With board approval the chairman can initial under the latest entry.

Control and security

The affixing of the seal to a document grants the authority of the company to the item and thus the seal needs to be adequately protected.

1 Is the seal kept secure?
2 Is the register of seals also kept secure, entries being made only (but always) when the seal is used, and submitted for authorisation to the next following board meeting?
3 Is every item sealed inscribed with the number given to the entry in the Register?
4 Is there a schedule of authorities, requiring adherence to levels of approval for prescribed value contracts (see AUTHORITIES, CONTROL AND DELEGATION)?

Abolition of seal

Under CA89, companies were permitted to dispense with a seal. If use of a seal is to be abandoned it might be advantageous to consider the following:

1 Are there adequate procedures for ensuring items needing the equivalent of the affixing of the seal do receive the degree of authority they require?
2 Are there procedures in place to provide evidence of the authority of those who will sign deeds instead of these being sealed?
3 Has explanation of the relaxation been given to those used to receiving a sealed document (for example those located overseas)?
4 Have we incorporated a rule such as the following to provide back-up authority for those actually signing documents which would otherwise be sealed?
   'Every six months, the board will approve a resolution authorising (named) directors and the company secretary to sign on behalf of the company, documents which otherwise would have been sealed. Copies of such a resolution, authenticated by the chairman, will accompany each document signed to avoid any questioning re. the authority.'
   This should also help avoid questions from those who are not aware of the option to dispense with the seal and have been accustomed to receiving documents that have been sealed. Requiring a six-monthly repeat/update of the authority itself, should negate any challenge as to its currency.
5 To ensure appropriate drafting all solicitors must be briefed to refer to documents as a deed if they are to be regarded as deeds and not to be sealed. A wording such as *'Executed as a deed, for and on behalf of Any Company Ltd by (two directors or one director and the company secretary or authorised countersignatory')* should be incorporated.

Further relaxations

Principles of the Regulatory Reform (Execution of Deeds and Documents) Order 2005 are that:

- sealing a document no longer makes it a deed;
- a third party can rely on a document signed by two directors (or a director and the company secretary);
- solicitors signing 'on behalf of the company' are now assumed to have the authority to bind the company in all transactions (not only transfers of land as they could previously);
- a corporate director (that is, a 'company that is a director'), can bind the company for third parties if a representative of the corporate director signs a deed (the company should retain a copy of the appointment of the representative).

CA06 allows the sole director of an LTD where there is no company secretary to appoint an 'authorised signatory' so that a second signature is available for documents requiring dual signatures, whilst under s.47 the company can by deed empower a single person (either for a specific purpose or generally) as its attorney to execute deeds or other documents on its behalf.

Register of seals

There is no legal requirement to keep a register of seals (or sealing) although many companies do so since it not only provides a record of the commitment to the contract, but also requires brief details of the content, date of approval and signatories, and the destination of the item after sealing/signing. If entries are numbered in the register, subsequent approval of the board to the affixation/signing can be achieved by a simple board minute:

'Approval was granted to the affixation of the seal (signing as a deed) of items numbered [X] to [Y] in the Register of Seals. The Chairman initialled the register under item [Y].'

Cross referencing can be obtained by inserting the register number against the seal impression.

WARNING

 If conducting business with Brazil, Russia, India and China (the BRIC four countries with the fastest growing economies), UK companies may find that their opposite numbers not only prefer contracts to be under seal but also require confirmation by a Notary Public. Retention of the seal may avoid a considerable waste of time trying to explain the diluting legislation referred to above. Usage of the seal is simple, time efficient, inexpensive (a seal can usually be obtained for less than £25) and subject to few challenges. Removing it negates these advantages and may create time-consuming – but wholly avoidable – problems.

Shareholders' agreements

INTRODUCTION

A company's Articles are made publicly available by being filed at CH. However, the shareholders may wish to agree items between themselves privately by entering into a shareholders' agreement which does not form part of the publicly-available information. Care is needed to ensure that provisions in the Articles and the shareholders' agreement are not in conflict, or, at least, to state, if there a conflict, which will have precedence.

Agreement to discuss the possibility of selling the shares

The agreement could stipulate that should one or more member(s) wish to withdraw from the company, the other members should have the right to purchase, or find purchasers for, that member's shares (i.e. a right of pre-emption or first refusal on the shares), rather than them being sold to an outsider. Reference should first be made to the Articles as some degree of protection may be included there. For example, many LTD companies' Articles give the directors powers to refuse to register a transfer of shares to an 'unacceptable' new shareholder (hence these companies being described as 'private'). However it might be preferable to address the possibility in advance as the following draft illustrates. This version does not, subject to the wording of the Articles, prevent the actual barring of any sale or transfer of the shares (as the board of an LTD usually can) but requires the member to discuss it with the other members.

Example	Deed of agreement
	This Deed of Agreement is made this day of 2XXX between XYZ, ABC, DEF and GHI, all of whom are shareholders in ANY OTHER COMPANY LTD (a limited liability company registered in England under number 1112223334).
	It is hereby expressly agreed by and between all four parties hereto that none of them will sell (individually or collectively) all or any of the shares he holds in the company without first discussing it fully with, and to the satisfaction of, the other members. ➡

Example	Deed of agreement – *continued*
	In witness whereof this Deed of Agreement is signed this day of 2XXX
	Signatures of all members and witnesses

Since an agreement is unenforceable unless there is a consideration, such a document (and the following alternatives) should always be described and signed as Deeds or alternatively incorporate a nominal consideration.

Right of pre-emption

Effectively this is a right of first refusal given to the other members to buy any shares that a member may wish to sell.

Example	Deed of pre-emption
	This Deed of Pre-emption agreement is made this ... day of ... 2XXX between all the members of ANY COMPANY LTD (the company) a limited liability company registered in England No 112233445566, whose registered office is at [address] namely XYZ (owning approximately 70 per cent of the issued shares of the company) and ABC (owning approximately 30 per cent of the issued shares of the company).
	Both the parties hereto, Messrs XYZ and ABC, hereby voluntarily, mutually, separately and expressly agree that in the event of either wishing to dispose of his shareholding (or any part thereof) in the company, he will first offer it for purchase by the other party hereto.
	The offer must be in writing specifying a price per share, and any other conditions of sale and must be posted by recorded delivery to the last known private residential address of the shareholder (the recipient). The recipient will have 56 days to make a decision whether to accept or reject the offer. If at the end of 56 days from the date of posting of the offer (as evidenced by the recorded delivery slip) no agreement or rejection of the offer has been received then the offer will lapse and the offering shareholder will be at liberty to offer the shares elsewhere at a ➜

Example	Deed of pre-emption – *continued*
	price not below that used in the offer to the other shareholder. In the event, and on each and every occasion, if the shares have subsequently to be offered at a lower price than that originally calculated, the shares will first be offered to the other shareholder (in the manner, and under the time restrictions, set out above). In witness whereof, etc. Signatures of both parties and witnesses to each. Date

It is important that the exact basis of the appointment of a valuer of shares is set out in the agreement or Articles and that those requirements are strictly adhered to.

Agreement allowing for calculation of value and veto on alternative member proposed

This version involves the auditors as witness to the negotiations which may help clarify the events in the event of dispute.

Example	Deed of agreement for calculation of value and veto on alternative member
	This Deed of Agreement is made this day of 2XXX between XYZ and ABC (the parties) both of whom own and control shares in ANOTHER COMPANY Ltd, a company registered in England No 111122223333. It is hereby expressly agreed between the parties that should either party wish to dispose of the shares held in their name or the name of their spouses as their nominees, or of any of such shares, that they should first offer such shares to the other party, and will only be able to dispose of such shares elsewhere after the other has indicated in writing that he does not wish to acquire the shares. The valuation to be placed on the shares shall be calculated by the auditors to the company, Messrs Accountant & Auditor, ➔

Example	Deed of agreement for calculation of value and veto on alternative member – *continued*

or such other valuer as the parties may jointly agree, or in the absence of agreement, by a person appointed to carry out such valuation by the president for the time being of the Institute of Arbitrators.

In the event of such shares being offered at the price stated by the auditors, the member will have 56 days (from the date that the disposing member confirms the intention to dispose in writing to the other member, a copy of such offer being sent to the auditors) to consider the offer. If at the end of this period no acceptance has been received, the member may offer the shares elsewhere. On receipt of an offer from a third party full details of such third party will be given to the remaining member, who shall have a right to veto in writing the person to whom the shares would otherwise be transferred. Any veto shall be sent by post within seven days of the remaining member being made aware of the identity of the third party, a copy of the veto will be sent to the auditors.

In witness wherefore the parties have signed this Deed of Agreement this [number] day of [month] 2XXX

Member   Member

In the presence of

Witness   (Name) ....

            (Address) ....

            (Occupation) ....

Case study	Costly ignorance

In *T A King (Services) Ltd Cottrell v King*, Mr King's motor business needed capital and Cottrell agreed to refinance it, taking 75 per cent of the shares in consideration. When Cottrell died, the company gave the shares under a transmission arrangement to Mrs Cottrell. Mr King objected, since the company's Articles stated that if one shareholder died their shares had first to be offered to the surviving shareholder. After a costly High Court action the shares had to be transferred from Mrs Cottrell back to her husband's estate, the executors of which then had to ➔

Case study	Costly ignorance – *continued*

have the shares valued and offered to King. If King wanted the shares he would have to pay for them, the money going to Cottrell's estate; if not the executors would then be able to deal with the shares in accordance with Cottrell's will.

Ironically, whilst he was alive Cottrell (since he had 75 per cent of the shares) could have passed a special resolution changing that requirement. However, there might have been a clause in a shareholder's agreement under which Cottrell undertook not to seek to change the Articles in this way.

Other clauses

Clauses could also be included covering:

- the granting of enhanced voting rights to some directors if the board is deadlocked. This device is sometimes used in Joint Venture companies, but, since one of the principals effectively has board control, can mean that the results of the joint venture subsidiary have to be consolidated with those of the principal with it;
- other methods (than the foregoing) whereby a member can realise the value of the shareholding;
- situations where unanimity of shareholders is required before action can be taken;
- a mechanism whereby if the shareholders are deadlocked, a decision can be arrived at.

This last item reflects fairly numerous instances where there is an equality of votes (e.g a 'quasi-partnership' with two shareholders each holding 50 per cent of the shares). This seemed fine when the company was set up and the parties were in agreement, but should there later be a dispute, deadlock can result – which is even more problematic if they are also the only directors. The logical result here would be for one shareholder to sell his holding to the other, although that in turn may give rise to a dispute as to the value to be placed on the shares. Without agreement at the time and/or in the absence of a shareholders' agreement regarding share price valuation, it may be necessary to apply to the Court for determination of the situation. The Court has wide-ranging powers – it can order that the company's conduct be regulated; require the company to refrain from certain activities; or authorise civil proceedings to be brought in the name of the applicant. The Court could also order that one party's shares should be bought by the other, and, if the parties cannot agree a valuation, the Court will determine this. Alternatively, the party in dispute could apply for the company to be wound up since obviously the 'quasi-partnership' has come to an end. Court action tends to incur expensive legal fees, so some kind of negotiated settlement would probably benefit everyone.

WARNING

I Experience indicates that in some cases shareholders' agreements, whilst freely entered into, may create a situation which breaches the law. One Agreement sought to indicate that certain directors would be 'special' directors and only they would have a vote at a board meeting even though all directors were 'statutory' directors (i.e. their details were registered at CH!).

2 Any agreement which allows the shareholders to change the Articles in certain circumstances will probably need to be lodged at CH (since it overrides the provisions in and thus effectively changes the Articles).

INTRODUCTION

Company law requires details of those who own and direct companies etc., to be entered in registers – collectively known as the statutory books – which must be protected and made available for inspection. The obligation, usually of the company secretary, is to bring them up to date 'on occurrence' and to notify the changes to CH within specific time limits. The statutory books are the official records of the company – CH's records are copies.

The registers

Register of members into which must be entered, the name and address of each member. A company limited by guarantee must enter the amount of the guarantee given by the member whilst a company limited by shares must enter the number/types of shares held (and transfers into and out of their holdings), calls on, and the nominal value of the shares. If it is a single member company (see TYPES OF COMPANIES) the register entry relating to their sole holding should bear the phrase 'this is a single member company'. Companies with large numbers of members usually keep their register in a computerised form in which case CH must be informed of this.

Details must also be filed with CH (i.e. in the ANNUAL RETURN). However, because of fears of identity theft, unwanted mailings etc., public information is restricted. Thus in listed PLCs, addresses of shareholders with less than 5 per cent of the shares are not disclosed, whilst for LTDs no private addresses of shareholders are shown.

Register of directors and secretaries. Full details (name, and any former name, address, date of appointment and date of resignation/removal) must be given for both directors and secretaries. In addition, dates of birth and nationality must be stated for the directors. Under CA06 all directors can opt to conceal their private address and nominate a service address to be made public. Both company and CH must, however, be told the private address.

Register of directors' share interests. Although holdings of shares in the PLCs of which a person is a director must be recorded, this register is no longer required for LTD directors. However, if an LTD director has an interest in a third party which does business with their company then that interest should be recorded (and could usefully be placed in this register – omitting the word 'share' from the title). If the interest arises after appointment then as soon as the director is aware of it, they must declare it. Similar entries could be made for any indemnities or loans etc. given to the director. PLCs might need a separate register for potential conflicting interests.

Register of substantial interests. Where a member of a listed PLC holds a beneficial interest of three per cent or more, a non-beneficial interest of 10 per cent or more, or a combined (beneficial and non-beneficial) interest of 10 per cent or more, this must be disclosed to the company and recorded in this register. Changes through each percentage point (up or down) must also be notified. Non-beneficial interests of 5 per cent are also now required to be disclosed (but not the variation of percentage points between 5 and 10 per cent).

Register of debenture and/or loan stockholders must contain details of name, address, holding (and changes thereto) of every stockholder.

Register of charges. Regardless of whether or not the company has created any charges (e.g. has mortgaged company assets), a register of charges is required. It must contain full details of all charges over assets of the company and by whom they have been taken.

Register of seals (or sealing). There is no legal requirement to maintain such a register but it is an efficient way of recording details of how and when the seal was affixed to deeds, who witnessed the seal's affixation, a brief synopsis of the content, and the document's ultimate destination. Even where a company has dispensed with the use of a seal, such a register may be a valuable method of recording such salient details of documents signed on behalf of the company as deeds – not least as a means of exercising control of authority delegation.

Compilation

Traditionally these registers have been held in hard copy format – and many still are, particularly in LTDs. Combined registers giving all the required rulings are available from law stationers or can be supplied by formation agents when they form a company. Formerly some registers were required to be held at the registered office which would mean, if using a combined register, that it had to be held at that office. A problem may arise when the place of work of the company secretary (or whoever is responsible for their updating and security) is not at the registered office. Under CA06, if the company notifies CH of a SAIL (using form AD02), the registers can be held there.

The registers can be held in electronic format which, if there are linked computers in the office where the books are kept and the registered office or SAIL, this would both comply with the legal requirement as well as meeting the administrative requirements of a choice of inspection locations (although anyone wishing to inspect would probably opt for electronic inspection of the records at CH).

Access and charges

Charges for inspection and copies are now:

a) Registers of members, overseas branch register, directors' share interests and members' significant share interests (PLCs only),
Inspection: £3.50 each hour or part thereof
Copies: £3.50 for the first 50 entries, £31.50 for the next 950 or part thereof, £20 for the next 4,000 or part and £25 for every subsequent 5,000 entries or part thereof.
b) Directors' service contracts and/or indemnity provisions, resolutions and meetings, report under s.805: 20p per 1,000 words or part thereof.

Retention and inspection

All these registers must be kept safely by the company and preserved for at least the life of the company (but see also RESURRECTION OF COMPANIES). Historically for two hours every working day, any member of the public could walk into the registered office of a company and demand to see its register of members. The creditors could demand to see that register and the register of charges, and the members could demand to see all the registers.

However, the right of inspection of the register of members has been curtailed by CA06, although much of the data is available at CH, since it is included in the annual return. The inspection rights of the other statutory books are unchanged (see RECORD RETENTION AND INSPECTION).

Certificate of Incorporation

The Certificate of Incorporation bearing the company name, date and place of incorporation, and company number is issued by CH when the company is placed on the company register and evidences its incorporation. If the company changes its name a fresh certificate bearing the new name will be issued. However, the Certificate (which no longer needs to be displayed) should be kept safely, as it evidences the existence of the company, and, if, for example, the company wishes to borrow money, a bank will insist on seeing it. If the Certificate is lost CH can issue a duplicate.

Types of companies

INTRODUCTION

Most UK corporate bodies are formed under company law which originated in the mid-nineteenth century when, for the first time, entrepreneurial (i.e. risk-taking) owners' liability was limited to the amount of their shareholding. Prior to that, owners could only escape personal liability to creditors if and when their company failed, if it was constituted under Royal Charter or an Act of Parliament (a statute company). Examples of all types of companies still exist and new types of corporate bodies have recently been made available.

Unincorporated businesses

Sole trader

This is the simplest form of business – and the most numerous – often operated from the trader's home, keeping overheads low and enabling lower prices to be charged. Approaching four million people work from home in the UK. As an unincorporated body a sole trader has personal unlimited liability for the debts of their business should it fail.

Committees

Those elected to a committee (for example of a social or sports club etc.) have personal liability for the debts of the business – a situation often not appreciated by them. If employing bar staff, gardeners and others, breaching employment legislation could create personal liability on such committee members including unlimited compensation if the offence was discrimination. The committee members' personal position could (and should) be protected by making such a body into a company, limited either by shares or guarantee.

Partnership

If two or more people go into business together they form a partnership whether or not they enter into a partnership deed (which is advisable). Individually their situation is similar to the sole trader and the club committee – that is they have joint and several personal liability for the debts of their business should it fail. Since 2001 partnerships have been able to limit the liability of their principals by becoming a Limited Liability Partnership (LLP) of which there are over 10,000 registered with CH; most being used by professional firms (e.g. solicitors). LLPs are hybrids, being neither companies nor unincorporated partnerships; they are not required to have a 'company' secretary but since the filing requirements (including the need to file accounts within set periods) are similar to the filing requirements for LTDs there is an obligation for someone to perform very similar duties.

Business names

Formerly anyone (e.g. a sole trader or partnership) using a 'business name' or trading name rather than the name(s) of their principals had to comply with the Business Names Act 1985 (BNA85). CA06 repealed BNA85 but replicates its requirements in ss.1200–1208, stipulating that, in running a business, if individuals use a trading name other than their own personal name(s), then on all notepaper, orders, invoices etc., the name(s) of the principal(s) 'behind' the business name must be stated. This is required so that those that deal with the business know the identity of the person (real or legal) with whom they are trading since legal action cannot be taken against a 'name'. Repealing the separate Act and inserting its requirements into CA06 seems odd in terms of requiring legal compliance – after all, a sole trader or other unincorporated organisation is unlikely to think of looking in a Companies Act for legal requirements affecting their organisation.

Incorporated bodies

There are some very large sole trader businesses. As businesses grow larger, however, so too do the debts of the organisation and to protect personal liability many sole traders, club committees, and partnerships decide to incorporate as limited liability companies.

(a) Private company limited by shares (LTD)

LTDs constitute the largest proportion (around 98 per cent) of the companies registered at CH. The company can issue from one to many million shares although around 80 per cent of such companies have a share capital of under £100 and around 90 per cent have five or fewer shareholders. The shareholders' duty (and legal obligation) is to appoint officers to run the company and to delegate to them the day to day control and operation of their company. Very often the Articles of such companies allow the directors to restrict who owns the shares (that is the directors have the right to block a share transfer to a person they do not wish to be a shareholder) meaning the directors control the company ownership – hence the reference to LTDs as being 'private companies'. Unless they act fraudulently, once a shareholder has paid for his shares in full he cannot be asked to pay more into the company – even if it fails with massive debts.

(b) Private company limited by guarantee

Where there is no real need for a share capital (e.g. for a company which will not trade in the normal sense of the word and/or is thus unlikely to fail in an insolvent manner – a Chamber of Commerce, flat management company, etc.) this entity can be formed by members who do not subscribe for shares (and thus create a fund of share capital) but simply undertake that should the company fail they will contribute the amount of their guarantee (say £1 each) to 'pay off the creditors'. Normally the company will be required to state 'Limited by Guarantee' at the end of its name although, with permission, the last two words can be dispensed with. The word 'Limited' can also be omitted from the name under s.60 CA06 by submitting form NE01 to CH. Since there are no shares, there are no dividends.

However, some pre-1980 Guarantee Companies do have a share capital. Thus there might, in older companies, be a few shareholders who have contributed capital to the company and, in addition, a number of guarantors who have not contributed. Since 1980 a guarantee company has not been able to be a PLC.

(c) Company with unlimited liability

Such a company (normally formed to take advantage of tax concessions available to UK subsidiaries of USA owners, or for businesses involved in farming or forestry work) does not limit the liability of its members – hence in any insolvent failure, unpaid creditors can sue the shareholders themselves. Thus, in failure, the shareholders have the same exposure to debt as have sole traders, club committee members or partners of an unlimited liability partnership. Unlimited companies are not obliged to file accounts at CH unless they are members of a group which also comprises limited liability companies. In addition, such a company can reduce its share capital without the authority required of other types of companies.

(d) Royal Charter companies

The Royal Charter is the oldest type of company – used since the 13th century when obtaining a royal charter was the only method of incorporation and of limiting the liability of its members. The first two Charter companies were the Universities of Oxford and Cambridge, although the concept was quickly taken up to 'create cities' – raising them from town status to one where they could 'conduct commerce' in their own name. There are now just under 1000 such companies formed under a charter signed by the monarch. They are often used by professional bodies (e.g. the Chartered Institute of Secretaries) which do not trade in the accepted meaning of the word, although they may often have trading subsidiaries.

(e) Statute companies

These are companies formed under an individual Act of Parliament. Such companies mainly pre-date the innovation of limited liability company law in the 1850s since (other than by Royal Charter) this was formerly the only method by which members' liability could be limited. Whilst they must comply generally with company law, they are also bound by the particular terms in their Constitution.

(f) Single member company

Since 1992, under the Companies (Single Member Private Limited Companies) (SMC) Regulations companies can have just one member (previously they were required to have two). When incorporating an SMC only one signature is required on the Memorandum and there is obviously only one member's name in the register of members. If additional members are generated by an ALLOTMENT or transfer of shares, not only do new accounts need to be opened in the register of members, but also the fact has to be drawn to the attention of anyone inspecting the corporate records. Thus in the share account of the original single member, a note must be inserted reading 'This company is no longer an SMC' with a note of the effective date.

Conversely, should a company with two or more members become an SMC, then in the account in the register of members for the remaining member, a note 'This company is an SMC' needs to be entered together with a note of the effective date.

At general meetings of an SMC, the sole member is a quorum, and decisions taken at such 'meetings' should be recorded. Contracts between the sole member and the company (particularly if the sole member is also the sole director which is very common) should also be recorded in writing or set out in the minutes of the board meeting(s). There are initial and daily fines for every officer in default of these requirements. Where a company which is not an SMC carries on trading with only one shareholder, after six months the remaining shareholder loses their limited liability protection and has potential personal liability for the debts should the company fail.

The danger for a company where there is one shareholder and that person is also the sole director is that should the sole director/shareholder be killed (or be unable to act e.g. is declared bankrupt or sectioned under the Mental Health Act) there is no-one with capacity to appoint someone to appoint a new director. The company will be unable to continue to trade until the ownership of the share(s) is determined – a process subject to considerable delay during which it could fail. For CA06 companies this is to some extent overcome since in the new draft Articles, item17 states that *'personal represen-tatives ... have the right ... to appoint a person to be a director'*. This implies that it would not be necessary to wait for probate or letters of administration to be granted to such personal representatives. It would be wise for the company to check the authority of the 'personal representatives' claiming to act. If there is a Will this is relatively easy, however, if the shareholder has died intestate there may be difficulties proving the authority of the person wish-ing to act. Where there is a company secretary at least there is an officer of the company who could carry out these checks – without this appointment the situation is even more problematic. The company might be wise to insist the person claiming to act signs a form of indemnity protecting the company should they act on his instructions which turn out later to be unauthorised. Legal advice should be taken.

The situation for single person guarantee companies is even more prob-lematical. Where a sole shareholder dies, at least the shares still exist and can be passed to the inheritor(s), but a guarantee cannot be transferred. It might be preferable to form an SMC limited by shares but with just one share so that the amount to be invested is small. Alternatively it might be suggested that the guarantor find a substitute who could step into the position should anything happen to them. The substitute would have to sign the same guarantee as the original guarantor (presumably made in advance but only coming into effect in the event of the original guarantor's death).

The same proviso referred to above for companies limited by shares applies to guarantee companies where a sole guarantor who is also the sole director dies. Article 17 similarly states that *'personal representatives ... have the right ... to appoint a person to be a director'*. Once again this implies that it would not be necessary to wait for the grant of probate or letters of administration. Legal advice should be taken.

CH state there are around 650,000 companies where the same person is both sole shareholder and sole director.

(g) Public limited company (PLC)

Subject to a company having:

- an issued share capital of £50,000 of which at least 25 per cent (i.e. £12,500) is paid up; and
- excluded from the Articles any directors right to reject a share transfer (which otherwise gives them control of who can be shareholders); and
- a certificate or licence to commence trading from CH evidencing satis-faction that the required share capital has been subscribed;
- appointed a company secretary; and
- changed its name to end in 'PLC' or 'Public Limited Company'.

then an LTD can RE-REGISTER, or a new company can be formed, as a PLC.

The external perception may be of a corporate body of considerable value and prestige although in fact its share capital is tiny. Such a company should not be confused with a listed or quoted PLC, although it must be said this confusion is very widespread – and is often the reason some LTDs become unlisted PLCs (i.e. seeking to give to the outside world an impression of the company being far more substantial than it is). They have all the legal obligations of a listed PLC (e.g. must file accounts within six months of their year end etc.) but not the Stock Exchange's listing agreement requirements.

(h) Listed or quoted public limited company

A PLC formed as above can apply either for a full 'listing' on the Stock Exchange (i.e. a traded company) or for a quotation on the Alternative Investment Market (AIM). To join either, the share capital will have to be increased considerably and the company will have to commit itself and its officers to the listing rules applicable to each market. Obtaining a listing is termed 'flotation' and is a route chosen so that either existing shareholders can realise their investment and/or so that the company has access to additional share capital other than that sourced by existing owners.

(i) Community interest companies (CIC)

Any LTD or PLC company formed for social enterprise and/or those entities which intend to use their profits for the benefit of the local community or public can (unless they are charities) become a community interest company or a 'CIC'. A CIC is:

- subject to objective and transparent eligibility tests;
- required to produce an annual report placed in the public domain (via filing at CH) showing how they are attaining their objective(s); and is
- allowed to transfer assets to other similar bodies.

It can issue shares, pay its directors and pay dividends subject to limits set from time to time by the Bank of England, since most of its profits are expected to be ploughed back into attaining the company's social activities.

If a company becomes a CIC its name must be displayed everywhere as (for example) 'J Bloggs CIC PLC' or 'J Bloggs CIC LTD'.

(j) Charitable incorporated organisations (CIO)

This concept (similar to a CIC) was enacted in the Charity Act 2006. These are now available in England, Scotland and Wales. They are not yet available in Northern Ireland pending the setting up of a Charities Commission there. CIOs can be used by charities and have to register with the Charity Commissioners (CC) but not with CH (which might simplify matters for those running charitable companies since charity and company law have conflicting requirements). A CIO must adopt a Constitution, and have a trustee body, and members. Whether the members will have an obligation to contribute on winding up as members of guarantee companies do, may be optional. A CIO must:

- keep registers of its trustees and members;
- make the above details available publicly;
- file accounts and annual returns with CC;
- advise CC of any charges it has created over the charity's property.

Although designed for charities a CIO may not be an appropriate vehicle for charities whose work entails giving grants and/or which do not enter into significant contracts.

(k) Foundation Trusts (FT)

This corporate entity was devised for the around 100 foundation hospitals which have their own regulator (a Monitor) and emerging requirements which are very similar in many ways to those applicable to companies. Recently the Government has stated that directors of foundations are to be required to comply with the explicit duties of directors in CA06. Governors of FTs have an explicit duty to hold directors to account and can require them to attend governors meetings. However, directors do not have to ask the Monitor for permission to change their Constitution although they must adhere to a core of items under the NHS Act 2006. An FT must hold an AGM for members so that the annual report can be discussed and they have to account separately for public and private money.

(l) Societas Europaea (SE)

Since October 2004 it has been possible to form an SE which is a European PLC formed under the European Company Statute (ECS). The ECS contains a regulation allowing the formation of such a company under core company law provisions which apply throughout the European Union. An SE must have a minimum share capital of €120,000 and is available to commercial bodies with interests in more than one European country. An SE allows UK companies to engage in cross border mergers with companies from other EU member states. Thus, rather than taking over a company in another member state, a UK company can agree with the other company to form a jointly owned SE subsidiary or holding company.

(m) European Private Company

SEs are only available for PLCs. Paralleling that development, however, is a proposal for private companies – set out in the European Council Regulation on the Statute for a European Private Company. Assuming the proposal allowing such a new legal entity goes ahead, it is unlikely that it will be available before 2013.

(n) Oversea company

Under s.1044 CA06, any 'company incorporated outside the United Kingdom' is an 'oversea company' and within one month of it establishing a place of business here it must send the following information (using form BR1) to CH:

- its Charter or Articles;
- names of the directors and secretary;
- list of persons in the UK authorised to accept service of notice on behalf of the company etc.

Under CA85 a 'place of business' was usually deemed to be one where only administrative functions are conducted. Any other activity (e.g. 'trading' or functions central to the operation of the business) usually meant that the location was defined as a 'branch'. Under CA06 there is no difference between the two definitions – any place of business is required to register as a branch.

(o) Dormant

Around 20 per cent of all companies registered at CH are not trading – they are dormant – sleeping and inactive. They are nevertheless required to submit an annual return and accounts each year (although instead of an actual set of accounts – which might be fairly skeletal – they can submit Form DCA). At any time the company can be re-activated.

It is widely thought that keeping a company on CH's Register (active or dormant) automatically protects its NAME. Whilst it may stop another company with an identical name being registered as a company (although even this is not impossible), this does not prevent someone using the name without 'Ltd' at the end. In this instance company law is of no assistance, and the recourse is an action for passing off or possible trademark infringement. Companies using names etc. as trade marks may find it advisable to also register a private company with that name.

Within the UK the protection given to companies whereby another company cannot have the same name may actually be of limited protection. For example, a company registered in the separate jurisdictions of the Isle of Man, Jersey, or Guernsey etc. could have the same name as a company registered at CH at Cardiff. The mainland CH is unable to prevent this provided the 'externally registered' company does not establish a place of business on the mainland (in which case it would be required to comply with the 'oversea' company provisions) but merely operates via third parties (solicitors, agents etc.).

(p) Joint Venture companies

To develop a new product or concept, two or more bodies (not necessarily companies) may agree to set up and operate a jointly owned subsidiary company. In addition to framing the ARTICLES OF ASSOCIATION they will normally enter into a SHAREHOLDERS' AGREEMENT setting out their relationship and the relationship they may have with those nominated to serve on the board. Most Joint Venture companies are LTDs although there is nothing to stop one being a PLC.

Voting and taking a poll

INTRODUCTION

The proceedings at the General Meetings of most companies are decided by show of hands and, since consensus is usual, only rarely may there be even a need for hands to be counted. Occasionally, however, there will be opposition to a proposal and it is as well to be prepared. Several listed PLCs have altered their Articles so that all general Meeting business requires ratification by poll (not by show of hands) which, since it reflects the true voting power of the shareholders, is democratic.

Authority to vote

There are three ways in which shareholders' powers can be exercised:

1 By attending and voting in person. Such attendance gives the shareholder complete freedom of action to speak and vote at the meeting.
2 By appointing a PROXY which may be able to speak but (subject to the Articles) may not be able to vote on a show of hands. The proxy can, however, demand (or join in the demand for) a poll. For members of a listed PLC usually the proxy cannot speak but can only vote.
3 By a corporate body appointing a representative. A representative is for all intents and purposes a member (since effectively the corporate shareholding body is actually 'present') and can exercise all the rights of an individual member.

Preparation

If antipathy is expected (and it is rare that there has been no indication in advance) preparation is essential. Thus the board could ensure:

■ the impact of opposition is negated by advance discussion;
■ there is sufficient support so that opposition can be out-voted;
■ only those entitled to speak do so – but are allowed to do so with courtesy;
■ meeting administration is sound; and
■ the media are given an adequate (and accurate) briefing.

Media

It is important that those who are to deal with the media are coached in such work, particularly in dealing with hostile or critical questioning. Unless well-prepared and well-briefed for this type of examination, reputations can be irreparably damaged and poor impressions created.

Out-thinking the opposition

Not only should friendly shareholders be canvassed to obtain their proxy (and thus support) if they are not attending, and to arrange tame 'proposers' and 'seconders' to avoid silences at the meeting when the chairman invites them, etc., but also it is essential that if hostility is expected, it is prepared for.

CHECKLIST   Preparing for hostility

✓ Identify source and extent of support and of opposition.

✓ Check if 'hostiles' have a right of attendance (if not, seek to exclude them).

✓ If time allows, consider possibility of an advance private meeting to avoid public confrontation.

✓ Monitor arrivals and arrange for security forces to be nearby to deal with any physical disruption. Ensure visitors sit apart from shareholders to aid accurate 'show of hands' counting.

✓ Canvass proxies sufficient to ensure overcoming any potential opposition.

✓ Prepare a list of the questions least wished to be asked – and, more importantly, a crib of suitable answers. Take advice.

✓ Brief the directors about the problem and steps taken to control/deal with it.

✓ Brief media contacts and provide media trained spokesman to answer follow up queries.

✓ If hostile shareholders wish to make a point they should be allowed such a courtesy, answering the points made as far as possible and offering subsequent discussions if this is feasible.

Voting

1 The Articles may give guidance re. QUORUM requirements, rights of attendance, who is to chair the meeting and any special rules re. voting.

2 If a large number attend it may be helpful to arrange shareholder seating in blocks of (say) 20 or 50 and to arrange for the auditors to act as

scrutineers for a block of seats each. The use of scrutineers (announced by the chairman at the commencement of the meeting) seeks to show that an independent force is available. The scrutineers could also act as receptionists, asking shareholders to sign in, checking voting strength and ensuring only shareholders sit in 'shareholder areas' to aid ease of counting votes (if necessary).

3 If a show of hands is required, each scrutineer should note the result from his section and hand it to the chief scrutineer (two such persons may be advisable for checking purposes) to provide the chairman with totals.

Poll

Reference should be made to the Articles for guidance regarding calling and administering a poll which can usually be demanded or called by:

- the chairman;
- any two members (which includes representatives of corporate share-holders); or
- any member(s) holding one tenth or more of the share capital.

The chairman needs to:

- check that the member(s) making the demand has/have the required authority;
- appoint scrutineers to administer the poll; and
- set the date, time, and place for the poll to be taken.

Administration

1 Since proxies are usually required to be deposited 24 hours or more prior to the meeting, the scrutineers' first task should be to check the proxies for authenticity and voting strength for each resolution. Proxies should provide a space for the insertion of the number of shares/votes applicable.

2 At the meeting the list of proxies lodged must be compared with those shareholders present to ensure there is no double counting. Although a shareholder has a right, even having lodged a proxy, to attend the meeting, clarification of the status of the proxy must be sought (i.e. is the proxy to act or will the shareholder act in person, or are they each to act in relation to part of the holding (although this would only be possible if the lodged proxy did not cover the whole holding)?

3 On receiving a demand for a poll to be taken, the chairman usually has authority to require it to be conducted immediately, or at the end of

the meeting or at some other date (in which case the meeting may have to be adjourned). Once again the Articles should be checked.

4   If a poll is demanded, the proxy cards provide evidence of the preferences of those not present. Additional voting cards (identical in most respects to the proxy card) need to be made available for those shareholders present at the meeting. Each scrutineer should distribute voting cards to shareholders present and not represented by a proxy (whose intentions will be known) – and, after voting, collect and total them. The results from each area should be passed to the chief scrutineer(s) who will summarise the returns and pass the result to the chairman, to declare the result. Shareholders have a right to inspect details of a poll vote.

The future

Companies (having checked that there is no prohibition in their Articles) can now use email to communicate with shareholders and to do so must submit a resolution to them for permission to communicate electronically. If the resolution is passed, shareholders must be advised that they have the option of continuing with hard copy or opting for an electronic version, and that if they do not reply within 28 days they will be deemed to have opted for the electronic option. However even if they do not reply (or do not give an electronic address) they must still be sent a hard copy notification of a meeting with reference to the company website carrying full information re. the meeting. They would not be sent (for example) the report and accounts – the shareholder would need to request these. Those who do not opt for electronic communication can be re-invited to do so once a year.

Case study	Using technology
	In *Byng v London Life* the Court stated that a general meeting could be validly held in several locations provided there were *'fully functional mutual audio-visual links'* – i.e. so that everyone could see and hear and interact with all others. Whilst holding the meeting in two or three locations might be feasible, attempting to use more locations and trying to ensure everyone can see and hear everyone else must be virtually impossible.

It is possible to foresee a situation where General Meetings could be held with shareholders remaining in their homes (connected via the internet to the location where the meeting is physically being held) and being able to exercise their voting power in 'person' having heard any points made in favour or against a particular proposal rather than signing a proxy well in advance of the meeting and without the benefit of such arguments. However, this would only be realistic if everyone was able to see and hear everyone else which poses a logistic/practical difficulty at least with current technology.

INTRODUCTION

Around 100,000 companies are removed annually from CH's register. Some are removed by default, e.g. if all the directors and the secretary resign simultaneously CH has no-one to chase for filing documentation, and after a certain period, and advertising the fact, may strike the company off. Similarly if it does not file an annual return the company can be struck off. These are not ideal methods and should only be used for dormant companies which have never traded and thus there is no possibility of subsequent claims from creditors, employees and other injured parties, etc., leading to a need for RESURRECTION. Most companies are removed following a winding-up order or for failing to file accounts.

Types of orders

Members' voluntary winding up

Where the purpose(s) of the company has/have been achieved and the assets are such that they are able to meet all claims likely to be made, and the directors can swear a declaration of solvency, this method of ceasing the company's existence can be utilised. Within five weeks of the directors swearing such a declaration, the members must pass a resolution winding up the company and advise CH accordingly.

Procedure: The directors swear declaration of solvency and convene a(n) (E) GM at which a liquidator is appointed. A notice regarding this event is posted in the *London Gazette* and details are given to CH within 14 days. The liquidator proceeds to sell the assets and settle the debts. A director has liability for the debts of the company (regardless of resignation) for 12 months from the date he signed a solvency declaration.

Creditors' voluntary winding up

If the directors are unable to swear a declaration of solvency, the company decides to wind itself up and calls a creditors' meeting.

Procedure: A(n) (E)GM is convened to pass a winding-up resolution. The meeting nominates a liquidator, and authorises the convening of a meeting of creditors giving at least seven days' notice including in the *London Gazette*. At the creditors meeting, those present appoint a liquidator whose appointment terminates the powers of the directors. The liquidator proceeds to sell the assets and settle such debts as are possible.

The Court orders a winding up

This occurs when:

- the company passes a special resolution to this effect; or
- a judgement creditor has a debt of £750 or more and has petitioned for the winding up; or
- the company has failed to comply with a certain requirement; or
- the Court feels it is just to do so.

Procedure: In this instance the Official Receiver becomes the liquidator.

Striking off

Under the Deregulation and Contracting Out Act 1994, provided a company has not in the previous three months:

- changed its name;
- traded or conducted business;
- engaged in any activity (other than that connected with this application); and
- made a disposal for value of property rights,

then the directors can apply to CH for it to be struck off.

Procedure: A form DS01 (under s.1003 CA06) must be filed, with copies sent to any director(s) not signing the form and all other interested parties.

Notice re. intent to strike the company off is inserted in the *London Gazette*. Three months later, provided there are no objections, CH can strike off the company.

Administration

The Enterprise Act now requires most companies approaching insolvency to apply for administration and as a result of the credit crunch there have been a number of well-publicised and household named companies – particularly retail chains – that have done so. Under this arrangement an Administrator is appointed (usually by the creditors) to try to save the company (and sell the whole or part as a going concern); or to sell assets (often at a discount to their true worth) to raise cash to keep it going. Should the Administrator be successful, the (often slimmed-down) company may be able to emerge from Administration. Voluntary arrangements (i.e. agreements with the creditors) are also encouraged under the Enterprise Act. Wherever the name of the company is used, the words 'in Administration' must be added to bring the situation to the attention of all third parties – particularly current and potential creditors. This is also important to customers – after all a customer wishing to return goods (e.g. if faulty), needs to be made aware of the state of the company, since it may not even exist in the near future.

'Pre-pack' administration (PPA)

Under PPA arrangements any potentially profitable part of a failing company is *'hived off'* (in advance of failure) and sold (often to the directors of the original company), whilst the *'rump'* is allowed to fail. Since unsecured creditors may be involved in both, they may have an incentive to go along with the concept in the expectation of continuing to benefit from trading with the continuing business. During the current recession there have been around 2000 *pre-packs*. To some extent PPA blunts the purpose of insolvency legislation which placed personal liability on directors, faced with the possibility of failure, should they not regard as 'paramount' the creditors interests. That was devised to deter directors from running companies into the ground knowing they could walk away without liability.

This scenario may not continue unabated following the *Wind Hellas* (WH) case. WH was registered in Greece but two weeks before it collapsed it re-registered as a UK company purely (state some of its unsecured creditors) to gain the benefit of the UK's 'pre-pack' concept, with the original owners and management continuing to run the profitable part of the business. One unsecured creditor, Hedge fund SPQR Capital, which lost £1.3 billion as a result, described the UK's situation as akin to running *'an insolvency brothel'*. Whilst the pre-pack concept has been criticised, it saves jobs, albeit at the expense of the unsecured creditors. In 89 pre-packs effected in one month, 4846 out of 5478 jobs were saved. When HMRC (a major creditor of one company) tried to block an Administrator setting up a pre-pack, the judge held that the plan seemed the best way of saving 50 jobs – in the process saving the State paying unemployment benefits, as well as notice and redundancy pay.

Administrative Receivership

Since the aim of current insolvency law is to try to save companies (via Administration), this alternative is now rarely used. The aim of an Administrative Receiver (AR) is to generate as much cash for the assets of the company as quickly as possible, which will entail the cessation of the company trading whilst the assets are sold – often at a considerable discount since purchasers, knowing the urgency may be able to strike a hard bargain. This was certainly the case in the recession of the early 1990s and banks (who under a CHARGE had the right to appoint an AR) were criticised for 'pulling the rug' from organisations which might have survived had they been supported. The AR pays his own fees and the organisation (usually a bank) with a charge over the assets, and then, (if possible) pays the unsecured creditors and shareholders (usually only a few pence in the pound – and often not even that).

Voluntary arrangements

Under a voluntary arrangement the creditors agree to support the company – normally by agreeing not to press for payment of their debt for a set period to relieve pressure on cash flow etc. This may allow the company time to 'trade out' of its current solvency problems. Very often the creditors may be in the position of being virtually forced to agree to a 'voluntary' arrangement simply since otherwise (i.e. if the company fails) they are likely to receive next to nothing of their debt. Alternatively, should creditors really wish to avoid the company failing they may even be prepared to exchange their debt for shares in the company – a 'debt-equity swop'. Should the company survive they can share in its recovery whereas if it fails they have probably lost no more than their, already incurred, debt.

Case study	Saved by the creditors
	The Queens Moat House Hotel group was saved from insolvency in the late 1980s by the actions of its bankers mainly since the credit they had advanced to the company was so great they could not afford to let the debtor go under – in which event the credit they had allowed would have become a bad debt, affecting their own accounts.
	Similarly in 2003 the Marconi Group (formerly the highly-respected GEC) was saved from insolvency by its creditors who agreed to a debt:equity exchange and finished up owning over 99.5 per cent of the share capital of a listed PLC.

WARNING

 If directors' personal liability is to be avoided it is essential that legal and audit advice is sought.

Wrongful and fraudulent trading

INTRODUCTION

During the expansion of the British Empire in the mid-19th century it was claimed that unlimited liability of shareholders inhibited the growth of commercial entities. To offset this, CA1856 and CA1862 introduced the concept of a limited liability company whereby the shareholders (who were very often also directors of the companies) liability on failure was limited to the amount they had invested in the company – i.e. their shareholding. Almost immediately this was criticised as being a little more than a 'rogue's charter' and 'encouraging overtrading' – allowing some unscrupulous directors to walk away from a failed company without any personal liability for the debts, the cost of failure having been passed to the creditors. To rectify this imbalance, the Insolvency Act 1986 introduced the concepts of 'wrongful' and 'fraudulent' trading for which directors of failed companies can be fined, imprisoned and/or required to make good any deficiencies personally.

Wrongful trading

A director is held to have traded wrongfully if he knew or, (critically), *ought to have concluded* that there was no reasonable prospect of his company's creditors being paid on their due dates or within a reasonable time thereof, or of the company avoiding insolvency and yet he allowed the company to continue to trade and take on more credit. If guilty of wrongful trading, a director can be made personally liable to contribute to any deficiency in assets available to satisfy the creditors of the company, and disqualified from acting as a director for a maximum of 15 years. Whether a company is insolvent (and should, therefore, cease trading rather than continuing to trade 'wrongfully') may be able to be judged fairly accurately with hindsight but may be difficult to assess at the time, particularly as the directors may genuinely be working to try to save the company. The following tests are no substitute for taking competent advice:

1   Is the company capable of paying its debts as they fall due (or shortly afterwards)?
2   Do the assets of the company exceed the value of its liabilities?
3   Would the realisation of assets be sufficient to pay all liabilities?

If the answers to any of these questions are 'no', then, unless it is known that the situation will improve before the debts become overdue, the company is almost certainly approaching insolvency, and unless the situation can be, or is reasonably expected to be, rectified swiftly, it should cease trading. To do otherwise may involve the directors being made personally culpable. In assessing culpability, the Court will bear in mind the expertise of the persons concerned. Liability can be reduced or avoided if it can be shown that everything that could be, was done to minimise the potential loss.

Case study	Qualifications enhance liability
	In *Dorchester Finance Co Ltd v Stebbing* there were three directors (all qualified accountants), two of whom left the running of the company to the other. The former often signed blank cheques for use by their colleague and made no enquiry of how the funds were used by him. When the company failed owing substantial sums to its creditors, all three directors were prosecuted. The Court found that the two 'sleeping directors' had failed to apply the necessary skill and care in the performance of their duties (and indeed that they had failed to perform *any* duties in their positions as directors).

The Court stated that a director must in the exercise of his duties:

● show the degree of skill and care reasonably expected from a person of his knowledge and experience (hence the expectations of three qualified accountants would be high in view of their professional qualification);
● take such care that a man might be expected to take on his own account;
● use the powers granted to him in good faith and in the interests of the company of which he is a director.

Directors must be proactive in the exercise of their responsibilities (inactivity is not an option if personal liability is to be limited).

Action required

Immediately it is known that a company is insolvent, or it appears that it is approaching this state, the directors must take action – inactivity is not an option. Whenever a company is wound up, an insolvency practitioner must investigate the position and the records and the actions of its officers. Each officer MUST complete a very lengthy questionnaire – the answers to some of the questions (e.g. *'When were you first aware the company was trading wrongfully?'*) being potentially self-incriminating. If transactions were effected at under-value or at preferential rates, or a creditor was given preferential treatment this can result in a report being made to the Director of Public Prosecutions who will decide whether to prosecute for fraud. If the company is being wound up under a Court order, the report must be made to the Official Receiver. If the insolvency practitioner or the Official Receiver feels that the conduct of a director has been such that he is unfit to run a company then a report must be made in case legal action should be taken against those culpable.

Case study	Fraudulent concealment?
	In *Contex Drouzhba Ltd v Wiseman*, W caused the company of which he was a director to enter into an arrangement with a creditor whereby the company promised to pay the creditor within 30 days of invoice. However, the company's financial position was so poor that the director knew there was no way in which such a promise could be kept. The judge held that there had been deceit on the part of the director and that it was 'inconceivable' that the status of director should protect him from personal liability. Accordingly, the director was held personally liable for the creditor's debt.

If insolvency threatens the board could:

1 **Cease to trade and call a creditors meeting to consider a voluntary arrangement** (see WINDING UP). Whilst this may remove what confidence remains in the company, in many respects the last thing most creditors would wish is for the company to fail, as often they have a great deal (more possibly than directors or shareholders) at stake. If there is a chance that the company could trade out of the position, the creditors (or a 75 per cent majority of value of them whose wishes could be binding on all creditors) may be prepared to accept a moratorium on their debt (or even a debt:equity exchange, that is taking shares in the company in exchange for extinguishing part or all of their debt).

2 **Appoint an administrative receiver.** However, this right belongs to a creditor – usually a bank – which has a charge over the company assets. The directors can invite the creditor to appoint an administrative receiver. As a result of the Enterprise Act 2002 this course of action is increasingly discouraged in favour of trying to save the company by means of a voluntary arrangement or administration.

3 **Petition the Court for the appointment of an administrator.** This is only possible if the company has access to funds and it is thought

possible that the company – or a profitable part of it – might be able to trade out of the situation. Using this alternative is encouraged under the Enterprise Act 2002.

4 **Raise loans** (i.e. additional capital).

5 **Source additional shareholder** (i.e. risk) **capital or loans.** Although sourcing loans may be a solution to the immediate cash situation, taking on a loan creates a further liability and may increase the company's inherent insolvency. New capital for an LTD could be sought from family and/or friends of the officers. If considering inviting employees to invest, the company should offer to fund financial advice for them, since the risk of failure may be high. When the former Rolls Royce company failed in the 1960s, its employees suffered a 'triple loss' since as well as losing their jobs, many had invested in the company shares, and the company pension fund had also invested heavily in the company.

Other sources of funds include loans from national and/or local government and even the EU; by advertising in the media for investors or even, if it is the only way the company can survive, approaching a competitor or supplier with a view to a merger.

6 **Try to amalgamate with another business.**

7 **Seek a 'white knight' to take over the company as a going concern.** ('White knight' is a term mainly used when listed PLCs are subject to a hostile takeover bid and depicts a company whom the board of the target company feel would be an acceptable parent – more welcome than the predator.)

8 **At all times, record (on an ongoing basis) full details of every action taken,** by whom it was taken, the date on which it was taken, and the result. Whilst the recording of such actions may not save the company, it may, since it is evidence of the positive action of the directors to regard the interests of the creditors as 'paramount', save the officers from being required to contribute to the assets available to the creditors. Advice should be taken.

If genuine re-financing steps are being actively taken (even if these subsequently prove unsuccessful), the directors' liability may be minimised or avoided. If it is thought that a company might be nearing the point at which it could be held to be trading wrongfully, it is *essential* that the directors take action and daily record details of their actions.

Case study	Creditors' interests are paramount
	In *Gwyer & Associates v London Wharf (Limehouse) Ltd*, a director made no effort to ascertain what were the interests of his ➔

Case study	Creditors' interests are paramount – *continued*
	company (which was approaching insolvency) before voting on a board resolution. The Court held he was not only negligent but also in breach of his fiduciary duty to exercise his discretion independently and bona fides in the interests of the company. It went on to state that where a company was on the brink of insolvency the directors owed a duty *'to consider as paramount'* the interests of the creditors.

Under recent initiatives, a company in financial difficulties can use a process under which creditors' claims can be frozen for 56 days, during which period efforts can be made to save the business. At the end of 56 days a creditors' meeting must be held at which the creditors could (subject to gaining a 75 per cent agreement) extend the moratorium for a further month.

Directors and officers' liability insurance policies should be checked to ensure that if found guilty of wrongful trading (which almost certainly would involve a degree of dishonesty) there is any cover under such a policy. The best policies may cover the defence costs – even of those then found guilty.

Penalties

Although, compared to the number of company failures, there have been relatively few such actions, a recent court case found two directors personally liable to contribute £75,000 each to the assets available to the creditors of their insolvent company because they knew before the liquidation that it was likely to happen and yet continued trading to the obvious detriment of the creditors. In similar cases, a husband and wife had to contribute £431,000 to the creditors of their failed company, whilst in one of the greatest value cases, a director was required to contribute £2 million to help pay off his failed company's creditors. It is expected that the number of actions should increase mainly since the responsibility for action has been passed from DBIS to an independent company – Forensic Investigation and Recovery Services.

Fraudulent trading

The essential difference between wrongful and fraudulent trading is intent. Whereas under wrongful trading the director could be held culpable by negligence or even ignorance, under fraudulent trading there must be proven intent to defraud the company's creditors – i.e. the company fails owing the creditors and it can be proven that those responsible were aware of the situation and rather than protecting the creditors, exploited them. Those responsible can be:

- held personally liable to an unlimited extent;
- disqualified from acting as a director for a maximum period of 15 years;
- fined and/or imprisoned for fraud (for a term increased by CA06 to 10 years).

Index